CITIES FOR PEOPLE

PRACTICAL MEASURES FOR IMPROVING URBAN ENVIRONMENTS

RONALD WIEDENHOEFT

VNR Van Nostrand Reinhold Company
New York   Cincinnati   Toronto   London   Melbourne

To Renate,
without whose encouragement and unflagging support neither
this book nor all that led up to it would have been possible

Copyright © 1981 by Van Nostrand Reinhold Company
Library of Congress Catalog Card Number 80–27992
ISBN 0–442–29429–8

Printed in the United States of America

Designed by Scott Chelius

Published by Van Nostrand Reinhold Company
135 West 50th Street
New York, NY 10020
Van Nostrand Reinhold Limited
1410 Birchmount Road
Scarborough, Ontario M1P 2E7, Canada

Van Nostrand Reinhold Australia Pty, Ltd.
17 Queen Street
Mitcham, Victoria 3132, Australia
Van Nostrand Reinhold Company Limited
Molly Millars Lane
Wokingham, Berkshire, England

16 15 14 13 12 11 10 9 8 7 6 5 4 3 2 1

Library of Congress Cataloging in Publication Data
Wiedenhoeft, Ronald V
  Cities for people.
  Includes index.
    1. Architecture—Human factors. 2. Architecture—
Environmental aspects. I. Title.
NA2542.4.W52   711′.4   80-27992
ISBN 0-442-29429-8

Contents

Urban Repair, Not Urban Removal

This book is about reclaiming cities as viable living places for people. It points out specifically how some cities have grown monotonous, ugly, and dangerous and also identifies techniques used during the past two decades to transform cities into far more hospitable places. This book is thus an amalgam: criticism of urban renewal practices still current coupled with an analysis of ways that have proved successful in cities around the world to achieve safer, more attractive, more economically sound urban environments.

Since the ideas and planning concepts in this book have succeeded in many different countries and under a great variety of circumstances, the validity of these concepts has been duly established. Yet, until the application of these principles is more thorough or more universal, the ideal synthesis of the positive measures for urban improvement re-mains to be achieved. True quality in urban life—achievement of an attractive living environment for people of all income levels—remains an unfulfilled but worthy goal. The optimistic message of this book is that steady and perceptible progress *has* been attained and that positive experiences *are* transferrable.

Problems of the urban environment fall into three major areas: environmental, economic, and sociocultural.

Problems of environmental quality have to do with damaging air pollutants: general dirt and other emissions, noise, and smells; damage to the ecosystem, including plant life, animal life, and water; problems of aesthetics, including ugliness, monotony, and barrenness; and problems of spatial relationships: whether urban functions are integrated and supportive or severed and disjointed.

Economic problems of the urban environment center around the general decline as it becomes visible in the form of blight or decay, specifically:

Loss of customers, decline in sales, small business failures, or companies moving out
Decline in real estate values and income, high vacancy rates
Loss of tax revenues
Sense of barrenness, loss of security
Inability of established companies to hold good employees permanently
Inability to attract new company headquarters
General loss of jobs and revenues to the suburbs
Loss of the city's attraction as a regional center
Inability to attract major conventions

Finally, malaise, alienation, and anomie are some of the terms used to describe sociocultural breakdown. Breakdown may start with a loss of a sense of identity, of community, of belonging, or may be imposed by hostile outside forces, such as highway or urban planners, over which one senses one has no control. To counter this tendency, communication must be established and maintained, people must be involved, and concern for the quality of their daily environment must be convincingly demonstrated. It is obviously crucial to our national health that urban environments be made vital again, that we enhance and create rather than destroy important linkages, and that *cities for people* be accepted as today's primary imperative for the organization and design of the urban fabric.

Two pervasive urban trends, more than all others, have progressively eroded the hospitality of so many of our cities during recent decades:

1. Unrestrained, speculative development of real estate
2. Unlimited accommodation of cities to automobile traffic

Fortunately, the problem has become apparent within the past few years, and solutions have begun to emerge. International congresses, government commissions, local bodies, and planning experts have come to the same general conclusions:

Uncoordinated sprawl of business, industry, and housing must be restrained, and development must be subject to more thoughtful standards of planning and urban design.
Widespread destruction of existing buildings and urban spaces must cease, and the identity and physical resources of the built environment should be conserved, encouraging new development that harmonizes with the old.

The wholesale relocation of people and its attendant disruption of social fabric merely to achieve the economy of large-scale urban renewal must cease; instead, families and individuals already living in cities should be considered as the single most significant resource for tomorrow's urban re-formation.

The gross accommodation of urban land to automobile uses must be redressed, and the expensive sterility of excessive motorized traffic must be eliminated.

Problem: Low-Density Sprawl

"The Great American Landscape" could be the title of Figure 1-1, since it represents what one is so often likely to find across the country in urban and suburban America: this is Niagara Falls, New York. Low-density sprawl, with low-level infrastructure and low-quality aesthetics, sets off tall utility poles, unrestrained advertising, and high consumption of energy and land resources. Unhampered speculative development of land and total motorization of society has produced this condition in every part of the nation. Any indictment of the free-enterprise system of land development could use pictures of this sort as damaging evidence against it.

From the air, the ubiquity of sprawl, with its low level of services and high level of cookie-cutter aesthetic, becomes apparent. The aerial view in Figure 1–2 happens to be a suburb of Detroit, but its like can be found strangling any large city in the United States. Low-density sprawl of single-family detached dwellings as far as the eye can see has turned the suburban dream of getting away from it all into a nightmare. Low density forces commercial strips, whose profitability depends on the economics of size, to spread even further. Every store must be surrounded by asphalt to cater to an automotive clientele spread thin across a vast landscape. And utility companies can only afford to run their wires such distances through the air rather than underground.

The postwar urban dwellers' wave of migration from the cities to the beckoning greenery of the countryside has broken against other "green waves" moving outward from other urban centers, leaving behind an asphalt wasteland. Disillusionment with the cultural isolation and enforced automobility of suburbia has finally fostered a reverse migration to the urban centers—where the action is and where

Fig. 1–1. Niagara Falls, NY. Unrestrained advertising, low-density sprawl, and low-quality infrastructure add up to nonexistent aesthetics.

Fig. 1–2. Detroit, MI. The suburban nightmare: asphalt and low-density sprawl as far as the eye can see.

one is not forced to drive to everything—a significant movement of the late 1970s. The trend is now toward reversing the trend.

Urban Renewal: Euphemism; Urban Removal: Reality

The English town of Guildford in Surrey once had a closely knit, highly attractive, historic urban fabric. Yet its picturesque main street and a significant portion of its low-rise but densely massed buildings and functions were recently cleared for new construction (Figure 1–3). Destruction has become as familiar in the small city as in New York or Chicago. Tear down to build anew, perhaps leaving a church or two standing for sentimental reasons. Inevitably the new lacks the scale, the texture, or the character of the old, to say nothing of the humanizing personal associations.

What happens to the homes, to the delicate web of social interrelationships when such wholesale clearance is carried out? How many people who lived there before can ever move back again (Figure 1–4)? And if they could, how much of what they knew of their city would still be there for them? What happens to the people who see their neighborhoods, stores, shops, places of recreation, and acquaintances disappear? Is the march toward bigger and better taking them anywhere they want to go? Are they considered? Does anyone care? Both buildings and people have been treated too much as expendable items: no deposit, no return.

And finally, who benefits from all this transformation? When, in fact, renewal rather than mere clearance eventually takes place, how much of what gets built is for an entirely different purpose and for an entirely different clientele?

The very enormity of recent renewal projects is awe-inspiring in its power to obliterate even the memory of what has come before and transform whole sections of functioning cities. The area of Les Halles in Paris is representative of the scale, at least, of recent projects (Figures 1–5 and 1–6). The public, informed that the idea of central markets for the region located in the urban core was obsolete, was persuaded that the valuable land in the heart of the city should be better used for more up-to-date purposes. But the excavation grew and grew to encompass an area far larger than the market halls and far deeper than neighboring buildings were tall. The extraordinary urban character of central Paris, shaped by an organic growth process over the centuries, was suddenly dynamited from French soil to create . . . a mixed-use development: very modern, very profitable

Fig. 1–3 (top left). Guildford, England. The characteristic approach of urban removal despite the historic town's organic fabric.

Fig. 1–4 (bottom left). Guildford, England. What happens to the delicate web of social relationships when residential areas are bulldozed?

Fig. 1–5 (top right). Paris, France. Les Halles, where the central markets once stood, has become an excavation of truly messianic proportions.

Fig. 1–6 (bottom right). Paris, France. A modern mixed-use development in the historic setting of Les Halles. What will rise above the surface is yet to be determined.

Fig. 1–7. Lansing, MI. When the urban core is considered obsolete, what will prevent its total removal? The automobile benefits, but what is lost? (Photo: Courtesy of Michigan Department of State Highways)

(presumably), with underground roads, garages, and trains and a subterranean shopping center focused on a central open space called the forum. By 1980 aboveground development, other than a large, bleak power plant, had not been finally determined, but very expensive housing, offices, and many other new features are likely to be built.

After the pit reached an incredible depth and breadth, it was gradually refilled with reinforced concrete. The entire process took so long that, by the time the concrete reached ground level, presumably no one would recall what spatial relationships had existed before. Everything would be all new, all different. This modern way exploits an important urban site, wresting maximum commercial advantage from a particular location. But the particular location in this case has won its advantages largely because of what had developed there over the centuries. Is it urbanity or barbarism to ignore the responsibilities of rebuilding in historic surroundings? Wise city planning cooperates with the past, instead of totally obliterating it.

Thus, the matter of scale alone in urban development, as we shall presently see, requires a new and greater sensitivity if the human factor is not to be sacrificed along with the older buildings.

Problem: Loss of Image, Destruction of Functions

Ironically, widespread inner city devastation has occurred only through the unlikely marriage between the high purpose of renewing city centers and enormous financial support from the central governments. The urban renewal program inaugurated in the United States in 1949 presupposed that urban decay had its roots in obsolescence, that the only way to stop blight was to uproot and build anew on a larger scale, that new uses would always be better uses. An aerial view of Lansing, Michigan's capital city (Figure 1–7), illustrates the lamentable results.

Outsized structures, the most pernicious result of urban renewal, were spawned from the basic assumption that bigger is always better, that real progress could only be achieved by replacing many smaller buildings with fewer large ones. The aerial view of Lansing shows that virtually all of the blocks in the near distance, once covered with detached dwellings, were cleared to make way either for monolithic state office blocks or nothing more productive than automobile parking lots.

Thus, massive clearance was one of the foundation stones of urban renewal: governmental initiative enabling private enterprise "to rebuild . . . deteriorating parts of the city's structure to meet changing needs and functions of urban areas." Federal condemnation aid was required to overcome the problem of economically assembling "a tract large enough to support efficient, modern development and at the same time to withstand effects of adjacent blight."* The Urban Renewal Administration's muscle could avoid the acquisition costs of private development, which would all too often reflect inflated, speculative values.

A number of other underlying assumptions also characterized the heyday of urban renewal, and although we will discuss them more fully later, it is helpful to gain an early familiarity with what has devastated the fabric of the inner city, both in the United States and abroad.

The private entrepreneur played a major role in determining what was to be built and where.

The substance of cities was assumed to be deteriorating, apparently irreversibly, and their structures were therefore worthy of destruction.

Anything that might slow down the process of demolition was removed by government action.

The needs and functions of urban areas were assumed to be changing, i.e., always significantly different than what they had been.

Efficient, modern development was assumed to be automatically more desirable than whatever had been there before.

Modern development would always require larger parcels of land.

These reckless attitudes and the federal funds that gave them their impact caused the unholy combination of massive construction and great amounts of urban-center barrenness that characterizes Lansing, Minneapolis, Seattle, and so many other cities across our nation today. Countless numbers of sound, older structures that were making positive contributions to their communities and could have been easily rehabilitated to meet contemporary standards of usefulness were needlessly torn down. It was an easy way to liquidate older real estate assets at federal expense. Programs of urban renewal, including the so-called model cities in 1966, have resulted in nothing so much as a net loss of buildings, commerce, and economic viability.

* James Q. Wilson, ed. *Urban Renewal: The Record and the Controversy* (Cambridge, Mass.: The MIT Press, 1966), p. 190.

This net loss has continued unabated throughout the 1970s. Many more hectares of urban land in America were devastated and drastically altered in their functions, shape, and appearance by urban renewal than in the war-ravaged cities of Europe, some of which had their downtowns bombed to the point of almost total destruction.

Two cities in the United States have been widely considered exemplary in fending off decay and achieving a high degree of reinvestment in their downtown areas: Minneapolis and Seattle. They are also therefore particularly useful for our discussion. Since each has high-rise renewal structures, providing convenient observation platforms from which to photograph the character of its redevelopment, we are also fortunate to be able to graphically document trends in urban renewal that have become widespread.

Figures 1–8a, b, and c are views to the east, southeast, and west from atop the Investors' Diversified Services Tower, the tallest building in the center of downtown Minneapolis. As in most other sizable American cities, the streets of Minneapolis are arranged on an efficient grid pattern. The streets are wide and straight and, in Minneapolis, have been made even more efficient for heavy traffic by making them alternately one-way.

Despite the fact that Second World War hostilities never reached the American continent, the vast majority of buildings that stood in downtown Minneapolis until then have simply disappeared. The inordinate amount of building land the illustrations show devoted to surface-area parking lots is euphemistically called "land banking"— parcels assembled under urban renewal intended for supposedly efficient, modern development at a later date. Lest you hope that the older buildings still seen here have been selected to remain as a nucleus for the renewed city, let me add that most are scheduled to come down as "higher and better uses" are found for their sites.

The multistory parking garages, naturally, are scheduled to remain. In fact, as developers are found for building sites where cars are now stored, a great many *more* parking structures will be needed in the center of the city to accommodate the growing number of cars entering the central business district. There are no plans to limit or restrict the use of private automobiles for commutation into the center. With a population of only half a million, Minneapolis in a cordon count of 1975 showed a daily accumulation of 28,000 automobiles in the central business district. Yet there are more than 48,000 parking spaces available.

Fig. 1–8. Minneapolis, MN. Views to the east (8a), southeast (8b), and west (8c) from atop Investors' Diversified Services Tower. Surface-area parking is called "land banking."

The horrendous extent to which the automobile overwhelms a relatively small central business district is merely suggested in the views of Figure 1–8; indeed, land used solely to accommodate vehicles exceeds 67 percent.

Essentially nothing of venerable age or tradition has been allowed to survive; the few exceptions are surrounded by a sea of cars. One of the few surviving clusters of trees is directly in the path of expressway construction; the other remnants of nature have been systematically obliterated and paved over. The retail and office core has shrunk to a narrow bastion along the axis of the Nicollet transitway-mall, and the vast barren areas surrounding it on all sides allow very little possibility of reinforcement of commerce through continuity. Places of employment that somehow survive in the no-man's-land surrounding the high-value portion of the core have few non-work-hour attractions for employees besides ample parking.

It would appear that the good intentions of ur-

Fig. 1–9. Seattle, WA. View from the Space Needle. Moving and storing motor vehicles can become the primary use for urban land.

ban renewal advocates to remove deteriorating and obsolete urban substance dovetail with the good intentions of advanced traffic planners to relieve congestion and provide ample parking. One must conclude that both parties have here achieved their goals with remarkable effectiveness. But why did no one anticipate the degree to which achievement of those goals would conflict with other environmental, economic, and human goals so essential to the fruitful functioning of cities?

Unlike that of aerial pollution, the burden of visual pollution and physical obstruction is visible everywhere. The achievement of certain myopic goals has been used to justify vast devastation by incremental stages. Human factors of identity, in-

terest, pleasure, an attractive environment, and places of residence in direct relationship to the urban core have been overwhelmed by the bulldozer approach: sanitize the city and provide more space for cars. It is not only a matter of human concerns; such misuse of urban land is also uneconomical to the highest degree.

Why, then, have we so long tolerated a program of urban development with such drastic effects on human interests, social welfare, the quality of the environment, and the economy? The answer, initially, is that the original owners of the now unproductive properties have been bought off with government funds so that their parcels could be assembled and held for future development. They have had the windfall: their real estate holdings unexpectedly turned into cash with very little effort. They are not complaining. Nor are there any complaints from all of the voters who are able to use these cleared sites as inexpensive, handy parking places almost anywhere they wish, not only in Minneapolis, but throughout the United States.

The Space Needle built for the 1962 World's Fair in Seattle provides another opportunity to look down on portions of a city and examine an urban renewal far better suited to cars than to people. Figure 1–9b, a detail of 9a, shows that redevelopment of cleared land has progressed much further in Seattle than in Minneapolis. Yet the net effect is largely the same: an agglomeration of isolated buildings that are prevented from adding up to a city. All possibilities of connections and integration of civil functions have been preempted for the purposes of moving or storing vehicles. Streets have been expanded and connectors cut over, under, and through to such an extent that circulation and parking become the nearly exclusive land use. Where do people work? Off on the edges somewhere. Where do they live? The people's response is likely to be "As far away as possible."

Problem: Cities for Cars, Not for People

Every city dweller is familiar with congested streets; everyone now knows the intimidating force of four solid lanes of cars steadily flowing through a city center on one-way arterials. Most of us also have occasionally experienced skyways and concourses, with unhampered flow of pedestrians above or below the level of traffic. But how many people have seriously thought about the impact of all three of these familiar elements together? Congestion, four lanes moving on a one-way arterial, and pedestrians in skyways overhead: the main implication is that all street space belongs to cars. People, on the other hand, belong in buildings, and in order to let them pursue their various functions in those buildings, we need to build little tubes above grade so that they can get from one closed environment to another without interfering with the cars. Cities are for cars, not for people.

That is the message of this type of planning. It looks like the view west on 8th Street in Minneapolis, past the I.D.S. Center and across the Nicollet transitway-mall in the very heart of the city (Figure 1–10). This is not to say that conditions

are particularly bad in Minneapolis; bad is a relative term. But all physical evidence in Minneapolis demonstrates incontrovertibly that one of the highest goals of planning in that city, as it is in many others—with or without malls—in North America, is to achieve a maximum flow of private automobiles into and through the downtown area.

Throughout the 1960s it was widely assumed that planning to maximize movement and storage of automobiles in central urban areas was necessary, inevitable, and worst of all, desirable. Many people still cherish those views, although the recognition that cities are better with less traffic has grown substantially. One of the central purposes of this book is to demonstrate the nature of this new knowledge and to explain how the concepts work in application. Dominance of urban environments by automobiles, even were there no ongoing oil shortage, is neither necessary nor inevitable; it certainly is not desirable.

Even without the presence of four solid lanes (or six, eight, or ten) of moving traffic, even with an empty street to contemplate, the degree to which our urban environments have been transformed to accommodate automobiles is appalling. North State Street in Chicago (Figure 1–11) typifies the problem. The mythical utopia Shangri-La, here merely an "adults-only" movie house, competes with asphalt and many-storied parking garages. The modern residential complex first begins twenty stories up in the air, after all the needs of automobiles and "adults" have been first served below.

Yet, even before the gasoline crunch of 1979, an awareness that things ought to be different gradually developed in America. Principles of planning and urban development that actively oppose automobile movement and storage in central cities have been in formulation for several years. Characteristic of these are the following five principles articulated for downtown Denver.

1. The central city must have high-quality environment, transportation, employment, public safety, recreation, and public facilities to assure a quality of life adequate to attract and hold the people upon which its long-term success depends. The central business district must continue its development as Denver's most important resource.

2. Increased transit ridership to and from downtown should be encouraged and accommodated with improved waiting facilities, added bus routes, park-and-ride facilities, pro-

Fig. 1–10. Minneapolis, MN. Contemporary development practices seem to grant all street space to cars.

Fig. 1–11. Chicago, IL. Shangri-La on North State Street. The modern residential complex first begins twenty stories up.

Fig. 1–12. Los Angeles, CA. Introverted, nonkickable buildings impose their bulk on the city in the manner of fortresses.

visions for exclusive bus lanes, and planning for the integration of future transit guideways.
3. Internal pedestrian movement downtown should be developed with higher standards of design for walkway areas, street furnishings, planting, and surfacing, and with the careful placement of added plazas, arcades, and pedestrian bridges.
4. The efficiency of auto movement and related parking should be increased by routing major high traffic volumes around the high-density central business district core areas.
5. Air quality is a growing problem in the life of the metropolitan area. Every effort should be made to improve air quality and emission controls.*

The principles are excellent, but the political climate in America is still not yet sufficiently hospitable to a fundamental economic shift to realize these goals. Politics is all-important, since

powerful economic interests currently deriving benefit from the status quo are predictably opposed to changing the rules of the game. Public education, however, can be used to generate political support for improvement. Since no program will work if the business community is united in opposition, particular attention should be devoted to demonstrating that change will bring strong economic as well as social and environmental benefits. Successful programs in Germany, the Netherlands, Japan, Sweden, Great Britain, and many other countries have been carried out using essentially these tactics, as we will shortly see.

Problem: Destruction of Scale

One of the most serious problems of urban development has been its persistent obliviousness to the human scale in new construction. While scale can be considered in terms of sheer size—height, width, and bulk of buildings and the impact of spaces—it is also a matter of psychological response to the environment depending on variety, interest, and amount of sensory stimulus. Color, pattern, rhythm, texture, and a sense of density are all

* Denver, Colorado, Denver Planning Office, *Policies for the Development of Downtown Denver and Adjacent Areas,* 2nd rev., prepared by Downtown Denver, Inc., Central Area Development Committee, January, 1976.

URBAN REPAIR, NOT URBAN REMOVAL

aesthetic devices to achieve visual interest and a heightened sense of human scale. Vegetation, moving water, changes in elevation, and variety between openness and a sense of containment are among other vitalizing design devices. The most important factor of all, undoubtedly, is plain human activity.

Figure 1–12, a view in downtown Los Angeles, illustrates some of the worst abuses in current architectural and urban development practices. High-rise buildings impose their enormous bulk on the city in the manner of fortresses: completely inward-turning, uninviting, and highly protected against presumably hostile influences threatening from without. With a multistory parking garage on the right, barren concrete walls on the left, and closed protective surfaces everywhere, these are perfect, nonkickable buildings. Access is extremely limited, so that all one needs to do is to let down the portcullis and pull up the drawbridge at the first sign of danger. A few trees, of course, are added to screen the ominousness of this posture.

What this does to a sense of human scale and interest at street level is indicated in Figure 1–13. The hostile barrenness of an entire block of unrelieved concrete wall warmly invites the liveliness of obscene graffiti. Exterior architecture of this nature speaks of callousness to human needs, buildings as sculpture, not shelter, revealing a total disregard for the quality of the urban experience. Barrenness generated by the hostility of such architecture discourages pedestrians so much that people are forced to traverse the urban environment in cars, simply for the sake of security. Cause and effect become a vicious cycle reinforcing the interiorization of human activities and abandonment of street spaces to motorized traffic.

It is highly ironic that this interiorization should take place in Los Angeles, where the natural climate can be enjoyed year-round. Yet another irony lies in the fact that the new Bonaventure Hotel was designed by John Portman, who in 1978 was given a national award by the American Institute of Architects for his innovative hotel designs. The Bonaventure's interior incorporates all the innovations of exciting people-places made famous by Portman in his series of Hyatt-Regency Hotel designs of recent years: interesting variety of materials, patterns, textures, vegetation, pools and fountains, changes of elevation, contracting and opening spaces, and an interesting integration of many human activities—but all on the interior. The exterior is barren at street level.

What, we may well ask, are the reasons for the conscious design choice expressed in so many buildings today? Are those blank walls turned on the street for security reasons? Does it reflect a belief that the urbanity of street life is irretrievably lost?

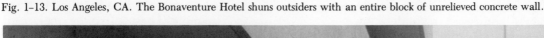

Fig. 1–13. Los Angeles, CA. The Bonaventure Hotel shuns outsiders with an entire block of unrelieved concrete wall.

Fig. 1–14. New York, NY. Is GRACE the right word for this empty space that replaced the shops once lining the streets at this corner?

Or is it a form of elitism, reserving architectural benefits only for paying customers? Does it reflect a conviction that streets indeed are for cars, not for people? Or is it merely a reflection of an insensitive developer and an uncaring planning commission? Or all of the above?

Whatever the case, to save the city from the developer, these tendencies should be strongly opposed by city planning commissions, chambers of commerce, citizens' groups, individual architects, and by everyone else convinced that cities must be hospitable environments for all social activities, high and low. Fortresslike buildings of concrete, steel, or glass that impose their bulk on the urban environment, exploiting the benefits of contact with urban density but giving little in return, must not be tolerated. Buildings today, as in the past, should be required to give in full measure for that which they receive from the urban environment. Developers and architects must be made aware of their larger responsibility to the best interests of the community.

A peculiar feature of American city planning is the existence of so-called zoning bonuses, financial inducements to encourage what are seen as socially desirable civic amenities, which will be nonincome producing, in the plans of commercial buildings. In return, developers are allowed greater height and greater rentable volume than would normally be possible to build under existing regulations. Such amenities—tree-lined pedestrian plazas, waterfalls, fountained courtyards, or galleries of pedestrian

ways lined with shops leading through a building from one side to another—are not always a good bargain. A logical result of such provisions is that whatever is required to obtain the bonus is done and frequently no more. Depending on the care with which the bonus regulations were written and the goodwill of the developer, the amenities provided may contribute much or little to the quality of the immediate urban environment.

A plaza attached to the Grace Building in New York is a good example of how mixed the results can be (Figure 1–14). While the admittedly handsome building soars on high, the northwest corner of the block has been left open to provide a large plaza, unfortunately largely devoid of sunshine. The space is, however, paved in travertine and another material to break up the vastness, and there are numerous trees in large pots. Positive design elements, yes? But does it add up to urbanity? Is this graceless, empty space really an amenity for people? Or is a single long row of expensive travertine benches, merely the fulfillment of a regulation, installed in a forecourt to serve the public-relations and zoning-bonus needs of the company? Can this emptiness be considered more desirable than the shops that once lined both intersecting streets at this corner? Clearly, mere open space alone is not an amenity and should be used judiciously in city planning.

Another imposition on the scale of urban spaces is oversize advertising. Attractive cityscapes can be ruined as easily as the countryside by the crass in-

URBAN REPAIR, NOT URBAN REMOVAL

Fig. 1-15. New York, NY. The colossal Winston ad north of Madison Square Garden characterizes the presumptuousness of nonrooted advertising.

general public. Signs of this type can be considered as desirable public communication, since they aid the finding of necessary goods and services. When signs attempt, however, to attract attention through visual dominance in size, shape, location, color, flashing lights, or other incongruities, a distinct transgression upon the aesthetic rights of urban citizens occurs. For this reason, many cities of the world have developed sign ordinances that forbid anything with the overbearing nature of the Winston sign.

Among the basic concepts underlying sign ordinances is one forbidding unrooted signs in particular types of urban spaces. A rooted sign appears on a building to represent a company, service, product, or activity directly associated with that building—in other words, a form of communication: here is the place. An unrooted sign, on the other hand, is any sign unrelated to the place where it is located. American billboards are classic examples: visual pollution that degrades any quality environment. They should be banned.

Many types of sign ordinances are designed to improve the visual quality of urban environments. They employ rules concerning size, shape, configuration, height above the street, illumination, and even relationship to other aesthetic elements in the space. It is impossible to set up any but the broadest standards for many different situations; nonetheless *some* standards must be established for each situation and procedures for aesthetic control must be instituted. Signage regulations are an integral part of every program to improve high-density urban areas.

Problem: Speculative Development and the Debasement of Older Buildings

Cities are vital entities that constantly grow and develop. Change is inevitable; yet it makes a great deal of difference to the quality of urban life if change takes place according to a plan intended to benefit the community or if it is at the mercy of the self-interest of developers and speculators operating with the perfect assurance of federally sponsored legal and financial backing. Speculation in real estate, i.e., buying or building in anticipation of making a profit, is a firmly rooted element in the capitalistic countries and is by no means a negative or unproductive activity. But, unrestrained, it can have devastating effects on existing urban environments and can completely vitiate planning efforts.

trusion of someone's advertising message. The aesthetic accomplishments of architecture and planning can be totally overwhelmed by out-of-scale signs, as in the case of a Winston cigarette ad north of Madison Square Garden in New York City (Figure 1-15). The sheer size and dominance of this type of message is one good reason to ban it altogether from the central city. No one should be forced to have a commercial message so insistently intrude upon his or her experience of a city.

Commerce is the central element in almost every city, and every business should have the right to use signs to identify itself and/or its product to the

Fig. 1–16. Boston, MA. The results of speculation alone as the principal determinant of city building: haphazard, coarse-grained urban texture.

Totally unrestricted enterprise within a coercive urban redevelopment climate inevitably brings seriously negative changes for the community.

Overbuilding goes hand in hand with speculation. In times of prosperity the market demand for buildings for all activities tends to increase at a faster rate than population growth and even at a faster rate than monetary inflation itself. A prime example is the enormous boom in office construction over the past two decades. Overbuilding of a similar nature, including increased use of spatial volume per person, can be observed in residences, schools, commercial buildings and other quasi-public buildings such as hotels and sports arenas as well. Prosperity leads to overbuilding; the call for more building means an overly rapid change of urban environments that in turn accelerates the demolition and removal, rather than rehabilitation and preservation, of the civil fabric.

Figure 1–16 is a graphic illustration of this insidiously circular process in action in Boston. The relative height and bulk of the new structures correspond to no concept or rational plan but reflect instead the speculations and land dealings of the developers in each case and in each particular period. The result is a haphazard, coarse-grained texture to the city: low-rise, medium-rise, and high-rise buildings bearing no supporting relationship to each other and interspersed with random open spaces such as the handsome parking lot in the foreground that is being transformed into a bus

depot in 1980. Chaotic results of this nature, the opposite of sound urban development, can be avoided. With careful analysis of need, accurate demographic and economic forecasting, and subordination of private interest to long-range urban development planning, the inner city can live again. Speculation alone as the principal fuel for city-building enriches individuals but impoverishes the community.

While the concept of building tall buildings was rationalized during the first flush of urban renewal as a means of concentrating development on limited amounts of land in order to open cities to grand landscaped open spaces, the reality has been quite different. Far from retaining the same or similar density arranged in a different, more humane pattern, high-rise construction has brought about radical changes in land use that have rarely resulted in net gain in urban amenity for people, although it has usually resulted in net gain in the developer's bank account. Plazas, galleries, trees, and fountains, where they have been provided, have usually been a form of tokenism designed to distract attention from great increases in floor-area ratios, i.e., intensity of use on particular building sites. In downtown areas of major cities, most notably in New York City, high risers have primarily resulted in great increases in density of land use.

Commonly, however, high-rise buildings have had an additional blighting effect on land in the immediate vicinity. Once it becomes possible to use land for tall buildings, the value of contiguous urban land soars and the value of neighboring low-rise buildings plummets. Inducement to maintain or upgrade older, low-rise structures tends to disappear in view of the windfall profits to be realized from sale of sites for high-rise development. Neglect and decay are the inevitable results, speeded by massive federally funded urban renewal programs enabling owners to liquidate their assets even where there are no immediate prospects for new development. The sad result across the United States is an incongruous mixture of high-rise and low-rise buildings or high-rise and empty land, instead of rationally planned development.

A view from the Trade Center (Figure 1–17) in downtown New Orleans shows the effect of this process. Older commercial buildings simply mark time in the shadows of new skyscrapers, decay from neglect, and wait to be razed for new development. Concentrating so much new building volume on limited amounts of land in a very low-density city that needs repair of vast areas is certainly not justified by city-planning considerations; the practice is designed to maximize profits for major capital investors: benefit for the few, but at the expense of the many.

And in the case of New Orleans, as can be seen in this particular view, another gross example of space inflation looms in the distance: the hulking new Louisiana Superdome, spanning an incredible two hundred meters. With the subsidiary structures and huge parking facilities associated with a public-events center of this size, it is apparent that many square blocks of existing urban fabric had to be wiped off the face of the city to provide room for this behemoth. While an occasional mammoth event on the scale of a Super Bowl football game, such as that of January, 1981, may pump many millions of dollars into the city's economy, this vast area is desolate most of the time. In terms of its impact on continuity of functions and urban linkages, a project of this magnitude is sheer folly, another example of throw-away city.

The structure is of enormous bulk, serving as an effective blockage to urban connections over a very large area. Most of the time the spaces around this facility are totally dead, since it can be used only for intermittent events. And at times when the events are scheduled, the deathly emptiness is transformed into an environmental burden of enormous proportions due to the influx, storage, and egress of endless numbers of cars. Placing a large stadium in an urban area is the equivalent of writing off that area as a total loss for any other useful function in the city. Downtown stadiums are

Fig. 1–17. New Orleans, LA. Neglect and decay result when high rise is coupled with low density. The mammoth Superdome, devouring acres of valuable urban space, only compounds the problem.

an abrogation of the responsibility to repair and rejuvenate urban fabric. They epitomize the approach of urban removal.

A northerly view from the same vantage point (Figure 1–18) shows the famed Canal Street of New Orleans, the beginning of the historic French Quarter that extends further east (to the right). The Marriott Hotel, with its forbidding fortresslike lower surfaces of blank concrete extending higher than adjacent buildings, is spoken of with subconscious defensiveness as being not *in* the French Quarter, merely *adjacent* to it, implying that a mammoth new skyscraper is somehow not infringing on the architectural fabric of historic New Orleans. Actually, the area east of Canal Street *was* the French Quarter until infringed upon by such insensitive, scale-demolishing concrete-slab buildings. And the Marriott didn't stay lonesome for long. A cleared, 23-acre site beginning at the lower right corner of this view has had a thirty-two story office tower built as the first part of an enormous, mixed-use development including several towers and a 500-room luxury hotel.

Fig. 1–18. New Orleans, LA. The Marriott Hotel on Canal Street is supposedly not *in* the historic French Quarter, but only adjacent to it.

Thus does speculation in the sheep's clothing of urban renewal change the face of American cities at a pace unequaled by anything since New York's building binges of the late 1920s. And by far the greatest impact on our cities results from the massive office towers built by controllers of large capital resources: banks, insurance companies, oil companies, multinational conglomerates, oil-producing countries, or combinations of these. Because an influx of capital in any form is welcomed by the money-starved cities of the United States, such gift horses are almost always welcomed by municipalities, regardless of their impact on urban environments. And all too often even the cities themselves naively function as developers of monumental scale-destroying projects.

Interesting parallel views of hopelessly outsized new building sore-thumbing its way across the country are to be seen along Broadway in Denver (Figure 1–19) and along Fourth Avenue in Minneapolis (Figure 1–20). High rise/low density is the best expression for this increasingly common feature of our urban skylines: tall, massive buildings surrounded by large open spaces used primarily for moving and storing automobiles. Formerly impressive civic and religious monuments with their exuberantly designed sculptural towers are overwhelmed by huge, barren, new monuments to commerce. Actually, in the case of Minneapolis, the new building is merely a bloated substitute for the old, housing the same city and county legislators, administrators, and courts. While it does provide some landscaped public open space around it and has a decorative atrium running the full height of the building within, why has there been such numbing repudiation of all human scale? Is enormous size, after all, an inescapable principle of American urban planning? Are there no more sensitive ways to satisfy spatial needs—even if inflated—than to erect skyscrapers amidst the bulldozed wastelands of once vital urban areas?

Before we, temporarily, leave the subject of scale, let's take a quick look at Madison, the state capital of Wisconsin, with a population of about 175,000. Like Minneapolis and Denver it has gone through a devastating period of urban renewal that

Fig. 1–20. Minneapolis, MN. Part of the new city-county building contrasted with the old—a numbing repudiation of all human scale.

Fig. 1–19. Denver, CO. Formerly impressive civic and religious monuments are overwhelmed by new monuments to commerce.

Fig. 1–21. Madison, WI. More results of urban renewal: "land banking" in the foreground and modern, up-to-date land uses in the background.

Problem: Excessive Transfer of Land Uses

The appropriation of central urban areas, particularly residential ones, for parking lots and telephone facilities has a serious impact on the character and viability of the city as *home*, with its integration of comforts, associations, facilities, and activities. Any total transfer of uses from integrated civic functions to heavily one-sided commercial, industrial, or purely utilitarian use means a loss of the very human qualities cities should be trying to foster.

Even a transfer to public open space from such formerly integrated commercial, industrial, and residential uses can cause a loss of urban quality, as we can see from the gross mistake that was once the heart of downtown St. Louis—the area between the Mississippi riverfront, the cathedral, and the courthouse. This area, once throbbing with life as a major outfitting and jumping-off point for the westward expansion of America, is now a lifeless monument to itself—an empty grassy plain at the base of the Westward Expansion Memorial Arch (Figure 1–22). Here, too, urban renewal has taken the clean-sweep approach, removing everything, then justifying the emptiness by calling it a park. Quite aside from the fact that the park is unimaginative in design and extremely poor in plantings and furnishings (recently improved), the area itself has almost completely lost any natural relationship to the fabric of the city.

Figure 1–23 is a view from the top of the same Memorial Arch, giving some sense of the spotty development of St. Louis's downtown area in recent years. Interstate highway construction, extensive road widenings, construction of isolated highrise towers, and the introduction of the disruptive new land uses of a downtown stadium and extensive parking facilities have left the cathedral (at the right in Figure 1–22) and courthouse sitting high and dry, bereft of the last vestiges of an urban setting that gave their architecture meaning. This token historic preservation retains the urban remnant of a few individual buildings as if they were quaint but interesting Christmas tree ornaments, but leaves them no healthy civic functions or attractive spatial relationships with which to draw people.

Large open spaces, great volumes of motorized traffic, a large stadium, oppressively boring modern architecture: as if these weren't enough to disjoint and distend the urban body, a new grassy mall the full width of the old courthouse is to ex-

removed residential population and small businesses from large chunks of its central area and replaced many older buildings with vast areas of "land banking"—parked cars. Figure 1–21 is a detail view showing the characteristic change in scale. The architectural environment must now be viewed above a plinth of cars. Older houses and apartments, many of which had been allowed to deteriorate while being rented to students at the state university, have been bulldozed away. The modern, up-to-date land uses the urban renewal program was intended to encourage are frequently those that strip the city of its former appearance and scale. Some of the resulting buildings—telephone company facilities in this case—have the grace and inviting attractiveness of a concrete iceberg, to which they bear a distinct similarity. Is it any wonder that many people are beginning to feel that if this is progress, they would prefer to remain old-fashioned?

Fig. 1–22. St. Louis, MO. The park of the Western Expansion Memorial Arch along the Mississippi replaces the once throbbing heart of St. Louis.

Fig. 1–23. St. Louis, MO. New highways, road widenings, high-rise towers, and parking facilities leave the historic cathedral and courthouse high and dry.

tend from there west to the new courthouse (peaked roof in the distance) and beyond. This empty axis, approximately as attractive in design as the park beneath the Arch, will further separate main functions downtown, virtually enforcing the use of cars to overcome the unrelieved distances between functions.

Problem: Antipedestrianism

The excessive change in scale accompanying the transfer of land uses in St. Louis is not unique at all; indeed it typifies most modern development, certainly in the United States, and often in other countries as well. The pedestrian scale has usually been so forgotten that linkages and interesting paths from place to place have been all but totally disrupted by the insertion of lengthy, monotonous stretches, barriers, and hazards. The monotony of new buildings is not *meant* to be looked at and contemplated, but merely driven by, ideally at a good rate of speed to avoid congestion.

Most important of all, we must remember that the loss of attractiveness due to loss of interest and human scale in urban spaces and buildings has distinct economic repercussions. It fosters a whole cycle of negative social effects: successful price competition from suburban shopping centers, decline in numbers of central business district shoppers and sightseers, declining retail sales, bankruptcies, loss of revenues from real estate, reduced tax revenues, and increase in crime.

The reverse is a city perceived by its citizens as being attractive, in which they can walk and expect to find an interesting variety of sights and pleasant discoveries: humanly scaled spaces with interesting structures and public examples of the builder's art and craft, a richer variety of goods and services located more closely together than anywhere else, a sense of uniqueness of place, and an atmosphere of comfort, security, and relaxation. Bigger is not better, shinier is not nicer, and a free parking place is not the ultimate good in a truly humanistic city plan.

Converting street spaces from car to pedestrian use most effectively returns a sense of scale to urban environments. While this measure obviously does not affect the height of buildings, it does make all contained urban spaces that are still worth it more capable of being experienced, their details and interesting features more readily observable. But there must be a relatively continuous progression of building frontages interesting to people, without

tedious "land banks," parking garages, or block-long concrete walls.

Bonn, the capital of Germany, is only one of over five hundred German cities that have now *pedestrianized* significant portions of their central areas, most of them since 1972. The concept in Bonn involves the development of an extensive interconnected network of streets for people covering almost the entire central business district. One can sense the liveliness that develops even on ordinary working days in pedestrianized urban spaces. Pedestrianizing, which has caught on like wildfire in Europe within the past few years, has been likened by downtown merchants to the finding of a philosophers' stone—the very paving blocks turned to gold.

Although planning such a radical conversion of a downtown area from heavy use by cars into primary use by pedestrians requires careful consideration, the results in hundreds of cases the world over have been no less than phenomenal. Rather than depriving one group in order to benefit another—so often the case with so-called improvements—pedestrianization has been accepted as a boon to all groups, all ages, all income levels. In Chapter Three, we will see exactly how this miracle is wrought, but for now we must finish our discussion of urban repair and its effect on the scale of streetscapes.

In Germany, where planning for pedestrians has advanced to a quite sophisticated level, the character of the recent architecture of Bonn's Remigius-strasse (Figure 1–24) has received strong local criticism for its lack of scale and its destruction of a sense of unique local character. By American standards, interestingly enough, the buildings would be considered quite small and their facade treatment quite reasonable in contemporary urban environments. Many Germans, however, want to correct the tendency toward blank, modern, anonymous, "anyplace" architecture generally preferred by chainstores, developers, and large corporations.

Local color sells well, and apparently people in our modern, impersonal, mechanized western society are in constant need of externals with which they can identify. A growing popularity for things old, including especially older architecture, seems to be an encouraging cultural development of recent years. Older buildings seem more inviting, perhaps because of interesting detail, craftsmanship, color, texture, or other artfulness that satisfies basic psychological needs.

In one of our own most historic cities, we do not have to search far to find the scale-destroying

Fig. 1–24. Bonn, West Germany. Only one of over five hundred German cities that have pedestrianized their central areas: a boon to all citizens.

Fig. 1–25. Boston, MA. Pedestrianized since this photo was taken, Winter Street still must contend with the scale-destroying qualities of the Provident Building.

Fig. 1–26. Philadelphia, PA. If the sky is the limit for development, does the historic city with which people identify stand a chance?

come to see. Notable examples of such spaces exist in Boston, why not in its central business district? Certainly the great success, almost next door, of the Faneuil Hall-Quincy Market restoration should demonstrate the many possibilities for financial gain in sensitive rehabilitation of older architecture.

Unfortunately, neither a Faneuil Hall, nor even Boston's Old City Hall, now successful in its new role as prestige office space, can compete in financial terms if a far larger building can be built on the same site. If maximization of financial gains is the goal and the sky is the limit for development, no amount of human scale, interesting detail, or potential usefulness for a variety of significant purposes can preserve the older architecture. The potential financial benefits from this type of development are simply too great to withstand.

Therefore, urban decision makers in every city must confront the issue of whether urban development is to be left to investors or seen as a legitimate concern of the guardians of the people's larger interest. If the latter, building regulations and guidelines must go beyond mere tokenism—a plaza here, a public sculpture there, and some scattered trees in pots in exchange for massive high-rise developments of very high floor-area ratios. In the case of the area in Philadelphia immediately adjacent to City Hall (Figure 1–26), for instance, development of this type is unquestionably highly efficient and likely to give a very high return on the investment dollar. But this is definitely not the type of environment that can easily rouse citizens' affection for their city or their desire to pursue leisure-time activities there. Instead, this type of psychic environment fosters anomie and alienation, foreshadowing the mechanized world of George Orwell's *1984*, complete with Big Brother watching via closed-circuit television.

The fact that certain parts of such cities as London and Paris—and many others—are no better than the Philadelphia situation is no reassurance. Modern architecture, touted as the molder of a more perfect urban society as seen in the once new monuments to world order and enlightened commerce as the United Nations Secretariat or the Lever Building in New York City, has become with the years a crashing bore. Take the case of the London Wall area near St. Paul's Cathedral in London (Figure 1–27). This photograph was taken on a Saturday and is characteristic of the civic desert that exclusively commercial office districts become when business is closed. Yet there is a hopeful sign here, visible in the tower and balconies at the far

qualities of modern building design—dull facade coupled with sheer height and bulk—such as that of the Provident Bank Building on Boston's narrow, old commercial Winter Street in the very heart of its central business district (Figure 1–25). To commercially exploit a small urban site, a building soars into the sky. This type of impudent disregard for the larger interests of the central city violates fundamental rules and principles of city planning. In most of the countries of Western Europe such a gross clash with established street scale in a downtown area would not be tolerated. Perhaps the time will come in America too when preserving the scale and architectural qualities of existing street spaces will play a major role in urban planning, conserving attractive, recognizable urban environments that people come to love and visitors

Fig. 1–27. London, England. Inventive commercial redevelopment can quickly become hackneyed, but the walkway system and the new Barbican housing development are hopeful signs.

right. A significant area of this commercial heart of London has been reserved for housing in the Barbican Development. Although the project was incomplete at the time this photograph was taken, the integration of high-density housing with high-density office concentration is an excellent attack on the problem of urban sterility resulting from excessive separation of functions. Steps in this direction are being taken in many cities, notably Battery Park City next to New York's World Trade Center, and should be strongly encouraged.

Another encouraging characteristic of the more enlightened developments is apparent in the foregoing view of London Wall: the presence of continuous linkages for pedestrians. A concept already realized in the commercial/office complex of New York's Rockefeller Center of the 1930s, continuous linkages for pedestrians, separated from street traffic, have been largely neglected since the Second World War and are only lately being incorporated again in urban design. In London, Minneapolis, and Cincinnati the new systems are walkways above grade; in Toronto, Montreal, and Philadelphia the continuous pedestrian movement is below grade at the concourse level; in Munich, Copenhagen, and Rome, however, complete networks of walking spaces are provided, where they should be, at grade level.

Fig. 1–28. Paris, France. Overwhelming scale, paucity of ideas, and lack of humanity on a modern pedestrian plaza at La Defense.

With the almost universal provision of central air conditioning and sophisticated artificial lighting in new construction today, more and more extensive areas reserved for pedestrians are being created in entirely closed architectural environments. The huge new development of La Defense in western Paris is a prime example of this: massive towers rise from an enormous pedestal filled with commercial and communication spaces linking the various towers. The space within the pedestal makes no use of daylight or the natural environment, but the area on top of it is designed as a large-scale pedestrian plaza, with trees, benches, flowers, and a monumental sculpture by Alexander Calder.

Figure 1–28, however, illustrates the extent to which such good concepts as pedestrian areas can miscarry. Overwhelming scale, paucity of ideas, and lack of humanity could hardly be more appalling than in parts of the La Defense development. The marvelous qualities of vibrant urbanity that have made Paris beloved of countless generations of natives and visitors alike are here voided with seemingly utter disdain. As if to add insult to injury, the barren wasteland has been provided with a (nonfunctioning) suggestion box. Anyone have any ideas?

Ten Guidelines: Positive Qualities of Historic Spaces

Rome has long been one of the great models of urban design, and its famous Piazza di Trevi has served as an urban focal point since it was built by Nicola Salvi in the eighteenth century (Figure 1–29). While not every plaza can be as artistically successful as the Trevi, some general principles of successful urban design can be derived from it.

First of such principles is a sense of place, recognizability. The central sculpture provides a unique character that makes it immediately interesting. Uniqueness doesn't have to stem from a Bernini or a Rodin or Calder, but a particularity, one might even say a peculiarity, helps.

Second is a sense of containment. Oxford University's Town Quad, Boston's Louisburg Square, the Alhambra Garden, have it. Psychological satisfactions are far greater in a space like the Trevi that is readily comprehensible and offers a sense of protective enclosure. Wide open spaces and endlessly long, straight streets tend to make people feel unprotected and uncomfortable. The spatial needs for efficient operation of motor vehicles are exactly the opposite of what urban spaces must have to make

them psychologically satisfying. No cars, obviously, in the Piazza di Trevi.

Consequently, the third principle is the separation of traffic from urban spaces to make them safer and more comfortable for pedestrians. An autoless Piazza di Trevi acts as an urban living room, a safe, enjoyable, contained urban space for relaxation and social communication.

A fourth design feature is the employment of elevation changes, which add, in this case, to the sense of containment, comfort, and focus. The soft, curving shapes of the stairs, benches, and pool rim provide amphitheatrical seating in great quantities, immediately available, while the walls and railings at different elevations are a constant invitation to pause and observe other people.

A fifth basic lesson to be learned from this historic space is that an urban place must provide reasons for people to want to go there. Many reasons here could be cited: the uplifting effect of monumental architecture and sculpture, the pleasant sensory stimulus of splashing water and a large pool, a chance to sit and have something to look at such as shops and restaurants or other people, or just the fact that the space is on the way between many destinations in the central city.

Sufficient places to sit is a sixth principle seen at the Trevi but is almost always an afterthought in modern urban spaces.

Seventh, already suggested, is the importance —belatedly discovered by restaurateurs with outdoor tables in the United States—of human activity to watch.

Shops and a source of food and drink are point eight, amenities that are always welcome everywhere. This satisfies not only psychological, but physical needs as well. The Trevi, incidentally, has several convenient spouts of the finest drinking water in Rome.

Relating directly to architectural design of the space are principles nine, materials and textures of aesthetic quality, and ten, plant materials and water. The emphasis at the Trevi is, of course, on aesthetic materials and water: marvelous textures in interesting combinations, a sensuous play of water over the carved rocks, and the lavishness of a pool that covers almost half the area of the square.

But what about those older buildings? Is not the contrast with these disheveled, irregular, ordinary, even ugly old houses also part of the composition? Do not the fountain (and the church, off the picture to the left) gain greatly from the containment and contrast offered by these seemingly unimportant buildings? One shudders to think what an ur-

Fig. 1–29. Rome, Italy. Many lessons on urban quality can be learned by studying the characteristics of historic plazas like the Piazza di Trevi.

ban renewal specialist would recommend: "Tear that old junk out of there. It's unsound and aesthetically worthless. And, besides, we need some room for the tour buses . . . and parking for tourists' cars and toilet facilities and cafeterias, and, and . . . modern functions for an up-to-date city."

While the suggestion that urban renewal as we know it would destroy the setting for the Fontana di Trevi may seem absurd, it isn't that far-fetched: that is precisely what renewal programs have done in city after city in the United States. The net loss of culture, comfort, and community has been a national tragedy greater than the removal of the entire Piazza di Trevi, fountain and all. The chipping away at America's urban cultural heritage in the name of progress and renewal has caused a loss of unimaginable proportions. And the destruction continues today.

In place of the countless small local equivalent Piazzas di Trevi that have been swept away (typically the statue or monument left standing but its architectural setting destroyed, its base diminished, and asphalt lapping at its feet), Americans have had to make do with malls, plazas, and assorted other nondescript, sleek environments.

A notable exception, the Crystal Court, part of the Investors' Diversified Services complex in Minneapolis (Figure 1–30) is a strikingly good example of the principles of an ideal urban space discussed

above (save the decorative use of water and sufficient seating).

It is no coincidence, when one compares the Crystal Court to the Piazza di Trevi, that the principal design firm of the Crystal Court was Johnson & Burgee. Philip Johnson was an architectural historian before becoming an architect. Historical precedent has here been applied adroitly, and the Crystal Court has, in fact, become the most popular urban space in Minneapolis.

If only more architects could learn their lessons from history as well as Philip Johnson has, American city centers would become far more attractive places for pedestrians, workers, tourists, and businesses. The actual amenities of the Crystal Court, of course, are only one part of it. Such a major success stems from coupling these amenities with the character of an urban square for pedestrians. Crystal Court is a great meeting place, a crossing of routes coming from different directions, and above all conveys the feeling of a space sensitive to the needs and responses of individual pedestrians.

One must ask, however, whether such quality spaces can be purchased only at the price of removing everything from the past and replacing it with new high-rise development. Why must we create brand-new, commercially sponsored urban plazas in interior environments when the makings of genuine public urban plazas already exist in most of our cities? Instead of constantly removing and replacing, why not begin with more sensitive *repair-*

Fig. 1–30. Minneapolis, MN. If only more architects would follow the example of those who designed Crystal Court and learn their lessons from historic urban spaces . . . .

ing? The crucial first step is to stop the devastation, economically and politically profitable though it is to some entrenched interest groups.

A major and instructive distinction between the cities of Central Europe and those of North America should be borne in mind: whereas the former were destroyed by wartime forces from without, the latter were destroyed by peacetime forces from within. Urban blast has been a voluntary act in America and, therefore, not the object of reconstructive fervor to regain what had been lost, even with some sacrifice of money and effort. But a national sensitivity to irreparable loss is finally beginning to develop on these shores, and more and more Americans are beginning to realize that if we *want* to save something, we *can* save it. Decay is not an inevitable process, but rather the result of neglect.

We need to discard renewal rhetoric and begin to insist on the concept that old uses may indeed be the best uses, particularly when they involve people living in cities. Social and commercial interplay, not separation of uses, makes cities into vital places for people. Older buildings that have declined can be rejuvenated, frequently for exactly the purposes originally intended. Why assume that modern uses must be different uses, that small sites must be assembled into development packages, at great cost to the community, for uses that have sprung from the mind of a city planner rather than from the experience of the community? Why accept disruption of functions, destruction of relationships, major changes in scale, transformations of land use, dominance by cars and high-rise buildings?

There are alternatives. They have proven to be viable, economical, and environmentally sound. They may be difficult, they may require great effort and investment, and they will not lack opponents. But the destruction has gone far enough. At issue today is the saving of cities before the last testament to our predecessors' civility has disappeared. Repairing existing fabric of buildings, spaces, environmental qualities, infrastructure, and sociocultural interrelationships is the essence of the solution. Urban repair, not urban removal.

The most important first step is to free urban environments from the overwhelming burden of automobiles and the traffic structures necessary for their accommodation. Clearly, access to city centers and movement of both goods and people

Fig. 1–31. Munich, West Germany. Formerly a principal traffic route through the city, this axis is now a pedestrian's paradise.

can be greatly improved by simply reducing the absolute volume of motorized traffic in cities. Moreover, the environmental impact of remaining traffic can also be greatly reduced. But an overall movement strategy should serve only as the beginning of a comprehensive program aimed at repairing the physical fabric of cities and restructuring vital interrelationships of functions. Dividing cities into segregated functional zones has sterilized the life out of them. The secret of revitalization is reintegration.

A view of downtown Munich serves to point up some of the grander possibilities of traditional urban integration (Figure 1–31). We ask the reader to envision this "main drag," the Kaufingerstrasse–Neuhauserstrasse intersection, in its former state as the principal traffic route for east-west traffic through the city, filled with cars, buses, trucks, exhaust, and streetcars. Pedestrians were jammed on narrow sidewalks along the storefronts on both sides, and a trip to shop downtown was a matter of risking life, limbs, or lung disease. Today we see a pedestrians' paradise, without traffic accidents or pollution, with high levels of retail sales—a remarkable center of attraction for people of all

ages, walks of life, and income levels, and a far greater tourist attraction than ever before. The character *is* transferrable, as we shall see in the following chapters.

This urban repair magic can be worked in any city, of any size, anywhere. Such dramatic changes, however, do not come about through mere ad hocism or by following existing trends. Saving cities from the strong downhill slide so many are currently on requires strong remedial action. But age of buildings, size of population, nature of modal split, and/or job distribution do not preclude an urban environment's developing toward a city for people. There is simply no longer any question of what will and what won't work.

The balance of this book is an attempt to analyze, comment on, and gather, for the purposes of precept, examples of planned urban re-formation undertaken in a great many cities in a number of countries. Our ultimate goal in every case is to save the civilization of the city for the fuller use and enjoyment of its people.

Better Towns with Less Traffic

Enhance Environmental Quality, Improve Infrastructure

In recent years the proper role of automobiles in urban environments has been endlessly debated. From the end of the Second World War until the 1960s, cities and national governments everywhere saw vehicular traffic as the lifeblood of a vital economy, to be given every encouragement to flow freely and fully. But as an outgrowth of worldwide social unrest, increased environmental concern, and disenchantment with so-called progress, particularly the increase in numbers of cars per person as well as mushrooming urban sprawl and resulting public sanction for indiscriminate roadbuilding, the late 1960s saw the establishment in most major industrial countries of national Ministries of the Environment (in the United States, the Environmental Protection Agency). The oil embargo of

1973–74 further threatened the universal middle-class dream of personal automobility, while the 1979 OPEC escalation of petroleum prices has cast the automobile in the role of villain.

The first international conference of Ministers of the Environment, in Paris in 1974, laid the foundation for a substantive meeting of planning experts on the subject of better towns with less traffic, which took place the following year. These experts concluded that significant improvements in urban environmental quality could realistically be achieved through relatively quick, low-cost measures to reduce the volume of motorized traffic in cities.

The Paris conference urged planners to apply the following guidelines:

1. Seek a new balance between individual and public transport and urge authorities to im-

prove the quality of public transport facilities and promote their use where scope for this alternative existed

2. Initiate low-cost schemes for increasing the speed of buses, providing cycle tracks, promoting the sharing of private cars, improving parking arrangements, and establishing traffic-free zones

3. Introduce complementary low-cost improvements such as small squares and parks and pedestrian areas

4. Devise new procedures for putting the foregoing ideas into effect, to study their financial and town-planning implications, and to take part in intergovernmental exchange of views

5. Reduce the demand for transport by changing patterns of land uses and by altering patterns of human behavior*

To illustrate some of the concepts outlined above and to suggest their universal applicability, I have gathered examples from some fifty cities in a dozen countries over a three-year period. Although urban structures, levels of automobile ownership, and other physical and social conditions vary considerably from place to place, the major problems, their causes, and the methods most likely to succeed in solving them are often similar in industrially developed countries. The exposition of ideas and techniques that have proven workable in these major cities during the past fifteen years is a means of assuring that those early successes can be shared by ever more cities on a worldwide basis.

A view from the center of London (Figure 2–1) suggests some of the basic qualities at stake. A safe, pleasant, and attractive environment for pedestrians is fundamental to the successful conduct of human affairs in cities. Equally important for the support of human activities is the actual infrastructure of cities, the basic facilities, equipment, services, and installations needed for the growth and functioning of a community.

A number of factors determine the environmental quality of the space: the architecture that defines the containing walls and provides aesthetic interest; the horizontal surfaces, paved or otherwise, that form the floor; trees and other vegeta-

tion; lamps, fences, benches, telephone booths, and other furnishings; the people in the spaces; and the character, size, and number of motor vehicles passing through. Immediately apparent aspects of infrastructure include the amount and quality of lighting, availability of telephones, toilet facilities, a taxicab stand, public buses, and interrelationships among the various functions within the buildings. In London, as in other cities, pressure for increasing volumes of motorized traffic through such spaces provides a greater threat to the quality of the environment and infrastructure than any other factor. The concern of citizens and public officials alike should be to protect and enhance both environment and infrastructure in the face of this threat.

A contrasting view from the center of Naples (Figure 2–2) illustrates the effects of this threat in action on an urban space with considerable potential but well-advanced degradation. These effects are all too familiar in cities throughout the world: congestion, pollution, uninhabitable neighborhoods, disruption of walking and cycling, hampering of public transportation, and interference with many other functions of urban life. Many people now realize that the economic and social benefits of individual mobility have been bought at too high a price. The tradeoff has not been favorable: destruction of viable urban environments and disruption of vital social interrelationships have been the inevitable result. Nor have the results been more satisfactory when planners have merely provided more efficient methods for moving motor traffic more quickly through urban environments. Cities transformed to better accommodate cars have continued to decline in environmental quality, while infrastructure has had to be spread thinner over larger areas and supportive urban facilities have eroded. At issue has been the very survival of cities. Redesigning urban environments to best accommodate people has become the top priority of today's planning.

The Naples example graphically illustrates how undifferentiated vehicular traffic tends to dominate urban spaces and overwhelm other functions. Marketplaces become parking lots; courtyards become private parking garages; sidewalk spaces once used for social communication and exchange of goods and services are made ever narrower and more dangerous until even walking is nearly impossible. Even the functions of moving people and goods are hampered by the anarchic jumble of vehicles and the countless conflicts that arise. The need for relief has become universally apparent.

---

* Organization for Economic Cooperation and Development, Conference Proceedings, *Better Towns with Less Traffic* (Paris, 1975), pp. 13–14.

Reduce Conflicts, Reduce Accidents

The volume of urban space required by one motorized private vehicle is out of all proportion to the amount of space its occupants require to carry out meaningful activity in cities. Furthermore, people occupying automobiles are generally *en route* rather than accomplishing gainful or socially meaningful activities, which they usually perform as pedestrians at the end of their vehicular journeys. Thus, as the Ministers of the Environment suggested, long-term programs to change patterns of land use to create more activity and less meaningless movement in cities are amply justified. In the short term, however, quick relief must be sought from the enormous social and economic costs of excessive motorization in cities. Waste of lives, time, precious resources, and nonrenewable energy supplies deserve far more attention than they have received until now. When examined with regard to modification or redesign of urban spaces, these critical issues translate into a mandate to reduce

Fig. 2–1 (above). London, England. Attractive environments for pedestrians are fundamental to the conduct of human affairs in cities.

Fig. 2–2 (below). Naples, Italy. Characteristic view of urban degradation: congestion, pollution, disruption of vital urban functions.

Fig. 2–3. Paris, France. Serving the needs of motorized traffic, Saint-Germain and Saint-Michel along the Latin Quarter are no longer the elegant boulevards they once were.

conflicts and reduce accidents.

A view from the heart of the Latin Quarter in Paris (Figure 2–3), at the intersection of the venerable tree-lined Boulevards Saint-Michel and Saint-Germain, demonstrates the nature of some of the conflicts. (The view is toward the southwest, with the cars coming from the west along the Boulevard Saint-Germain.) Perhaps the first conflict is with history itself, since almost the entire space of this intersection adjacent to the medieval Cluny Museum has been asphalted to serve the needs of motorized traffic. Unlike other historic boulevards and intersections in countless other cities, these still have their trees, but just barely—and no one knows for how long. One can see that pedestrians at the time of the photo still asserted their rights to coexist in the space—but again no one knows for how long.

Saint-Germain and Saint-Michel are no longer the elegant boulevards they once were, each having been degraded to the role of half of a one-way pair of parallel arteries in the name of traffic efficiency. What this efficiency does to urbanity is clearly visible in the inconvenience and dangers to which pedestrians are subjected and in the destruction of a unique sense of place. From the standpoint of vehicular movement, the reasons for such transformations are understandable, but from the standpoint of urban spaces as places for human activity, the decision is incomprehensible. Internationally, the

middle decades of the twentieth century have seen a continuous history of resolving such conflicts in favor of cars and in opposition to pedestrians, leading one prominent city planner to formulate the following counterprinciple: "It cannot be emphasized enough that, when a contained, attractive area for urban experiences is threatened and the sense of scale of a people-place impinged upon, perfection of traffic techniques must be suppressed."*

Traffic signals, a policeman in the intersection, one-way systems, reserved bus lanes, turn restrictions, and elimination of on-street parking are some of the operational and regulatory measures intended to reduce conflicts: conflicts among the vehicles and conflicts between vehicles and pedestrians. Success is sometimes less than optimum, however. A next step would be to achieve vertical separation by channeling the pedestrians into tunnels (concourses, according to accepted jargon) under, or bridges over, the intersection. The repertoire of devices for facilitating the flow of vehicular traffic in cities seems inexhaustible. Yet the conflicts between traffic and environmental quality and between traffic and other more desirable human uses of the spaces remain.

* Harald Ludmann, *Fussgängerbereiche in deutschen Städten* (Cologne: Deutscher Gemeindeverlag, Verlag W. Kohlhammer, 1972), p. 10.

A more radical approach to eliminating conflicts than traffic measures that encourage ever higher volumes of vehicular flow has been suggested by the French Minister of the Quality of Life, M. André Jarrot. M. Jarrot, expressing the opinion that better solutions can be found by adopting the principle that the town should be made for man, has suggested guidelines for a new charter for the urban core, including a revolutionary proposal that we should "give the all-purpose motor car back the role it should always have kept, that of a transport facility relatively seldom used in an urban environment."

The nature of the optimum solution to resolve conflicts and reduce accidents in a space such as the intersection of the Boulevard Saint-Michel and the Boulevard Saint-Germain presents itself with the simplicity and directness of cutting the Gordian knot: remove the cars. Translated into the jargon of city planning and traffic regulation, the solution is called horizontal separation. Instead of having maximum-volume, one-way traffic arteries slashing through the urban heart in a crisscross pattern, dedicate the street spaces to the activities of pedestrians and remove the vehicular traffic to arterial routes further out, where they do less damage. After all, as Minister Jarrot asked rhetorically, "Is it really necessary to fill the center of towns with car parks to saturation point, to overendow them with broad avenues and underpasses, which only too often have the effect of disfiguring our cities, and

increases the number of cars in the streets without improving traffic conditions?"

A characteristic example is the one-way arterial leading out of the heart of Bergen, Norway, through a residential district (Figure 2–4). It brings to mind the thought process responsible for so much destruction of viable urban fabric: "Now, if only this artery could be opened up to allow those vehicles to flow more freely, the whole urban body would be healthier." Since trees were long since sacrificed to road-widening and the sidewalks shrunk to minimal proportions, only one answer remains: tear down the buildings. When older housing, no longer quite up to modern standards of comfort, is involved, the decision is all the easier, but yet another piece of the flesh and lifeblood of the city is irretrievably lost.

Fortunately, this section of Bergen has not yet been sacrificed on the altar of improved traffic, although one can foresee the effect of traffic turning these historic buildings into a slum and subsequently into fodder for the urban-renewal mill. Who, if anyone, still lives in these older buildings, bearing the burden of all this pollution, noise, and destruction of the street as a communal place? If they object to having their particular street exploited to serve the commutation needs of the rest of the city, do they have anyone on the city council to support their cause?

Yet there still may be hope, since officials are beginning to recognize that reducing or diverting

Fig. 2–4. Bergen, Norway. A characteristic example of the universal pressures of trend: "If only that artery could be opened up . . . ."

BETTER TOWNS WITH LESS TRAFFIC

the flow of vehicles is better than breaking through the bottleneck. High-density housing in walk-up buildings above shops in central areas of established character, convenient to numerous places of work, suddenly sounds like the description of an urban asset highly worthy of protection and rehabilitation. Reduce conflicts? Reduce accidents? Achieve a better town? Simply reduce the volume of traffic; eliminate the vehicles from this place.

Enforce Existing Regulations

But how does one eliminate vehicles from an urban space? One answer is through regulation. In fact, most cities already have rather strict regulations that are intended to protect the activities in useful urban spaces from excessive incursions by motorized vehicles. Graz, one of the largest cities in Austria, provides a demonstration of how poorly these regulations usually are enforced in our auto-oriented age (Figure 2–5). The sign on this rather narrow but active street in the historic core of Graz reads: *Halten verboten, ausgenommen Ladetätigkeit,* "no stopping, with the exception of loading activities." Some responsible body had determined that, while the street could appropriately be used for access, pickups, and deliveries, parking would be inappropriate; yet, within a forty-five minute period of observation, no vehicle was moved and no loading took place. Clearly the intended, more pro-

ductive uses of this urban place were being obstructed and existing regulations circumvented by a few individuals who had entered the city and needed a place to leave their mobility machines while they conducted their business. How many times each day is this perversion of priorities allowed to take place in how many cities the world over?

A simple answer is to enforce existing regulations, as was done on a similar street in Madrid (Figure 2–6). Priorities for using valuable urban street space would suggest that far more private automobiles ought to be towed away in order to make room for more desirable urban activities. Yet why rely on regulatory measures, when physical measures can be far more effective in achieving the desired results? Particularly in areas of commerce and housing, numerous physical deterrents have been successfully applied in many countries to prevent, restrain, or selectively screen through traffic and parking. These can range from simulated construction sites, through "sleeping policemen"— humps and dips in the pavement—to physical obstructions that prevent entry by certain types of vehicles. It is, of course, entirely possible to be very selective in choosing which classes of vehicles are screened out and which are allowed in. More and more municipalities are recognizing the futility of allowing every flat (and some not-so-flat) urban surface to be free game for the most daring of the persistent parking-space hunters. It is up to the

Fig. 2–5. Graz, Austria. One problem is the failure to enforce existing traffic regulations.

Fig. 2–6. Madrid, Spain. Removing the blockage can create room for more desirable urban activities.

municipality to set the ground rules for the hunt and to see that they are enforced.

Unfortunately, tow-zone ordinances have, until now, been seen primarily as devices for enhancing parking opportunities and improving the flow of vehicles through cities (Figure 2–7). As characterized by an example from downtown Philadelphia, automobile restrictions of the past have been most frequently applied to facilitate the flow of cars during rush hours. Destruction of formerly residential areas and their conversion into surface-area parking lots, as in this example, have been logical corollaries, and no one has complained, since it is always lower income groups who are driven out of the houses and higher income groups who find spaces for their cars. Nonetheless, the success of such programs has demonstrated that enforcement of existing regulations can effectively control the desired presence or absence of vehicles in particular urban spaces at particular times.

Differentiate Access and Through Traffic

Unquestionably, the most influential single document in the English language concerning design modifications of urban environments necessary to deal with the problems of a motor age was the 1963 study commissioned by the British Minister of Transport and entitled simply *Traffic in Towns*. It is frequently referred to as the Buchanan Report, after Colin Buchanan, British traffic expert and chairman of the working committee for the report. The main study is preceded by a report of the steering group, which includes the following references to the American situation. (Note: *motorway* is the British word for the American *expressway*.) "The American policy of providing motorways for commuters can succeed, even in American conditions, only if there is disregard for all considerations other than the free flow of traffic, which seems sometimes to be almost ruthless." Furthermore, "even with the advantages that their circumstances provide for the success of a motorway policy, many Americans are coming to doubt whether it provides a final solution. Each new motorway, built to cope with existing traffic, seems to call into existence new traffic sufficient to create a new congestion."

Among the major conclusions of *Traffic in Towns* are several which have had profound effect on policies implemented in many countries during the intervening fifteen years. Most fundamental— and most contradictory to transportation planning policies up to that time—was its conclusion that "some deliberate limitation of the volume of traffic in our cities is quite unavoidable." Although it may have taken twelve years, the title "Better Towns with Less Traffic," taken by a 1975 conference of official government delegations from the major

Fig. 2–7. Philadelphia, PA. But while removing violators of tow-zone ordinances may improve the flow of vehicles, quality of the residential environment will not always be helped.

western nations indicates that this concept had gained wide acceptance at influential levels of government. The fact that the meeting was held under the auspices of the Organization for Economic Cooperation and Development reveals that the romantic humanists have been joined by pragmatic economists in their concern that the automobile no further threaten the economic viability of cities. Regrettably, many business and community leaders of North American cities have not yet received that message.

To achieve their "inevitable limitation of motor traffic," the British conference steering group concluded that "any such organised attempt to solve the problem will necessarily involve very large-scale redevelopment of our cities and towns on a significantly different pattern. If we are to have any chance of living at peace with the motor car, we shall need a different sort of city."

While it is beyond the scope of the present study to analyze or develop the concept of "environmental areas" or "traffic cells" or "automobile-restricted zones," as defined in the Buchanan Report, a brief description is in order. A basic point of the Buchanan Report suggests that cities of the future should be divided into a pattern of many environmental areas from which all traffic, other than that which has specific business in the area, would be excluded. An analogy was drawn between cities and major buildings such as hospitals, where no

one would dream of trundling laundry, supplies, or dirty dishes through the wards or the operating rooms. Just as well-organized new building provides spaces where primary functions take place with corridors for communications and services, so, it was reasoned, could cities be organized in a similar manner to better facilitate both the principal functions in the "rooms" and the connecting and service functions of the "corridors." As simple as the concept appears, it provoked thoroughgoing reallotment of urban spaces in Europe beginning in the early 1960s, continuing at an accelerating pace in the 1970s.

The success of Buchanan's concept was subsequently considerably diluted by the narrowest implementation: excessive concentration on the one-dimensional central commercial district, frequently only the busiest portion of the main shopping street. The report explicitly stated that environmental areas could be residential, commercial, or industrial, and that many of them should be mixtures. In all cases, differentiating access from through traffic would be fundamental in order to facilitate the primary functions in each area. Pedestrianized shopping streets as they are now beginning to exist in hundreds of examples throughout the world thus must be recognized as only a first step toward realization of the broader concept as formulated in the Buchanan Report.

The North German port city of Bremen provided

an early model for northern European cities, notably Göteborg in Sweden, by developing its own system of traffic cells for its entire historic urban core. In the Bremen prototype the main shopping street, square, and intersection are retained as traffic routes through the center but only for pedestrians and public transportation in the form of electric trams (light-rail transit). Cars and trucks are rerouted into five traffic cells surrounding the central spaces. These cells, in turn, are surrounded by a ring road, which provides access to the individual cells. These inner-city areas thus do admit automotive deliveries and parking in department stores and garages, but they do not permit vehicles to cross over from one cell to another. For access to another cell, vehicles must drive out and around the ring rather than across the main square or shopping street via the most direct route. (For a 1974 view of Obernstrasse, Bremen's main shopping street, see Figure 3–17.)

Such a scheme works very effectively to reduce both absolute traffic volume and needless congestion. While pedestrians and public transportation are given the benefit of the most direct route, cars and trucks are detailed to a circuitous route. This plan has the dual benefit of eliminating the environmental burden of vehicles from the properly pedestrianized urban spaces and also discouraging unnecessary vehicular traffic.

The concept of unnecessary vehicular traffic is not an easy one to pin down, although perhaps all can agree that a drive of one hundred yards to buy a newspaper or a pack of cigarettes is unnecessary. A good way to make a distinction is to call traffic "unnecessary" that can be easily discouraged through physical barriers that reroute or make certain types of trips more difficult or circuitous. In Bremen, Copenhagen, Göteborg, and other cities that have tried such schemes and have conducted traffic surveys to check on the results, such traffic management schemes have effectively reduced the volume of vehicular traffic by 20 percent or more. Such positive results serve as telling rebuttal to pessimists who argue that traffic regulation will only serve to shift existing traffic volumes onto parallel streets.

Fig. 2–8. Bonn, West Germany. Since the 1960s a system of traffic cells has been developed to differentiate access and through traffic.

Fig. 2–9. Florence, Italy. Former routes for motorized traffic as in the Ponte Vecchio can become "filters," letting people in while keeping vehicles out.

A view along the inner ring road of Bonn, Germany's capital (Figure 2–8), is on a segment of street leading past the cathedral, across the cathedral square, and to the historic main post office building. The large traffic-regulation device at right illustrates Bonn's traffic-cell system. The route straight ahead, once the main route through town, now leads only a short distance to the garage underneath the cathedral square or to short-term access to the main post office. All other traffic is required to turn left onto the city ring around the central business district. In addition, access to both the post office and the subterranean garage can be changed at a moment's notice; lights indicate that the garage is full or that access to the post office is closed because of a public event on the cathedral square. It becomes apparent that such a traffic-cell system offers far greater flexibility in the use of urban spaces than the previous state of "autocracy."

Bonn has put a filter around its urban core to screen out the impact of motor vehicles and simultaneously encourage the far more enjoyable and productive uses of a high-density pedestrian concentration.

The medieval Italian city of Florence has taken a similar approach. The southern entry to the legendary Ponte Vecchio, a fourteenth century bridge lined with goldsmith shops and other tourist attractions (Figure 2–9), shows a similar filter at work letting people in and keeping vehicles out at one of the main approaches to the historic center of Florence. It is not difficult to imagine what a deterring effect these mopeds and motor scooters would have if they were let loose on the strolling crowds. Yet how many cities have allowed themselves to find out what kinds of crowds might develop if the lopsided competition with motor vehicles were eliminated?

Encourage Walking

Bologna has gone furthest among Italian cities in encouraging pedestrian movement and stimulating people to be more selective in the use of automobiles. The program in Bologna is particularly noteworthy in that it encompasses the entire city to its furthest limits rather than merely being restricted to the historic core. Bologna's pedestrianization has

Fig. 2–10 (left). Bologna, Italy. Encouraging walking, a major mode of movement, is essential in a comprehensive traffic management scheme.

Fig. 2–11 (right). Venice, Italy. Like other modes of movement, walking can have its principal distributors, district distributors, and local access routes.

come about as one result of an explosive increase in car ownership. From one vehicle for every 11.2 persons in 1960, automobile ownership increased phenomenally to one for every 2.6 persons—men, women, and children—by 1973. The desire to preserve historic urban fabric and to keep people living in all parts of the city led to a very extensive traffic scheme that embodied total prohibition of automobiles from many streets throughout the city.

A major effort was simultaneously made to encourage walking and the use of public transportation. While Bologna already enjoyed some thirty-five kilometers of arcades that provided covered walking environments partially protected from traffic, a characteristic view of a pedestrianized street in the center of the city indicates that the new scheme went far beyond the network of arcades (Figure 2–10). Despite the existence of at least one automobile for every two of the people in this view, this particular street space, although closely related to the primary urban spaces of the core, is not even a prime shopping area but is mainly a pedestrian link in a larger network of spaces designed to cultivate walking as a habit as well as a mode of transportation.

But encouragement of walking is only one part of the new comprehensive traffic management scheme instituted in Bologna during the 1970s. Expanding the idea of environmental areas or traffic cells throughout the entire city furthers another main goal: the preservation of high-quality living environments in all parts of the city, including its center. Instead of the chaotic use of all street spaces by all modes of traffic, the Bologna scheme provides for highly differentiated uses for particular purposes. Less than one-quarter of available street spaces are allotted to mixed public and private general traffic, while the rest are restricted to specific uses, including access to residential areas and even to individual dwellings. By 1975 the area reserved exclusively for pedestrians had already reached a remarkable 125 hectares (309 acres).

One of the models analyzed in the 1963 Buchanan Report was Italy's island city of Venice. As in the scheme more recently realized in Bologna, Venice had always had a highly differentiated system of principal distributors, district distributors, and local access routes. Differentiation not only expedites passage over the many kilometers of water routes that interlace the urban fabric but spectacularly enhances the considerably longer network of routes for pedestrian movement. A view along one of the main distributors leading from the railroad station to the Piazza San Marco (Figure 2–11) demonstrates some of the great advantages of walking in Venice: virtually complete safety for pedestrians, no noise, and relatively little disturbance from vehicle exhaust, except at bridges where the two modes of transportation cross. While the street clearly serves as a traffic route, this purposeful movement does not at all disturb—in fact it tends to enhance—other functions of the urban space: the rich aesthetic or psychological impact of the "outdoor living room," social communication, exchange of goods and services, relaxation, and extension of the residential environment.

The Buchanan Report concluded that the important lesson to be learned from Venice is that it *is* possible to contrive independent systems of vehicular and pedestrian routes, that the two systems can be completely separated physically, and that such a scheme actually works. A comprehensive redevelopment study for Tottenham Court Road in London in the early sixties used the Venetian concept of entirely separate networks; such ideals have remained a major principle of British planning ever since, for example in the new town of Milton Keynes in the 1970s.

Inauguration of pedestrian paths as a transportation network has never been opposed by the general public, interestingly enough. The business community has usually generated political pressure against change in the status quo. Part of this doubtlessly stems from merchants' desire to enjoy the comforts of driving to work, but the concern has always been expressed that well-to-do customers will take their business elsewhere rather than accept the inconvenience of being separated from their cars. In fact, such opposition has marked the early stages of nearly every city plan where systems of environmental improvements for pedestrians have later been successfully carried out. Bologna, Copenhagen, Minneapolis, Munich, and Norwich are only a few of many cases where pedestrianization, now seen as a boon to commerce, was once vigorously opposed by skeptics in the business community. Had there ever been cars on the streets of Venice, we would certainly have heard commercial anguish over their removal as well.

The success of temporary street closings for summer festivals, arts festivals, farmers' markets, flea markets, and a myriad of other special events has always demonstrated that urban residents are enthusiastic about walking and shopping in pleasant, attractive environments free from dangers and other environmental burdens. Such special events have increased greatly in public street spaces in Europe and America during the past decade, a trend that seems to swell with the number of automobiles available. An automobile-dominated daily life may even need the balance of a completely automobile-free urban environment.

But festivals and other special events are artificial and temporary. Although they identify a need, they do little to satisfy that need on a lasting basis. Photographs of masses of people using street spaces for special occasions have been widely used in recent years to propagandize for streets for people. Because such scenes are basically unreal, however, they distract from the real issue of quality civil environments for everyday life, and their use has been largely avoided in this book. Nonetheless, a view of Water Street in the Gastown historic area of Vancouver during a temporary closing in the summer of 1976 is highly illustrative of the concept of routes for walking (Figure 2–12). The Gastown area is the former heart of town left behind as the commercial center gradually moved west. Now the importance of Water Street is recognized as a vital pedestrian linkage between the two areas. Sans autos, its refurbished older buildings, sensitive infill, and upgraded furnishings transform it into an astonishingly attractive route.

The continuity of such routes over great distances, including the elimination of barriers, detours, and hazards, is an essential ingredient of systems designed to encourage walking in urban environments. Such continuity, of course, can be provided at levels other than the normal street level. Some cities have seen fit to avoid barriers and hazard by directing pedestrians over or under them, rather than eliminate the source of conflict. The skyway system in Minneapolis and the underground concourse system in Toronto are the two best known examples of such attempts in North America.

The skyway system in Minneapolis was conceived as a means of encouraging pedestrian movement throughout the downtown area (Figures 2–13 and 2–14). While encouragingly in favor of free movement of people and providing direct linkages of functions, the concept actually reflects a decision to allow automobiles virtual domination of all street spaces of the central city other than the eight blocks of the Nicollet transitway-mall, but including every intersection with Nicollet. A total of seventy-six bridges linking sixty-four city blocks were included in the original plan for a skyway network, intended for completion by 1985. A major component of this plan is a ring or collar of seven-story parking garages around the central business district. While this would alleviate the current gross misuse of urban land (more than two-thirds of all downtown surface area is devoted to movement and storage of motor vehicles), it would not stanch the current unrestricted flow of private vehicles on every downtown street but the transitway-mall.

Figure 2–13 shows the typical traffic load of streets crossing Nicollet, just visible as the cross street in the background beneath the bridge. This block of Seventh Street between Marquette and Nicollet at the very heart of the central business district has had everything possible done to it to encourage through movement of vehicles, including street widening, elimination of trees, narrowing of sidewalks, and introduction of one-way regulations, not to mention the discouragement of pedestrians. A logical next step to accommodate still higher traffic volumes would be to eliminate the sidewalks altogether, expand the street to extend from wall to wall, and *require* pedestrians to use interior passageways for access to stores. Although no one, to my knowledge, has yet come forward with that proposal, it is undoubtedly only a matter of time; the skyways will make it all possible.

The skyway concept has caught the fancy of many North American planners and developers precisely because it seems to satisfy the needs of all citizens, both in their capacity as pedestrians and in that as automobile drivers. "Free movement in a free society" could be the motto of this system, just as it has been for interest groups in Germany that have successfully prevented the establishment of any speed limit at all on expressways in that country. But just as totally free movement on highways leads to inordinate numbers of dead people, so does totally free movement of vehicles in cities lead to inordinate amounts of dead space. Just mollify the sensibilities of the pedestrians somewhat by getting them out of the way into air-conditioned overhead tubes.

The tubes themselves (Figure 2–14) are comfortable enough and lead directly into department stores, banks, office buildings, and other useful places for people to be. Crossing street spaces in air-conditioned or heated comfort under certain weather conditions is also an undoubted advantage. Nonetheless, the concept of skyways becomes pernicious when accepted as a valid substitute for a network of hospitable urban open spaces at grade level. Is the artificiality of the antiseptic, continuously closed environment justified by the protection

Fig. 2–12. Vancouver, Canada. Refurbished older buildings in Gastown coupled with temporary closing to vehicular traffic create a very attractive route.

Fig. 2–13 (left). Minneapolis, MN. Skyways encourage controlled pedestrian movement and surrender virtually all street spaces to cars. Fig. 2–14 (right). Minneapolis, MN. The heated, air-conditioned tubes of the skyway lead directly into department stores, offices, and banks.

afforded from the weather? It is also questionable whether significant problems of aesthetics, pollution, waste of energy, and misuse of urban land are not simply being avoided rather than solved. At any rate, skyways are certainly not a Venetian-type solution, as they superficially may appear to be. Despite the intention to create a network for motor vehicles and a network for pedestrians largely separate physically from each other, the two systems in Minneapolis do not enjoy the relative equality of those in Venice. Pedestrians are still being treated as inferior species in North America.

The same can be said of the concourse system in downtown Toronto or of the growing group of galleries and other through-block arcades in New York City. While they clearly encourage pedestrian movement as an important adjunct of central business districts, these more or less artificial environments do little to recreate the traditional life of urban streets. Their model is not the historic city, but rather the modern suburban shopping mall; their focus is not the complex bodily and spiritual needs of the urban dweller, but the pocketbook of the anesthetized and apathetic consumer. The result is a sea of asphalt and motor vehicles surrounding a limited, self-contained island dedicated to consumption.

Commerce, of course, is a vital urban element, but where it overshadows all else, its temple, the city, begins to crumble. A view of an entrance to the below-grade shopping concourse in Toronto (Figure 2–15) hints at how much of the traditional warmth, vitality, and scale of urban environments is being sacrificed to maximize exploitation of land and total consumerism. The towers are allowed to soar to great heights over bleak spaces of underused plazas that pass for some kind of tradeoff in amenity to the city. The entire block is a below-grade shopping center, linked under adjacent streets to yet other shopping concourses. But where, we can well ask, is the uniqueness of locale, the integration of a broad range of urban functions, the rich tapestry of tradition and identifiability? Where is what makes a city a city?

Save the Trees

The token trees visible in our view of the Toronto Dominion Plaza are a reminder of one of the shortcomings inherent in the bulldozer approach to urban redevelopment: disruption of all genuine relationships to nature. Too often in modern rede-

Fig. 2–15. Toronto, Canada. The shopping concourse is below-grade and linked beneath the street. But what has happened to traditional urbanity?

velopment programs, trees have been relegated to an insignificant role as decorative objects, and too often is the great potential of trees overlooked in redesigning public open spaces, including streets. To the great credit of the Minneapolis city planners, many trees were inserted into the commercial core through the transformation of Nicollet Avenue into a transitway-mall. Besides adding a delightful element of soft, living foliage to an otherwise hard environment, the trees gave a sense of closure and containment to the seemingly endless shaft of space defined by straight frontage lines of buildings.

But perhaps even more sensible than the insertion of necessarily young trees in modern design schemes is the prevention of the removal of mature ones in the name of progress. A view of the ring road on the eastern side of Bologna's historic core (Figure 2–16) illustrates the forces threatening the urban inventory of trees everywhere. In America, and in many other places in the world, a situation such as this would have long since been resolved by simply removing the trees. The pressure of automobile traffic is greatest where there is the greatest amount of vulnerable space, so that parks, waterfronts, and green boulevards are always in danger of being sacrificed to the greater good of moving traffic more efficiently. Stump removal is far less costly than removing buildings, and besides, no one will be dispossessed since the city already owns the trees.

Fortunately, the approach in Bologna has followed a different line. Which, the civil authorities reasoned, contributes more to the quality of life, parked cars or trees? Bologna's comprehensive traffic management program, with its emphasis upon careful preservation and nurturing of all positive elements in the environmental heritage of the city, is therefore planned to reduce the misuse of private automobiles for most journeys between home and work, home and school, and home and shopping. Since 1972 the declared philosophy of Bologna's City Council has been that the provision of ever more parking facilities for ever more cars is an out-of-date, limited concept that deserves to be rejected. The frequent requests that underground or multistory parking structures be built in the city center were turned down, and a systematic policy of encouraging use of public transit, walking, and bicycling in the city was pursued instead. Significantly, this policy makes careful distinctions between which types of journeys should be facilitated and which types should be discouraged through design and regulation. Accordingly, along with severe limitations on long-term street parking, new parking facilities are built not in the center but in fringe areas adjacent to major routes in the city. They can thus serve as transfer points to rapid and reliable public transit and absorb the long-term parkers who need to leave their cars for several hours or all day.

Fig. 2–16. Bologna, Italy. Powerful forces threaten the urban inventory of trees everywhere.

Fig. 2–17. Amsterdam, the Netherlands. Urban drivers tend to be self-centered the world over. Regardless of position or rank, they want a convenient place to park.

Perhaps because the anonymity of large-city existence allows it, urban dwellers tend to react in a self-centered way the world over, as a view of a charming urban square in front of the Stock Exchange in Amsterdam hints (Figure 2–17). Car owners, feeling entitled to drive to work, seek a parking space as close as possible to their final destination. Voluntary restraint for the sake of aesthetics or environmental quality should not be expected from individuals, no matter what their social status or official rank. In fact, the stock exchanges, city halls, state houses, and parliaments of the world are always the buildings most likely to have their forecourts or even interior courtyards filled with automobiles belonging to the highest representatives of society. The only solution is to undertake communal action for the communal good, to establish an environmental ethic in the interests of urban quality, and to undertake the necessary physical alterations that will make compliance with parking restraints the path of least resistance. The trees and fountains of the world's forecourts (and other urban spaces) must stay; the intrusion by cars must stop.

One such space in which the trees were just barely saved from traffic expansion measures is the historic market area known as Tombland in Norwich, England (Figure 2–18). In the early 1960s, when Norwich was studied by the working group preparing the Buchanan Report, this area, as well as many others within the medieval fabric of Norwich, was inundated with parked cars. The proposals of local traffic experts at the time advocated the

normal course of action taken by so many cities up to that time. In order to alleviate congestion and parking problems, many trees would be cut down, the two monuments in the space moved, and a higher capacity road built through this charming space.

But, fortunately, trend is not always destiny. More than a decade later, despite a quadrupling of cars in the city, Tombland is virtually free of parked vehicles. The trees have all been saved, and the monuments are still in place. The major change—a boon, could it be effected in cities throughout the world—came in Norwich when traffic planning was subordinated to city planning. This in turn led to the development of a Draft Urban Plan, now required for all British communities. Rather than simply developing cities in response to pressures as they arise, Great Britain has legislated a procedure whereby cities must design a rational plan for future development and have it presented, publicly discussed, and finally approved by citizens and various government agencies. All subsequent development and construction of traffic facilities must then conform to it. Such requirements for rational development are standard in many countries, including Great Britain, Germany, and Sweden, but in 1980 not yet in all.

A careful inventory of all existing assets in an urban region is one of the most important foundation blocks upon which an urban development plan should be based. In planning the new town of Wulfen in northwestern Germany, an inventory of existing arboreal assets played a major role. Part of

Fig. 2–18. Norwich, England. Before traffic planning was subordinated to city planning, a major road was planned to be pushed through here.

the rural site to be developed included a handsome old tree-lined road called Napoleonsweg (Figure 2-19). Although development of new towns these days is usually pursued with greater circumspection and planning than normal urban expansion, one can readily imagine what might have happened to these trees had they been left to the mercy of a dynamic new developer during the 1960s. In Wulfen, however, the former road was transformed into a recreational path and entirely removed from the vehicular circulation network. Although it was obviously the right decision in this case, in a great many less clear-cut cases, planners and urban decision makers should ask themselves whether existing roads or streets are not too valuable as spatial assets to be used merely for the circulation of vehicles. As in Wulfen, the simple conservation of trees can be one very good reason for deciding to pedestrianize.

Fig. 2-19. Wulfen, West Germany. Instead of widening, with inevitable consequences for the trees, an alternative use was found for Napoleonsweg.

Seek Alternatives to Maximum Through Traffic

Trees lining the banks of the Seine are among the hallmark attractions of historic Paris. Lovers strolling, the romantic flavor of the *bouquinistes*—the antique booksellers' stands—along the embankment, and such beautiful historic structures as the eighteenth century palace of the Mint (Figure 2-20) complete the charming picture of a left-bank scene in the eternal city. But what is wrong with this picture? There, sundering the charm and beauty of the river, the trees, historic buildings, attractive paving, interesting lamps, quaint benches, and old prints, come the thundering hordes of "city-cars," rushing in like cavalry attacking a china shop. The analogy is not inappropriate, since the urban amenities that determine the unique attractions of Paris are of an extremely delicate nature, while the civic authorities' measures to increase the flow of vehicular traffic have been insensitive and brutal in the extreme.

Quai de Conti is but another of the halves of a one-way pair, this marvelous invention of modern traffic experts to speed the poisonous roar of motorized traffic through the heart of the oldest of urban environments. Efficiency is the reason and destruction the result. Enough will never suffice.

The stubborn *bouquinistes* have long since covered their prints with plastic in a vain attempt to protect them from the dirt and pollution of traffic. The less stubborn have gone out of business, since the narrow space between the river embankment and the torrent of noisy traffic can hardly retain the magnetism for tourists it once enjoyed. Historic buildings are desecrated and physically destroyed by the effects of traffic emissions. Yet the expanded road is already inadequate and is becoming more so as traffic volume steadily increases. There can be only one solution: a radical shift in priorities. If the habitability of Paris, not to mention its magic, is to be saved at all, the goal of maximizing the flow of through traffic must be dropped entirely.

Paris serves as a good example because it is so well known and so much is at stake. Yet, despite the pronouncements of the national Minister of the Quality of Life, there has been less progress in France's capital than in the small provincial center of Besançon (population 135,000). This city in east central France was chosen as one of the study cases for the O.E.C.D. conference "Better Towns with Less Traffic" because of its successes with traffic

Fig. 2–20 (near right). Paris, France. The thundering hordes threaten strollers and *bouquinistes* on the banks of the Seine.

Fig. 2–21 (facing page). Paris, France. Efficient traffic schemes and drastic pruning along the Boulevard Saint-Michel seem to leave the grand old lady stripped naked.

management. Facilitating traffic movement through the center was considered in Besançon, as was the possibility of entirely closing it to all auto traffic. Finally, prohibiting only heavy truck traffic, leaving access for cars but preventing through traffic, was the solution chosen by the Council of Besançon.

Although the Buchanan Report cautioned that ring roads should not be seen as an automatic best answer to all problems, Besançon chose the approach of restraining traffic in the center by banning through traffic, providing a ring road to take all through traffic excluded from the core area, and creating extensive pedestrian-only areas and traffic cells in the center. This middle-of-the-road solution is of great interest to us because removing through traffic from central areas and placing it further out on ring roads seems to represent the limits of political feasibility of traffic restraint measures in most cities today, although clearly it does not strain the limits of advanced urban planning.

Nonetheless, removing through traffic to areas where it will do less damage and thus freeing many attractive street spaces from dominance by cars to serve more useful human functions does represent a concept that has received widespread trial, success, and acceptance. This is the precept currently being emulated most widely on an international basis, and it is to be hoped that Paris itself may close some of its one-way pairs through the heart of the city

before the damage has advanced too far.

A view north on the Boulevard Saint-Michel toward the most ancient historic land on the Île de la Cité in Paris (Figure 2–21) demonstrates just how far the damage due to enslavement by motor vehicles has progressed. One-way movement of traffic is now the prescribed patent nostrum for automotive atherosclerosis all over the world, although the early signs of sanity, reserved lanes for buses, are beginning to reassert themselves. Amusingly enough, we now find a contraflow lane (opposite to the general flow of other vehicles) at the left, as evidence of the *most* up-to-date thinking. Reserved lanes are now commonplace, enabling public transportation to attempt on-schedule transportation in these overly congested streets. The regulating signs say that these reserved lanes are restricted to buses, taxis, and ambulances between the hours of 8:00 A.M. and 8:30 P.M. Without physical barriers, enforcement becomes a bit of a joke. Moreover, a major exception dooms this well-meant device to considerable disruption from the beginning. Trucks are allowed to stop, stand, and make deliveries from this reserved lane any time between the hours of 8:00 A.M. and 1:00 P.M.

Conditions for traffic are not good, but it still moves. Pedestrians still move, too, but under considerable restraint (note the chains) and at considerable danger. Curbstones have been moved dangerously close to the trunks of trees, and one

wonders how many of the trees will recover following their drastic pruning this time. Transformation of the space into a honking, snarling sluice for traffic has robbed it of all charm and urban quality, despite its historic monuments and the area's concentration of so many vital urban functions. The example is crass, but the approach is typical: be ready to sacrifice everything if only a few hundred or thousand more vehicles per hour can be squeezed through.

The same approach had been planned for central Malmö, Sweden. In this smaller city, the older core area had become a bottleneck between the main place of work in the harbor area to the north and the main residential area south of the historic center. The logical solution from a traffic-planning point of view was to cut an expressway connector—the Englebrekt link—through an old, rather run-down portion of the central city. When word got out in 1971 that buildings were being condemned in preparation for a 30-meter (100-foot) right-of-way through this older section, the reaction from the people was spontaneously negative.

"Stop the Engelbrekt Link!" became the rallying cry for the city, and town fathers appointed a new planning group to study the situation and come up with an alternative solution. After innumerable discussions that served primarily the political purpose of creating a receptive atmosphere for the new proposal, a traffic-cell system was adopted in 1974.

In place of the goal of maximizing through traffic, the new plan eliminates all vehicular traffic from the main street, reduces traffic volume through the central area, and generally decreases total traffic volume and its impact on the urban environment. Instead of ramming a connecting link through the historic center of town, transportation planners were able to solve the problem by looping a bypass around it.

Underscoring the glaring difference between what could be and what actually is, Figure 2–22 shows the actual conditions on the Champs-Elysées in Paris on Wednesday afternoon, April 16, 1975, during the O.E.C.D. conference "Better Towns with Less Traffic." This was the same conference at which the French Minister for the Quality of Life called for establishment of a new Charter for the Urban Core, in which the automobile would assume the role of a transport facility "relatively seldom used in urban environments." The distinguished minister obviously has his work cut out for him.

Eliminate the Burden of Parked Cars

Although moving vehicles impose an incredible environmental burden on such streets as the

Champs-Elysées, they are perhaps difficult to eliminate altogether on a broad avenue of such generous dimensions. To tolerate parked automobiles in this monumental space, however, is inexcusable. Rational consideration of the economic or socially beneficial uses of urban land is bound to conclude that parking is one of the worst conceivable misuses of urban real estate. Besides sheer inertia, no small force actually, the only reason parking is tolerated on such an enormous scale is the politics of self-interest. No matter how upset one may become with the nuisance of other people's parked cars, the nagging question, "Where will I leave my own?" remains. Consequently, very little political pressure has built up against the habitual long-term private use, without charge, of desirable public land.

One such inappropriate place that will serve as a good example is the Quai Saint-Bernard in Paris, a street along the Seine bordering the Botanical Gardens. Figure 2–23 is a view west along the south side of this street, with the cast-iron fence of the gardens at the left, on an early Sunday morning before any visitors have driven to the gardens. The cars were parked all night and belong, presumably, to people living in nearby residential areas. Rising affluence, on the one hand, has brought with it a fashionable desire to live in attractive older residential areas near the centers of historic cities where one does not need a car but, on the other hand, simultaneously, the desire to enjoy the status of having a car available whenever one might want to use it. Because of the newly discovered desirability of having a mixture of income groups residing in the city, planners frequently feel compelled to allow, and even encourage, middle and upper income families to maintain automobiles even in the heart of historic cities. Conflicts between considering car storage a necessary adjunct to the better dwellings in cities and recognizing that just the presence on the street of the stored cars detracts significantly from the urban living environment pose problems of design yet to be solved.

Fig. 2–22. Paris, France. Characteristic view of the ten lanes of moving(!) traffic along the Champs-Elysées during the O.E.C.D. conference on "Better Towns with Less Traffic."

BETTER TOWNS WITH LESS TRAFFIC

The burden of parked cars is not only inimical to recreational and residential functions of central urban spaces, but it also destroys other traditional urban aesthetics, attractions such as historic architecture. Guildford, in Surrey, England, offers an example (Figure 2–24). Wide streets such as this in historic townscapes are usually an indication that either the space was once a market square or else an entire row of houses has been removed to make way for the needs of traffic. In either case, wide streets tend to be exploited for perpendicular parking to increase the capacity for this single use. Since historic buildings tend to lose something when viewed across a pedestal of automobiles, the historic qualities of the space tend to be undervalued and in time will be considered replaceable by out-of-scale modern chain stores or other examples of space inflation in reinforced concrete, as in Guildford. Removing the parked cars, on the other hand, would be an important first step toward restoring appreciation for the human scale of historic spaces.

When it comes to finding parking places in urban environments, the usual motto is "Enough will not suffice." Parallel parking, diagonal parking, and finally perpendicular parking form the usual progression toward using all that vacant

Fig. 2–23. Paris, France. Cars block the sidewalk at the Botanical Gardens on an early Sunday morning.

Fig. 2–24. Guildford, England. Transforming an old market street into a car park threatens the historic fabric and destroys a sense of scale.

street space. But why stop there? Figure 2–25 demonstrates the obvious best use of a former stately residential area with lavish promenades beneath an allée of mature trees in Stuttgart, Germany. Presumably no one will notice when the last trees, slightly quaint spatial furnishings at best, downright nuisances at worst, finally die and are taken away.

The problem is universal and by no means limited to France, Germany, or America. Left to their own devices, people will use every conceivable urban surface to park their cars for the entire day, and as we shall see, even graceful old Vienna is no exception. The capital of Austria is struggling to retain its jobs, its tax base, and its reasons for people to go to the historic central business district. Among the most important of many measures to keep downtown Vienna the vital and highly attractive regional center for a vast area is the construction of a new subway system. Rapid transit via a new underground heavy-rail system will bring great advantages to the city. Although Vienna has long been served very well by a highly developed network of light-rail trams, supplemented by an extensive network of buses, even this excellent network of public transportation did not convince enough people to leave their cars at home. Streets and squares of the historic core have been swamped in recent years by private cars, as can be seen in a view of Vienna's Neuer Markt (Figures 2–26 and

2–27). Both wide-angle and telephoto views of this historic square were taken from an incongruous multistory garage, which will be removed before too long. Progress is being made toward transforming central Vienna into a highly attractive pedestrian-oriented district with a traffic-cell system admitting vehicular access but eliminating the current dominance of automobiles. These views were taken when Vienna's main street, the Kärntnerstrasse, just behind the buildings to the right, had already been converted to a total pedestrian preserve but before the first subway line had been opened. Thus, even in a city already growing accustomed to the concept of a pedestrianized core, even in a city where merchants who had opposed the elimination of cars from the main commercial street have long since acquiesced in the face of enormous increases in turnover and profits, even in Vienna it is too much to expect that individual citizens of their own volition will keep their vehicles out of prime urban plazas. The sad fact is that people will continue to drive and park as close to their destinations as they possibly can, even to the very edge of historic fountains and practically into the foyer of the opera and the court theater, unless stopped by physical barriers and visible transformation of the space. Why the cars were not banned during a transitional period before final conversion and redesign as a pedestrian space can only be understood in political terms. The auto-

Fig. 2–25. Stuttgart, West Germany. When it comes to finding parking spaces in urban environments, enough will not suffice.

Fig. 2–26 (left). Vienna, Austria. Despite plans to convert the Neuer Markt to a pedestrian zone, drivers exploit every opportunity for a parking space.

Fig. 2–27 (below). Vienna, Austria. Unless restrained by physical barriers, seekers of parking spaces show little respect for historical monuments.

mobile lobby usually can be overcome only by major projects that promise great economic and social benefits to the entire community.

Reduce the Impact of Parking Structures

At first blush, off-street parking, either in lots or multistory garages, would seem to solve some of the problems raised in the preceding section. Indeed, while surface building lots misused for parking are relatively rare in Europe, European as well as North American business communities continue strong pressure to provide adequate parking in multistory structures within the central business district. For many years it was official policy in many countries to require that new commercial or office developments provide or pay for such parking facilities in keeping with the number of people they were expected to attract. This attitude is changing, however, as the realization spreads that these very parking structures disrupt the continuity of downtown functions and generate high levels of pollution and spatial disharmony.

A characteristic example of the negative aesthetic impact of multistory parking structures on central cities is provided by a view of one very near the Chestnut Street transitway in Philadelphia

Fig. 2–28. Philadelphia, PA. *Park* can be one of the most insidious euphemisms in the English language when applied to such a structure.

Fig. 2–29. Lübeck, West Germany. Modifications to make the urban fabric up to date can drastically affect historic scale.

BETTER TOWNS WITH LESS TRAFFIC

Fig. 2–30. Lansing, MI. Despite the choice of aesthetic materials, provisions for automobiles will never substitute for more traditional urban qualities.

(Figure 2–28). The scale-destroying size and ugliness of the cheap utilitarian structure is compounded by the visible stacked cars and only aggravated by the irony of the Park designation for such a facility. Additionally, unattractive, gaping holes from entry and exit ramps have a disruptive effect on the usefulness of the sidewalk and tend to repel pedestrians.

A particularly glaring example of parking structures' tendencies to disrupt the existing scale of established urban environments is provided by an example in northern Germany, Lübeck (Figure 2–29). Following extensive bombing destruction during the Second World War, a decision was made to rebuild the historic city, but with modifications to bring it into line with modern requirements of dynamic urban areas. "Cities cannot be treated as museums" was an argument frequently used. To satisfy those who argued for maintaining existing scale, a concession was made to limit the height of this structure to the gable height of adjacent older buildings. While not entirely without aesthetic merit or justification in supporting important urban functions nearby, the building is generally recognized as having a disastrous effect upon the scale and spatial interrelationships that were to have been so carefully preserved. Urban conservation in Germany was pursued with a far more sensitive hand in the

1970s, so that a structure with this impact in an area of such strong historic continuity would be very unlikely and certainly would never receive approval in Lübeck today. Yet, although usually not as glaringly obvious as in this instance, multistory parking garages in cities always have a similar effect: they destroy scale and act as a barrier to important spatial linkages.

Of course, negative effects on existing scale and spatial relationships can be avoided by first eliminating all existing buildings and then building the multistory parking garage, or garages, as has been standard practice in so many American urban-renewal schemes. Figure 2–30, a view in the center of Lansing, Michigan, demonstrates the extent to which central business districts can be restructured to accommodate automobiles. It must be stressed that this is not a peripheral area but the very heart of the core. The opposite side of this block, marked by the concrete tower in the background, is the location of the new Washington Square, the pedestrianized main street of the redeveloped core. Thus within less than fifty yards of what is advertised as a pedestrian paradise is this monstrous parking structure covering 50 percent of the entire city block, and it is only one of several parking structures in the renewal area. It would seem that total automobilization of an urban core can go no further.

Yet, for those who would argue that the main problem of parking structures is their poor aesthetics, it should be pointed out that the Lansing garage is designed in impeccable taste, with pleasing proportions, an elegant combination of earth-colored brick and textured concrete, and planting beds adjacent to the sidewalks. It is certainly a handsome, well-conceived structure. One can well imagine the designer and sponsors requesting that this area be colored green and labeled "park" on maps of the city, completing the perversion of urban values. One-way pairs and adequate parking will never substitute for the qualities of a city.

Far larger cities than Lansing have demonstrated the same no-deposit, no-return attitude toward their existing architectural fabric. When it comes to intensive modern exploitation of urban land, little is so sacred that it cannot be sacrificed on the altar of adequate parking. Contemporary mixed-use developments, which are usually touted as examples of modern urbanity and as "a city within the city," are among the worst offenders in expressing disdain for the urban environment and creating a barrier of traffic approaches and parking garages around their periphery. St. Louis, at an intersection in its central business district, demonstrates a characteristic example of this gross callousness to urbanity (Figure 2–31). A reinforced concrete garage has taken on a symbolic significance

on a traditionally prestigious corner in an urban setting. Yet, lest anyone accuse the developers or city planning commission of insensitivity, please note the careful matching of cornice line with that of the neoclassical colonnaded building on the other half of the block!

The miracles of modern accommodation to automobiles in urban settings will never cease, and, if the offices of an organization calling itself Downtown St. Louis Incorporated can be located in a building that rises from a pedestal of five floors of parking, Chicago is certainly the city to carry that escalation a bit further (Figure 2–32). Marina City is the fanciful designation of a high-rise complex designed by Bertram Goldberg to bring luxury housing to downtown Chicago, directly at the intersection of State Street and the Chicago River. Since it was unthinkable to provide luxury housing without accommodations for luxury automobiles, the acrobatic solution of spiraling a continuous garage seemingly endlessly into the sky was hit upon in a moment of inspired imagination. What aridity this brings to the urban environment at street level can only be guessed at, a result obviously overlooked during the design process.

Reducing the impact of parking structures on urban environments is thus an ideal imperfectly realized in the contemporary world. The goal of reclaiming streets as spaces for people to carry on

Fig. 2–31. St. Louis, MO. An important intersection downtown is appropriated by a reinforced, prefabricated, multistory concrete garage.

Fig. 2–32. Chicago, IL. What happens to the urban street environment when a parking garage looms above for the first twenty stories?

Fig. 2–33. Minneapolis, MN. A parking garage designed to be recycled for other uses.

Fig. 2–34. Madrid, Spain. An urban plaza with a ramp leading to parking beneath. While the surface is regained for people, vehicular access remains a burden.

activities other than driving requires very sensitive design and careful placement of parking structures. One interesting development in the use of parking structures is demonstrated by an example from Minneapolis (Figure 2–33). The concept was to design a garage as a camouflaged mixed-use structure with built-in flexibility. The question, "When is a garage not a garage?" has been answered very cleverly here: "When it is a bank at street level and the rest of it looks like an office building." While this does not answer the problem of auto domination of the area, it does provide some pleasing aesthetics and eliminates the problem of brutality and boredom at sidewalk level so characteristic of earlier parking houses, such as that in Philadelphia (see Figure 2–28). A great advantage, flexibility, is provided for the day when this site actually becomes more attractive as office space than as a garage. Ample ceiling heights and the free-standing removable construction of the spiraling ramps will make it relatively simple and inexpensive to effect the conversion. This planned flexibility is an excellent means of reducing the impact of parking

structures and may be worthy of emulation in other locations.

Put the Parking Underground

As it seems that, one way or another, cars will always be with us, the preferred approach in Europe to avoid the negative impact of parking structures has been to build below grade and channel the flow underground. This has usually been more expensive than aboveground garages, but it has halted destruction of existing buildings, and existing public open spaces can be returned to the pedestrians. This solution has had great political appeal among voters, since it seems to give them the best of all possible worlds: attractively landscaped public plazas for relaxation and social communication plus a very desirable availability of parking spaces close to major urban functions.

One example characteristic of many throughout Europe—and increasingly also in America—is shown in Figure 2–34, a plaza in central Madrid.

The approach is typical: on the side of the square nearest the main traffic route through the space an unobtrusive ramp is led down into the subterranean space, usually only one story deep. The entire area of the square (but usually not including the adjacent streets) is excavated and developed for parking. Since this is almost always an open excavation, it is necessary to provide an entirely new roof surface to the space, replacing pavement, landscaping, and furnishings. Superficially the square resembles its former self, but in detail there frequently are significant changes, such as a less interesting pavement or the disappearance of some large trees. Popular satisfaction with such newly created spaces is usually positive though, due to the vast improvement over the former sea of cars.

Transformations of this kind provide excellent opportunities for generous public seating, attractive plantings, and areas where mothers can stroll with small children. Too often, they are not designed to encourage use of the space for children's play, and, as a result, conflicts between uses of the space by different age groups frequently occur. Although these conflicts are anticipated, the European garage-top squares are primarily paved in order to provide for the greatest flexibility of their use, including play, strolling, temporary markets, and political presentations or assemblies. American examples, on the other hand, such as Union Square in San Francisco, are quite often designed to avoid conflicts of use through formal designs including large, fenced-off expanses of lawn.

One disadvantage of garage-top squares is that their use, and thus their contribution to the quality of the urban living environment, can be very limited. Furthermore, if the space is essentially a square block without buildings in the normal grid pattern of streets, it tends to be separated from immediate connections to surrounding buildings and spaces by vehicular traffic on all four sides. Maintaining accessibility to the underground garage further strengthens the severing quality of surrounding streets.

Closed squares, on the other hand, have an entirely different potential when they have their subsurface areas developed as garages. The Plaza Mayor in Madrid is an example of a monumental closed square, i.e., one that is entirely or virtually enclosed by the walls of buildings and presents a logical possibility of having no traffic flowing through. The desirable aesthetic feeling of containment depends on both the configuration of architecture surrounding the space and the presence or absence of traffic flow. In the case of Plaza Mayor,

containment is complete, with all four walls continous and meeting at the corners. Archways through the buildings allow access from outside, and arcades along the sides provide covered passageways.

A detail view of this space conveys its sense of containment and its use as an urban living room (Figure 2–35). It has become a major social gathering point in the city and is so heavily frequented that it is difficult to imagine that vehicles could ever have been allowed into this space. Since it was built in its present form at the end of the eighteenth century, the Plaza Mayor has seen significant historical events as well as countless festivals and fairs. It still functions in this way today and now acts as a veritable oasis in the center of the city.

Figure 2–36 reveals the secret of how a major public open space like the Plaza Mayor can exist in the middle of the urban environment and yet be entirely free from cars: traffic is diverted underneath. Because the plaza is a contained space, it is freed entirely from the impact of through traffic and access to the underground garage. Only very limited spaces outside the plaza are affected by the environmental burdens of vehicles entering and leaving the traffic realm beneath the plaza. This distinction is of enormous importance. It suggests that many urban plazas could be transformed far more effectively into major people-places if routes for through traffic and access to parking could be placed underground at points outside the plaza rather than within. Entry points for underground vehicular spaces need to be removed to greater distances from spaces reserved for people if the full environmental benefits of putting parking underground are to be realized.

Underground parking is not new to the United States. Several cities have adopted this approach during comprehensive redevelopment schemes, including Cincinnati in the redevelopment of its Fountain Square area (Figure 2–37). This major historic square, like Union Square in San Francisco, is the number one urban space in the heart of the city. Because of this unquestioned prominence, a proposal was made in Cincinnati to eliminate all vehicles from the space by devising a suitable traffic management scheme. It would have been quite feasible to realize such ideal transformation of this space. Problems were not of a technical but rather of a purely conceptual nature: important civic leaders simply could not imagine this hub of urban activity without its traditional burden of vehicular traffic. Consequently, traffic still flows along two sides of the square, and the entrance to the parking

Fig. 2–35. Madrid, Spain. With an underpass and parking beneath, the Plaza Mayor benefits from having no cars visible from the pedestrian area.

Fig. 2–36. Madrid, Spain. Designing the vehicular approach well outside the pedestrian square suggests a way of creating major people-places.

Fig. 2–37. Cincinnati, OH. Despite redevelopment of Fountain Square, motor vehicles are kept in the space, reducing environmental quality.

Fig. 2–38. Mülheim, West Germany. The street, a major part of a pedestrian network, was excavated to provide a linear parking lot beneath.

garage is also served from the square. While Fountain Square is quite successful as an attraction for office workers during lunch hours, the environmental quality could well have been significantly higher had all vehicles been eliminated.

An interesting variation of underground garages is provided by the German city of Mülheim in the highly industrialized Ruhr area (Figure 2–38). Here, Schlossstrasse, the main shopping street, has been transformed into one of the main axes of a network of crossing pedestrian routes. The new design has been conceived in three dimensions, with terraces and a cafe terrace attached to a major hotel (at left in Figure 2–38). Planning in the third dimension extends to a one-way garage beneath the pavement, which is as wide as the street space. Entrance and exit for automobiles is via ramps at either end of this major axis, while pedestrians may enter or leave the garage via stairways at the very center of the pedestrian network. Such imaginative use of the space beneath the main street obviates the need for obtrusive parking structures aboveground.

Multiple use of space helps justify great expenditures on quality materials for paving and furnishings to make it genuinely attractive. A further argument for expensive underground garages commonly used until a few years ago was that a higher pedestrian count could be expected if people were able to drive their cars directly into the center. Actually, the percentage of people driving into downtown areas as a proportion of the crowds on downtown streets and squares has been universally exaggerated in the past because of an automobile bias among traffic planners and survey takers. While fairly accurate counts of public transit riders can be taken, numbers of people entering a central business district on foot or by bicycle are habitually overlooked altogether or grossly underestimated in traffic surveys, in which origins and destinations of trips in motor vehicles are the primary focus.

Thus it has been discovered through a long and painful process that many of the measures aimed at making urban areas more attractive by encouraging car owners to use their individual vehicles for access into central areas have been highly counterproductive. The numbers involved in trying to achieve satisfaction of potential demand are simply too great to be accommodated without causing irreparable damage to the unique architectural and social ambience that tends to attract the most people. Even subterranean garages, which can be photographed in a manner as to seem to deny existence of access or egress routes have significant negative effects, severing the continuity of attractive spaces for pedestrians at these crucial points.

On the other hand, it has been discovered in countless examples in cities all over the world that the numbers of people that can be attracted into urban areas through appropriate design measures and provision of attractive access via alternative modes are far greater than anyone had dared to predict. Although we live in a technological and automotive age, human need for hospitable spaces to encourage social interaction is very real. Consequently, the highest levels of government are recognizing that our excessive emphasis upon motor traffic in cities has been misguided. Current pedestrian zones in commercial areas are only the beginning of a transitional stage toward larger scale planning that will bring about major differentiation of the use of street spaces everywhere.

Recycle Street Spaces for Other Purposes

Figures 2–39 and 2–40 suggest the *nature* of changes that could be achieved almost anywhere, although the physical details will vary from case to case depending on local circumstances. The views are both north on the axis Weinstrasse–Theatinerstrasse in Munich and represent the transition between September 1974 and March 1977. In the first view the axis was already in a transitional period: the street had been closed to through traffic but was still available for taxis and cars belonging to individual properties. Markings in the pavement, however, reveal that this relatively narrow street space had served as the primary, one-way, north-south artery through the center of Munich. After the closing, the hectic, dangerous, and terribly polluted conditions of the preclosing phase had already disappeared, so that it was safe for mothers with little children to walk in the street space at leisure, but old habits, a lack of quality design, and continued perception of the character of a traffic way kept the space from attracting very many pedestrians.

By early 1977 people's habits had changed completely, even in cooler weather. People are resourceful and discover amenities that are provided for them. This facilitates their adjustment to new habits and movement simply through changes in the shape of their surroundings. While it may be absurd to compare people with laboratory animals, people do respond in fairly predictable ways to environmental stimuli. This should help to demon-

Fig. 2–39 (above). Munich, West Germany. The Weinstrasse–Theatinerstrasse axis in a state of transition hardly suggests what it was to become.

Fig. 2–40 (below). Munich, West Germany. The Weinstrasse–Theatinerstrasse axis after pedestrianization suggests the vast changes that can be achieved through thoughtful design.

strate the absurdity of arguing, as many opponents to pedestrianization have, that you can't generate people where there weren't any before. It is far more appropriate to realize that the people are already in cities and urban regions, but they need to be stimulated to come out into communal spaces and participate in positive social activities. However one may wish to define positive social activities, the activities evident in the March 1977 view of Munich would seem likely to satisfy most definitions. The examples of Munich and many others like it have shown that quality urban design stimulates good citizenship.

Results so far have been most spectacular in programs to eliminate traffic from heavily visited downtown areas. The implication of "Better Towns with Less Traffic," however, is that *all* areas of cities could benefit from a differentiation of traffic movement in order to reduce environmental burdens and better use the resource of street spaces. While some areas may not warrant the expense of transformation because too few people would benefit, residential areas certainly are among those deserving highest priority for reducing the impact of traffic. Even more important than the opportunity to shop in a pleasant, safe, nonstressful environment is the opportunity to live and sleep in such a conducive atmosphere. Traffic management schemes, traffic-cell systems, programs to enhance public transportation, encourage walking and biking, and discourage the use of cars for trips within the city are all among the measures that should be

Fig. 2–41. Stockholm, Sweden. A busy intersection in Östermalm can become a quiet plaza for relaxing, and the neighborhood a better place for living.

applied to all residential environments in order to further the healthy development of families.

The Östermalm section of central Stockholm, an area east of the central business district, demonstrates the application of these principles to central residential areas (Figure 2–41). The foreground in this view, where a group of elderly people can be seen enjoying the quiet security and interesting variety of an urban pedestrian plaza, was once a busy intersection, the Karlaplan. A traffic-cell system now facilitates the flow of vehicles on the major street (behind the camera), which is now disrupted less because traffic entering from these smaller side streets has been eliminated. The side streets that previously entered the main street at this point are now culs-de-sac, while the intersection itself has been turned into this simple but attractive plaza. The large, new, mixed-use development seen in this view is also directly affected by the traffic management scheme. The development is a combination of apartment units around landscaped courts raised above a modern, enclosed shopping mall. One can well imagine that this interesting combination of uses could result in serious conflicts if traffic approaching the shopping center were given complete freedom of approach

and circulation, as has been the universal practice for shopping centers in the past. A radical shift in attitudes toward traffic made it possible in this instance to integrate major urban functions in a highly favorable manner.

Practical experiments and extensive experiences of this nature show that selected traffic limitations and development of overall movement strategies incorporating all modes into well-balanced, integrated systems can have great impact in making cities better places for people. Limiting the use of cars has been proven to serve major goals of energy conservation, enhanced accessibility to urban centers, and improved environmental quality for all functions in cities, including the residential. Above all, these measures are appropriate everywhere and in many cases they can be undertaken quickly and at relatively low cost.

The most vital first step is to establish the principle that cities are for people while automobiles play a secondary service role. Cities are better with less traffic, when the great resource of street spaces can be adapted to a more productive urban mixture of human activities. The next important step is to find the most effective means of transforming this resource from streets for cars into streets for people.

BETTER TOWNS WITH LESS TRAFFIC

Streets for People

Revitalize Cities Through Better Planning

Revitalizing our cities by making them more attractive to people on foot is one of the crucial issues to be faced by city planners in the 1980s. Fortunately, significant progress in both principle and practice of city planning has occurred in the years since 1961, when Jane Jacobs began *The Death and Life of Great American Cities* (Vintage Books, 1961) with the words, "This book is an attack on current city planning and rebuilding." Her crusade to introduce a new set of priorities and attitudes, startlingly different from those found everywhere from architecture school curricula to the Sunday supplements and women's magazines, was joined in the 1960s by other voices and fledgling organizations. Benefits to many cities were visible as early as the 1970s. While much still remains to be done, today cities throughout the world are actively reassessing priorities, converting more and more street space from motorized traffic sluiceways to pedestrian uses. This process must be vigilantly continued.

The importance of vigilance, however, may not be immediately apparent to everyone. While such humanistic goals as comfort, convenience, safety, aesthetic elevation, and social enjoyment for the citizen both individually and en masse might seem sufficient in themselves to carry the day, one must recognize the weight of entrenched interests that resist any change from the present furthering of important auto traffic just to please mere pedestrians. The commerce of central cities everywhere has been declining, it is argued, and the automobile population has been increasing far more rapidly than the human population. We must therefore

Fig. 3–1. Paris, France. A high volume of potential customers stroll the Champs-Elysées in a prime retail area.

lure back from the suburbs the affluent customers who have been buying all those automobiles if we are to rejuvenate the economies of central cities. A more careful consideration of the intricate factors involved, however, suggests that panaceas and parking lots will not suffice. Rather a system of goals for urban development and improvement must be established, and conflicts between goals, as well as conflicts between goals and givens, must be carefully analyzed and rationalized before any definitive courses of action are determined.

Clarify Goals

Goal-oriented planning, then, is of the essence. Because nearly all cities the world over are established, developed, torn down, and redeveloped for economic rather than aesthetic reasons, economic considerations must be realistically weighed in the goal-planning process. If these considerations are ignored, the forces in charge, which inevitably have strong interests in the economic viability of the city, would simply not allow humanistic measures to be undertaken.

What goals are thus suggested? Two primary goals are (1) promote the retail economic structure of the central city; and (2) reverse the erosion of real estate values and, in turn, tax revenues from real estate. These issues need to be considered individually, in relationship to each other, and in relationship to other important goals.

A view of the Champs-Elysées in Paris (Figure 3–1) highlights some of the important steps in promoting a center's retail economic structure. Furthering an influx of buying potential is one cause that stirs the heart of every merchant. Business associations and municipal administrations everywhere exert great efforts to entice a high volume of potential customers to the retail area during business hours.

The Champs-Elysées does this very well: the Métro, a fixed-guideway, heavy-rail mass transit system, not only runs directly under the street, depositing people at three stations along the commercial strip, but it also collects people from all over the metropolitan region and brings them with speed, reliability, convenience, and a modest cost to this premier retail area. Furthermore, buses handle a considerable volume of local traffic, a bit more slowly, but still with relative comfort and convenience for the same price as the Métro. Attractive public transit is an extremely important factor in promoting an influx of buying power into a central city retail area.

Resolve Goal Conflicts

As is readily apparent beyond the main roadway on the north side of the Champs-Elysées, considerable attention has also been paid to facilitating automobile access to this area. Ten lanes of moving traffic at the center of the avenue (see Figure 2–22) feed into parking lanes at each side—intended to make it convenient for the individual motorist to reach his (commercial) destination. Congestion and delay, however, are the obvious results. Yet congestion and delay for motorists are not the only negative impacts on the environmental quality of the retail area. The photograph, taken on an average Wednesday afternoon in April, demonstrates that pedestrians are constrained to far too small a portion of the public space, are denied the attractive proximity of trees, and are subjected to noxious auto fumes—not only from the ten lanes of moving traffic, but also from many cars idling their engines while waiting for parking spaces. The goal of directing as many streams of traffic as possible toward an urban center clearly conflicts with the goal of enhancing the attractiveness of that area.

The choice of goals is all the more apparent when one compares the number of potential customers attracted to an area via each mode. Observations indicate that approximately 75 people can comfortably occupy an area the same size as that used by 15 cars. But, in terms of turnover, the relative difference in spatial productivity is even more glaring. On a normal weekday afternoon, the flow of parked—therefore potential customers'—vehicles through this space (at an average of little more than 1 person per vehicle) is about 30 per hour. By contrast, the constrained flow rate of pedestrians is 26 per minute per meter of walkway width,* or approximately 7,800 people per hour. The factor in this case would thus be a staggering 260 times as many people brought into the area by foot as by

car. Allowing for fluctuations and errors, a conservative estimate might still speak of a ratio of 100 people who have reached the space by other means and are walking to 1 who has driven a car into the space. Since no studies have been conducted to demonstrate that those who come to a space of this nature by car are more affluent or more willing to purchase than those who are walking, the conclusion from a strictly economical point of view must be that the presence of vehicles on this high-value urban land is overwhelmingly counterproductive.

Avoid Blight

In contrast with Paris, in many North American cities far too few people come downtown. The urban center here all too frequently already has lost its role as the major commercial center of the region. So before considering other aspects of goal planning to enhance the economic structure of the central area, one should note that an even more fundamental goal for inner cities should be reversal of blight—a state of decay or decline that may result from a great variety of negative circumstances. Its outward signs, however, are always the same: a sense of bleakness, evidence of creeping disrepair and neglect, gaping holes in the architectural fabric, and more cars than people visible on downtown streets.

Downtown Detroit serves as a good example of the failure to revitalize downtown areas caused simply by accommodating ever more automobiles (Figure 3–2). A view toward the Hilton Hotel during a convention shows a city in the process of sliding downhill. An area intensely developed with a landscaped boulevard and a church on a tree-lined square, in this view from the mid 1970s the sidewalk is in disrepair, four rows of parked cars line the boulevard, and a large surface-area parking lot disrupts the continuity of buildings. It is a street along which unescorted women do not care to walk. After dark no one would want to traverse it outside the protection of a locked automobile. Such are the indications of spreading blight. In fairness to Detroit, it should be pointed out that major steps to improve this area around Cadillac Square have been undertaken since the photo was taken. Since the changes—no matter how substantial—were undertaken in recognition of the pernicious effects of blight, the point made here is only corroborated.

It is no coincidence that Detroit was one of the first cities to develop a necklace of very attractive

* The mid-range for constrained flow of pedestrians is approximately 2.8 square meters per person, or 26 people per minute per meter of walkway width. Figures from Boris Pushkarev and Jeffrey M. Zupan, *Urban Space for Pedestrians* (Cambridge, Mass.: The MIT Press, 1975), p. 90. The narrowest portion of the walkway of the Champs Elysées is approximately five meters.

suburban shopping malls, milking away great quantities of buying potential from downtown, as early as the 1950s. Northland, Southland, Eastland, and Westland are major commercial complexes on the outskirts of Detroit, the product of the farsighted planning of the president of Hudson's Department Stores and his designer, Victor Gruen. Did these malls precipitate the decline of central Detroit, or were they merely another symptom of a process already under way? In either case, today Detroit is desperately searching for ways to revive its central area, although whether enormous, introverted, individual projects such as the new, mixed-use complex optimistically called "Renaissance Center" can ever fully accomplish the desired results is highly questionable.

To achieve such revitalization, a more organic approach is required: define and remove functions that give the central area its negative image and then loosen up the monofunctional nature of streets and entire districts. Concerning the first of these, quite radical steps may need to be taken to remove uses and appearances of uses that threaten the attractiveness of a pedestrian-filled urban core. Evidences of bleakness, barrenness, disrepair, decay, and garbage need to be counteracted and eliminated. Proliferating pornography and massage parlors have had pernicious effects on other, more urbane functions in core areas of many North American cities. Usually the necessary legal powers to remove, suppress, or regulate them are already available and only need to be enforced.

But pornography, decaying buildings, and garbage are only some of the more obvious outward symptoms of space misuse in the heart of our cities. Anything that produces combustion emissions, garbage smells, chemical air pollution and, of course, noise contributes to making central cities unattractive.

Functions that attract or generate a high volume of motorized traffic, either trucks or cars, are likewise culprits. Consequently, one of the aims of the Environmental Protection Agency in the United States and similar regulatory agencies in other countries is to control functions that generate heavy traffic detrimental to urban environmental quality. If major vehicle-generating functions can be removed to sites directly linked to major highways, the burdens on public space can be reduced and the urban sites returned to use by people rather than by their vehicles.

Encourage Use by People

An urban center's character depends upon high concentrations of people interacting productively throughout the texture of a finely woven fabric of

Fig. 3–2. Detroit, MI. Planning that favors the automobile over anything else almost inevitably results in urban decline.

Fig. 3–3. Malmö, Sweden. The kinds of environmental burdens here are found everywhere in our motorized century.

interior and exterior spaces. Goal planning toward revitalization thus should be directed toward regaining surface area in the center for such productive interaction. Functions that could be replaced include those that require extensive surface area but have little variety of goods or functions to attract people. Surface parking lots are a prime example but so are factories or any large buildings or spaces that present extensive areas of asphalt or blank walls to discourage pedestrians and disrupt the continuity of retail involvement. Barrenness itself can constitute blight and must be remedied.

Loosening up single-purpose or monofunctional streets and districts is another means to revitalization, spreading the attractiveness of variety and generating interest among wider circles of urban population centers. Areas drawing many employees but almost no one else need to be laced with shops, restaurants, and perhaps even tourist attractions which will draw different people to the area and generate activity beyond the nine-to-five working day and will provide employees with diversions during lunch hours as well. Similarly, excessive concentration of retail commerce on one main street is also a monofunctional use that should be loosened up with other functions. Offices, restaurants, theaters, other forms of entertainment, and, of course, housing can contribute to generating a more continuous use of the urban center over a broader span of hours in each day and of days in each week. Revitalization means to infuse life again, and life means people actively interchanging goods, services, information, and impressions.

Reduce Environmental Burdens

If two primary goals for reorganizing urban structure are enhancing the economic structure and counteracting blight, a third is improving environmental quality: identifying and ameliorating factors that negatively affect people, that tend to destroy building substance, or that create disturbances to ecological systems.

Factors negatively affecting people include particularly those in the psychological realm contributing to feelings of apprehension, danger, and stress. A view down the main street, Södergatan, of Sweden's third largest city, Malmö (Figure 3–3), prior to its pedestrianization, suggests the kinds of environmental burdens to be found in urban centers everywhere in our motorized century. The sheer bulk of the intruding vehicles, direct exposure to pollutants, and lack of protection from physical conflicts produce stress, discomfort, and danger of injury or death.

Malmö actually is an exception to the norm in this regard, since it has considerable numbers of trees in its center, its buildings hardly go higher than those seen in the photo, and it was able to avert the creation of a planned expressway link through the urban core. Major improvements in environmental quality were won in Malmö by converting Södergatan into a street for pedestrians, preventing cars and motorcycles from crossing the center, putting buses onto parallel streets, and devising special access routes for deliveries.

Malmö's success shows how almost nothing can be as beneficial for a commercial street as the establishment of a relaxed, pleasant environment free from stress. *

Conserve Existing Resources

Another of the primary goals for urban improvement is suggested by Malmö's success in averting highway construction that would have destroyed the historic urban fabric. This goal may be summarized as historic preservation, which means much more than merely retaining and restoring historic monuments. The goals of historic preservation are to retain a sense of place, to enhance local character, and to stimulate social identification with a particular locale. Thus preservation is particularly important, contributing directly to establishing or enhancing a city's positive image and improving its ability to attract and hold people and to develop in them attitudes of good citizenship.

Venice enjoys a unique ability to attract people from all over the world as tourists. Its image derives from a venerable history that lives on in its unparalleled concentration of historic buildings. Yet neither its famous churches and palaces, its bell towers, the Piazza San Marco, nor even the magnificent Grand Canal sufficiently accounts for the city's unique power of attraction. The explanation is best found in the total consistency of its appeal and its sense of continuity through time. Identifiability, local character, and a sense of place all exist in great force. Most appealing is a pervasive sense of an environment totally responsive to the scale of individual human beings.

Venice is not only a city heavily dependent upon boats for movement of people and goods, it is also the world's largest city designed for pedestrians, with a complicated but efficient network of routes linking all major parts of the city. Part of the main route from the railroad station to the important commercial district around the Rialto Bridge is shown in Figure 3–4, a characteristic segment of

* For a discussion of the process averting highway construction through the city and creating a new plan for revitalization and reorganization of central Malmö, see Ronald Wiedenhoeft, "Malmo: the People Said No" in the *American-Scandinavian Review*, Vol. 65 (March 1977), pp. 12–17; reprinted in Ronald Wiedenhoeft, *Readings in Architecture and Urban Design*, (Dubuque, Iowa: Kendall/Hunt Publishing Company, 1978), pp. 50–55.

the pedestrian network. The fine texture and uniform fabric of the city, as well as the continuous variety within a human-scaled pattern, make walking a pleasant and stimulating experience. Tourists from all parts of the world find no problems in adjusting immediately to walking, no matter how much they may have become accustomed to driving at home. Clearly, if Venice can teach us anything at all, walking should become a much more important element in the comprehensive movement plans for all cities.

Preservation of historic building ensembles contributes enormously to retaining a sense of character and continuity in time. Although none of the buildings in the view of Venice is an important monument in its own right, the totality of spatial impressions, integrated functions, and encouragement of social use demands preserving. As countless cities in Europe and a happily increasing number in North America have demonstrated, preservation can achieve very beneficial social and economic results. Luring people back from the suburbs to the urban core is a major part of these benefits. Attracting people to live in city centers, however, requires that a significant subgoal be established for urban redevelopment schemes: to conserve and improve existing structures wherever possible rather than to tear down entire sections for new development. Large-scale urban renewal virtually outranks blight as the prime enemy of urban conservation, the obliterator of the historic substance with which people most readily identify.

Maintain Attractive Residential Environments

Embracing historic associations and fostering individual identifiability through restoration are only two goals. Other reasons to conserve the existing qualities of cities include maintaining or re-creating attractive environments that enable all income levels to live in the historic core rather than letting older buildings deteriorate and trickle down to the lowest income groups. Restoration and rehabilitation should not, however, be so thorough and so expensive as to drive out all low-income people, creating a new ghetto for the wealthy—as was the case with the transformation of Philadelphia's Society Hill. Both social decline and social segregation of the core area should be avoided.

If the historic qualities of urban environments are to be preserved, and if a particularly attractive residential environment is to be created so that a

Fig. 3–4. Venice, Italy. Walking is a stimulating experience along this route in the historic city.

variety of income levels find it possible to live in the city, then another goal must be linked to that of preservation. To prevent the destruction of existing urban substance in order to create new roads, alternative, more socially appropriate modes of inner city transport than the private automobile must be found. The walking system of Venice provides a wealth of ideas that could be exploited by many cities once our fixation with the power and the glory of the automobile can be put aside.

Control Real Estate Exploitation

Conserving existing urban fabric and retaining existing urban qualities speaks directly to the major goal conflict in urban development. Certainly one of the most powerful forces, undoubtedly the one that has transformed more urban environments than any other, is that of achieving profits on real estate investments. Realizing a return on investments in land and buildings is a fundamental aspect of all free-enterprise economies and remains

an important element in the economies of all such societies today. To increase returns on real estate will always be one of the most potent motivating forces in transforming cities, for better or worse. Therefore, subgoals must be clearly identified, all ramifications analyzed, and the goal conflicts that arise be carefully considered and resolved.

A view of downtown Philadelphia from the tower of City Hall toward the west (Figure 3–5) shows the impact real estate development (and traffic measures) can have on transforming an urban environment. Even without raising the issue of whether such results are good, bad, or some shading of gray in between, one can recognize that the degree of transformation depends entirely on the particular set of goals operant in that particular case. If realizing a return on real estate is the primary goal of urban development, should the main subgoal be to maximize the profitability (and tax assessment) for individual investors? Has overemphasis on this subgoal resulted in the repression of other goals which may be perhaps even more socially worthy? Perhaps only the creation of a comprehensive catalog of the interests of all parties and then consideration and resolution of goal conflicts can answer these questions.

Questions that have recurred in discussion of these issues in many countries include the following. How much should private investors be able to profit from drastic changes to the urban fabric? When a community makes zoning changes or improvements in infrastructure that greatly enhance the value of certain properties without the owners having contributed anything, how can the community itself reap the benefits of these increases in value? By what means can such unearned increments be recaptured from the private sector in order to benefit the entire city? In what ways can major urban renewal best provide opportunities and capital to achieve major structural changes that are considered desirable or necessary? How much transformation of the centers of cities is desirable or necessary? How rapidly should changes be allowed to take place?

While these questions have no standard valid answers, asking them may help to find answers more satisfactory to a broader segment of the populace. If the implementation of major structural changes through urban renewal and the narrow financial interests of real estate developers are given highest priority, major conflicts with other important goals will inevitably occur and will remain unresolved.

Among the goals that seem to have been repressed or ignored, for instance, in downtown Philadelphia, are the following: the achievement of a uniform improvement over the entire central area, avoiding jarring differences and distortions in the competitive ability of the area's commercial locations; the achievement of an even-textured, steady upgrading of the entire urban substance through restoration and renovation of older buildings wherever possible; the rescue of monofunctional areas with a lively integration of many different land uses; the reintroduction of a wide range of housing possibilities for all income groups in the central area; retention of a refurbished historic urban substance to promote its unique architectural image; and finally, most important of all, enlistment of the active participation and personal identification of citizens with the process of developing their own city.

In all of these ways, the Philadelphia redevelopment story contradicts significant tenets of the best modern planning. To what extent these conflicts can be resolved frequently remains a strictly political question. Since no one can surely predict the politics of any local situation, it is difficult to

Fig. 3–5. Philadelphia, PA. The degree of urban transformation through real estate speculation can be awesome.

predict the precise outcome of ultimate planning decisions. Nonetheless, the wide range of possibilities should prompt a careful consideration of all possible development goals, and an early resolution of the goal conflicts revealed will yield results more satisfactory to a larger segment of the community.

Resolve Conflicts of Concentration

A period of prosperity such as that experienced in the entire western world during the 1950s and 1960s led to a great expansion of the supply of consumer goods and services. Because of the mutually reinforcing "market" effect of retail concentration, more and more shops aimed at the consumer market took spaces on main streets everywhere. This effect should be recognized and constructively channeled. It is a useful economic tool, since concentration tends to maximize pedestrian flow and thus draw a great amount of buying power into a particular area.

The problem arises, however, when market concentration lures pedestrians from other areas of the city or surrounding region. All too often they come by car. This situation arose in many of the world's cities as automobile numbers increased dramatically, even before the Second World War. The pre-energy-crisis economic advantage of car travel, as well as its socially attractive personal mobility, led to its acceptance everywhere as an essential element of the urban fabric. Messianic street widening to lead cars directly to the centers of cities was ubiquitously pursued during the 1950s and 1960s. It is still considered a major planning goal in all too many places. But as more and more devastation of the land and cityscape was undertaken in the name of moving ever greater volumes of traffic ever more efficiently, the many conflicts between the gains achieved and the losses incurred emerged.

The German city of Essen, part of the great urban agglomeration of the industrialized Ruhr area, has been a prime, because a notably early, example for other cities to follow in the conversion of downtown streets into places more hospitable to people. Disturbing conflicts between vehicles and pedestrians on the fairly narrow but very heavily commercial Limbeckerstrasse in downtown Essen led to periodic closing of the street to vehicles in times of heaviest pedestrian usage as early as the 1920s. The practice was continued in the 1930s and extended to another major street, Kettwigerstrasse. In both cases the intent clearly was to achieve better movement for both pedestrians and vehicles through horizontal separation—channeling the cars onto streets that could better handle the flow and giving the most heavily commercial streets to pedestrians at times of heaviest use.

The somewhat nondescript modern architecture in the photo of Limbeckerstrasse (Figure 3–6) is an indication that central Essen was devastated during the war. Because it had been a main commercial street, it was one of the first to be rebuilt in the postwar period. The architecture is of a fairly neutral character but interestingly restricted to the same height, bulk, and frontage lines as before the war. Such restrictions serve the laudable purpose of creating a distinct sense of an urban room. The intent—or goal—remained the same as before the war: to stimulate commerce through concentration and encouragement of a maximum pedestrian flow in direct contact with a maximum number of shops. As this photo from the mid-1970s shows, although the city planning measures seem limited to separating vehicular and pedestrian traffic and to repaving the street to a single surface wall to

Fig. 3–6. Essen, West Germany. Even a street of uninspired modern architecture can become appealing through differentiation of traffic.

wall, the space has been very successful in attracting both customers and investors with strong capital resources. (Most of the shops represent retail chains.)

Current experts on advanced city planning in Germany criticize this type of solution for its excessive fixation on the commercial element of urbanity. Social concern moves them to feel that creating attractive urban spaces only where the heaviest concentration of consumer magnets is to be found—as if the sole purpose of city planning were to stimulate sales—is somewhat venal. And, as has been demonstrated in more recent examples, true urbanity—or the design of urban spaces to better satisfy the needs of the people—requires far more than just comfortable shopping environments. Yet German cities in general and Essen's Limbeckerstrasse in particular offer spectacular working models.

Contrary to popular belief, motivating people to walk considerable distances, especially in cities, has not proven at all difficult if the pathway is interesting, pleasant, and safe. A pathway will have these qualities when it leads through a varied but harmonic urban fabric with human activity and vitality all along the way. Modest and unassuming buildings may even be advantages since, from the pedestrian's point of view, a sense of uniform texture and fine grain are often more important than outstanding individual buildings. Height, width, and detailing of the architectural space here is in keeping with the human scale and is therefore perceived as pleasant, even without additional amenities such as seating, planters, fountains, or other furnishings.

Not Malls But Routes For Pedestrians

In this view of Essen, shops usually occupy only the ground floor, while upper stories are used for a variety of purposes including workshops, office spaces, and even housing. The addition of these other uses enhances the space socially and provides a more steady population at all times of the day. The secret, in fact, of any market street is that much impulse buying occurs simply because the wares are attractively displayed and can be seen as people pass through. The street is designed not as a mall but as a route linking important nodal points: a department store with parking garage at one end and the pedestrianized Market Square with some major clothing stores at the other. Furthermore the distance that one walks—even though an uphill grade toward the camera—appears shorter because of the vertical banner configuration of most signs, pulling the space together. These signs are carefully controlled to avoid appearing "busy" and further contribute a decorative quality to the space. They are simple, straightforward, and easily recognizable, usually identifying each firm with a single word. One tends not to tire quickly in spaces of pleasant character, despite the substantial distances one might actually traverse.

Another street that represents an earlier generation of replanning downtown streets in Germany is the Holstenstrasse in Kiel (Figure 3–7). Planned shortly after the Second World War as part of the rebuilding program, Holstenstrasse was conceived

Fig. 3–7. Kiel, West Germany. An early example of traffic differentiation draws strollers on a Sunday afternoon.

not only to create a better environment for shopping but also, ironically enough, as part of a scheme to accommodate more cars in the center of the city. Similar to solutions in Bochum and Dortmund, the approach in Kiel during the 1950s was to create a new traffic thoroughfare parallel to the main shopping street. Initiating a car-free shopping axis was part of a program to reduce conflicts between pedestrians and vehicles and thus achieve a more efficient flow of traffic generally.

Furnishings and other aesthetic details are not of a particularly distinguished character in the early portions of the networks of pedestrian spaces in Essen and Kiel. Later portions demonstrate increasing awareness of the importance of appealing details and amenities, especially concerning materials, textures, and places to sit. Nonetheless, this picture in Kiel was, interestingly enough, taken on a Sunday afternoon when *no stores at all were open*. People are walking for pleasure and using the opportunity for some leisurely window shopping. Although no one considered it in the original planning of the 1950s, planning downtown streets to be significant magnets for leisure-time activities for people in the city is now considered important in reshaping central urban areas and revitalizing urban streets to achieve high pedestrian counts.

A Network of Attractive Shopping Streets

Attracting people to urban spaces over a larger portion of the day and major parts of the week has lately become a major goal in successful planning or replanning of downtown street spaces. Although this concept still is only grudgingly tolerated by many business (and planning) people in many cities, it was well understood by the Dutch planners after the Second World War in the rebuilding of central Rotterdam, where cars were clearly separated from pedestrian spaces. The area of Lijnbaan in the very heart of the devastated city became world famous as early as the 1950s for its dramatic new concepts of what a city center should be. Its extensive network of attractive shopping streets created *exclusively for pedestrians* was visited by planners and delegations from all parts of the world and may have contributed more than any other city center to the propagation of new concepts for pedestrian-friendly central cities.

The fundamental goal of the attractive shopping streets of the Lijnbaan has subsequently been applied heavily to a great number of other pedestri-

anized main shopping streets: dissipate the consumer's resistance to making a purchase. This goal, of course, relates directly to that of attracting economically strong groups of customers, but it should be considered separately for greatest effectiveness. A willingness to buy can be directly stimulated through the design quality of the physical environment. The means, or subgoals, include the following:

Present goods attractively in a pleasant setting
Provide an opportunity to contemplate goods in a relaxed atmosphere without stress or pressure
Encourage leisurely window shopping, even when stores are closed, as a means of reaching a broader potential market
Stimulate impulse buying by encouraging a prolonged stay and casual strolling in the area
Stimulate a greater willingness to buy through creating a generally positive mood of contentment, leisure, and an engaging sense of attractive urbanity
Provide improved opportunities for comparative shopping

These goals are more carefully differentiated and more dependent upon environmental quality than the more traditional merchandising nostrum: simply get the greatest number of people to pass a given point. The concept is also closely related to one developed in the United States at the same time, that of the suburban shopping mall. The effectiveness of stimulating radically improved sales through design of an attractively stimulating ambience has been so amply proven in countless cases in the intervening years that it hardly requires further elaboration here. Yet it is significant to note that Rotterdam was a rare exception among the world's major cities when its new urban core was designed to have streets for shopping separated from streets for cars.

A view of a characteristic shopping space in the Lijnbaan complex (Figure 3–8) shows some of the design elements aimed at achieving the subgoals listed above, including a pervasive sense of intimate human scale. By keeping the space narrow and immediately adjacent buildings low, designers give visitors a sense of containment and protection while still providing pleasant contact with nature. Trees and beds of flowers help to break up the regularity of straight street space and add color, fragrance, and other sensory stimulation. Overhead canopies serve as protection from the weather when needed, and a canopy crossing from side to side contributes

Fig. 3–8 (left). Rotterdam, the Netherlands. A major exception when built in the 1950s, the Lijnbaan demonstrates how delightful shopping streets can be.

Fig. 3–9 (below). Rotterdam, the Netherlands. Negative effects of progressive modernism around the Lijnbaan in what once was the historic city center.

to a sense of containment. A wooden bench provides a place to pause and relax, and the pavement, with its simple pattern and smooth surface, encourages both walking and use of nonmotorized wheeled vehicles including hand carts and baby strollers.

Although the forms were newly created in Rotterdam, the concepts were derived from traditional land uses in central cities. Among such traditional uses for central-city land, the residential function is included here in high-rise buildings just behind these shops (see Figure 6–15). Office buildings abound in the immediate area so that the rebuilt town center, although very different in appearance and structure from the old, still retains much of the traditional lively intermixing of functions in the urban center.

Yet, while the effects in most regards may be considered successful, some significant goal conflicts still remain in the Lijnbaan example. The architecture and pavement of the Lijnbaan carry a stamp of standardized modernity that could occur anywhere, preventing the citizens from identifying with this particular urban center. At a time when the cities of Warsaw and Danzig in Poland were going to great lengths to recapture the historic structure and substance of their equally destroyed central areas, Rotterdam chose to ignore completely the former urban fabric at its center and design a new complex unrelated to former streets and buildings. For the Dutch this decision was characteristic of the thinking of "progressive modernism" in the

1950s. No doubt in the 1970s this decision would have been entirely different.

The decision to concentrate heavy vehicular traffic in major arteries immediately adjacent to the Lijnbaan also would have been different in the 1970s. As success of the replanned central city continued unabated in the 1960s, pressure to enlarge it increased. Although new office towers, additional commercial buildings, and more housing were added in the course of the years, the system of high-capacity roads that had been planned right through the urban center proved to have significant negative effects on the area that had not been anticipated (Figure 3–9). Among these were physical severance, air pollution, noise, and danger imposed directly on the core area by large streams of traffic. Dutch planners now recognize that the horizontal separation of cars and pedestrians that seemed so progressive in the Rotterdam of the 1950s simply did not go far enough.

Improve Structural Relationships

Goals of progressive planning in the late 1970s designed to resolve segregation of functions and severance of physical and social linkages therefore included an important primary goal: improve the relationships of all central city locations. These concepts today would preclude creation of a tight commercial sector surrounded by high-capacity roads. Improved, integrated urban structure over as large an area as possible should be the goal; access and through roads need to be planned with this goal as major determining factor.

To achieve these structural improvements, the environmental quality over the entire area must be enhanced. This requires, perhaps first of all, reducing the burdens and emissions imposed by motor vehicles or heavy industry. Second, it means removing or correcting symptoms and sources of blight. Third, it means avoiding disadvantages of site through excessive clustering of major magnets. Planning two department stores close together, for example, simply reduces the amount of other spaces and activities that could benefit from their proximity. Creating new paths and relationships through midblock passageways, opening access to centers of blocks, and enhancing the attractiveness of non-commercial secondary areas are among the ways to expand viable possibilities for new retail locations and improve structural relationships of a central area. Main Street should not get all the attention. Origins and destinations—pedestrian magnets—

should be distributed throughout central areas, and barriers in the paths linking these magnets need to be removed. A differentiated network of high-volume pedestrian flow is a most direct method for achieving improved urban structure in cities. Yet businessmen everywhere, seeing that their clients with high buying power have automobiles, persist in the simplistic belief that the best way to induce these customers to spend more of their money downtown is to provide them with more free parking spaces—directly in front of the store if possible. This line of reasoning has resulted in countless programs aimed at converting downtown's main street into a replica of a suburban shopping mall. It doesn't work.

Do Not Suburbanize Downtown

Sacramento's K Street Mall is one such effort that demonstrates the futility of trying to suburbanize downtown. Sadly enough, California's capital city mall has been unsuccessful, as demonstrated by vacant stores, a vacant theater, buildings in a poor state of maintenance, and generally low pedestrian traffic. One basic problem was that this section of the former main shopping street of the region had already lost most of its business to suburban malls before an attempt to save it through conversion to a downtown mall was undertaken. Another problem was the nature of the attempt itself. The midsection of the street was originally treated as an island between the rivers of traffic in large, one-way pairs of streets. Significantly, K Street lacks direct linkages for pedestrians to the capitol, major office buildings, downtown housing areas, and other important magnets or generators of pedestrian traffic.

Instead of direct pedestrian linkages, K Street was given parking lots and a new image as a mall to which one could drive—just as in suburbia. As in suburbia, image, aesthetics, and parking were considered the crucial ingredients. Unfortunately, the new image and aesthetics, instead of substantively tying into the capitol building or other traditional elements, depended primarily upon the questionable abstract sculpture of large angular forms in concrete that have raised considerable controversy (Figure 3–10). Dubbed "the Maginot Line" by some, these foreign forms have been enjoyed mainly by climbing children. They don't seem to have encouraged many people to reidentify with downtown. Artificial aesthetics usually cannot compensate for a lack of local character and may,

Fig. 3–10. Sacramento, CA. Filling the K Street Mall with sculptural forms did not help citizens identify with downtown.

in fact, serve to obliterate familiar associations of long-established clientele.

Hopeful remedial measures, however, have been undertaken in Sacramento. The mall has been extended westward through new commercial development, under the freeway, and into the Old Town area along the river. Major reconstruction was undertaken as a Bicentennial project in this once almost totally defunct area. Actual replicas of several historic buildings were built and other buildings refurbished in a concerted effort to reestablish a sense of continuity with historic traditions. These efforts, coupled with a very thorough restoration of the State Capitol, hold promise of eventually providing Sacramento with a successful synthesis of tradition, commerce, entertainment, and a pleasant walking environment. Since housing areas and office buildings in the immediate vicinity are also included in the redevelopment scheme, the chances for establishing downtown Sacramento as a lively regional center are very good indeed.

Perhaps a street needs, above all, to retain its traditional character as a street space. One of the most striking differences between American and European pedestrianization programs aimed at revitalizing downtown spaces is that, while Europeans continue to call their upgraded spaces by the historic designations, Americans too often feel compelled to find a new, flowery appellation contain-

ing one of the magic words—mall, square, plaza, or court—wistfully hoping that saying so will make it so: a fancy new name will make up for lack of substance or weakness in the change.

Michigan's capital city, Lansing, took this approach in its 1973 major downtown redevelopment program (Figure 3–11). Three separate blocks of the former main street—cut by traffic at every cross street—were transformed into Washington Square with many new plantings, furnishings, concrete in relief, a $90,000 sculpture by Ribera, and massive new buildings. The transformation is almost total. With the exception of the stately bank building, style, scale, detail, and substance do not relate to what was there before. Even assuming that the sole motivation was commercial, one is moved to question the wisdom of blindly destroying any former association (or sentiment) with this particular main street in this particular city. Are the gains worth the losses? Who benefits?

The ultimate irony inherent in renewal rhetoric is revealed in a 1974 photo of a portion of the same street (Figure 3–12) that was not redeveloped and serves under the paradoxical designation of parking mall, a benighted euphemism if there ever was one. Placing the goal of individual private accessibility by car above all others is futile and destructive. Excessive numbers and excessive proximity of motor vehicles—both stored and moving—simply and

Fig. 3–11. Lansing, MI. An attempt to transform a street into a "square."

Fig. 3–12. Lansing, MI. Another section of the same street turned into a parking mall.

plainly degrade environmental quality. Clarification of goals is crucial. To revitalize the economy of the locale, buying power must be attracted into an area, but customers must also be stimulated to apply this buying power by actually spending their money. As many cities have learned to their dismay, filling the parking spaces does not lead inevitably to filling the cash registers.

Does the sidewalk in this parking-lot atmosphere provide an opportunity to contemplate goods in a quiet, attractive atmosphere free from stress or pressure? Does this environment encourage merchants to present their goods most attractively and to invest in upgrading their storefronts? Do weed-filled planters, small potted trees, and cold concrete benches suffice to encourage casual strolling, a prolonged stay, or window shopping . . . even when stores are closed? Hardly. Nor does the physical environment provide really improved opportunities to comparative shop or contribute to a generally positive mood of contentment, stimulated relaxation, or interesting urbanity. On the contrary, the inevitable conclusion is that goal conflicts here are resolved to the detriment of the customer and in favor of his car. Such a compromise can hardly be considered appropriate in a program intended to stimulate customers' willingness to buy.

Attract People Through Pleasant Stimulation

The sad but inevitable conclusion is that commercial goals have been better understood by the planners of Disneyland and suburban shopping malls than by planners and decision makers responsible for downtown rehabilitation. To stimulate economic vitality, it is crucial to attract and hold people frequently and for as long as possible. The proven philosophy is that the more people can be attracted through pleasant stimulation and the longer they can be induced to stay, the more money they will spend. The goal of advanced planning in the Disney enterprises is to develop Florida's Disney World in such a manner that families will want to come to spend entire vacations there, staying within the complex and spending their money for two weeks or more.

Ways to stimulate interest include contrasting and varying the elements of shape, color, pattern, rhythm, and texture; introducing the appealing qualities of natural materials, especially stone and wood; incorporating water into the design; using natural vegetation; and providing a variety of ways

Fig. 3–13. Madison, WI. Shopping malls are creating ever greater pedestrian spaces and are more concerned with aesthetics and comfort.

to experience these different elements through changes in elevation and variety in possible routes. A characteristic example of the application of such devices occurs in American suburban shopping malls. A view inside a mall outside of Madison, Wisconsin (Figure 3–13) demonstrates the trend toward steadily increasing attention to aesthetics and comfort. In a program of investing to attract ever more customers and to meet the rising expectations of those they already have, malls have been steadily upgrading the quality of their artificial environments by adding more surfaces in patterned tiles and other appealing materials, larger areas of real vegetation, splashing fountains, comfortable seating, and more roofed areas. Management has realized that increased contrast with the bleak realm of automobiles and asphalt outside will make people want to stay inside longer. This, in turn, stimulates impulse buying. The old merchant's adage of "Stop loitering, you're hurting business" has been changed to "Have a pleasant stay in our attractive shopping environment."

Controlled environments that enfold shoppers in a protective cocoon of comfort, buyable goods, and

Fig. 3–14. Cincinnati, OH. Amenities that ease walking over long distances are characteristic of many modern airport interiors.

Muzak also are intended to eliminate all distractions of the outside world including danger, stress, and pollution. Even the vicissitudes of the weather —hot, cold, wet, dry, too bright, too dark—are considered potential distractions. The fact that many people actually prefer the qualities and stimulations of natural climate often is considered less important than establishing a constantly controlled ambience in which the carefully calculated stimulus to buy is never disturbed. Thus we see an almost universal trend toward total enclosure of shopping malls.

One major result of extensive modern shopping malls—now being built in many countries of the world—is a seeming paradox: in a period of exploding automobile ownership, more people are walking greater distances than at any time in the past two decades. While only a decade ago accepted conventional wisdom said that normal, automobile-owning consumers would walk no more than three hundred meters from a parking place to their destination in a downtown or suburban environment, it is tardily being recognized that the limit is extremely flexible, depending upon the particular local conditions, especially the attractiveness and interest of walking environments between vehicle and destination.

Mending at the Seams

An interesting parallel between airports and central business districts is the need in both cases to encourage pedestrian traffic by making the route as attractive as possible. A view down a passageway-bridge at the recently built Cincinnati Airport (Figure 3–14) shows two of the simplest ways to generate attractiveness: carpets and windows. Whereas airport passageways of the past have almost always been bleak, boring, uninviting, and tiring, here the application of a pleasant surface underfoot makes walking a far more pleasant experience, while windows let walkers look out at the varied activities of the airport environment and also let the sun look in. Choice of aesthetic materials, concern for pleasant acoustics, and design of pleasant lighting all help lift the spirits of the pedestrian/air traveler. The same considerations hold true for the pedestrian/car traveler in an urban or suburban setting.

Lessons can be learned from the similarities between airports and urban environments, one such being a recognition of the importance of the transition between being a pedestrian and a driver. The airline industry needs the loyalty of passengers in the same way that cities need the loyalty of their citizens, and cities would do well to heed the way the airline industry undertakes to secure this loyalty. The city's pedestrian pathways also need to be made as comfortable, convenient, and pleasant as possible. Great advances have been made in airports during the past thirty years. What was frequently an adventurous dash through wind and weather, up or down slippery stairs, is now most commonly a pleasant stroll through a contained environment linking plane and terminal, with little or no change in elevation. Compare that with the comforts provided by most bus stops, subway stations, and parking facilities in North America! Streets for people, if they are to encourage walking or shopping, badly need to provide attractive interfaces with the vehicles that bring people to the urban space.

One such interface is the cathedral-like covered-street network in the redeveloped area of Östranordstan in downtown Göteborg, Sweden's second-largest city. The blocks were rebuilt with four-story buildings, and street spaces were covered over (Figure 3–15). Since part of this redevelopment includes a major multistory parking garage, the covered-street network provides an immediate interface with a vehicle-free commercial area and also leads directly into the network of pedestrianized streets in the historical core of the city. Furthermore, this redeveloped section of several city blocks is linked directly via a short pedestrian route (under a major road) to the main railroad station and the regional bus terminal. This interface with two other modes of vehicular access to the central business district really plays the major role here, rather than the glossy concept of the covered street. In fact the bland International Style architecture of the redevelopment combines with the roof system to diminish a sense of locality. This space could be anything, even an airport. Although protection from the weather is undoubtedly appreciated at certain times of the year, the great success of Göteborg's Kungsgatan and other uncovered portions of the pedestrian street network suggests that total insulation from the weather is not central to a program of revitalizing commercial streets.

Strengthen a Unique Sense of Place

Comparison between Göteborg and Copenhagen suggests some alternatives to all-new weatherproof development. One of these is a desire to strengthen a unique sense of place. To attract and hold people, cities should cultivate a strong, independent image for which people can develop strong identification and affection. Modern redevelopment, unfortunately, must usually be aimed at the efficiencies of large-scale construction and maximum use of site, goals which tend to create a monotonous, standard, "anyplace" image rather than enhancing a sense of heritage and tradition that builds citizen identification and pride.

Pride of place, quite to the contrary, is best achieved by retaining the scale and space of streets and squares and enhancing the character and quality of buildings, as in the case of Copenhagen's famed Strøget (Figure 3–16). Conserving existing architectural fabric is one of the best, and usually cheapest, ways of developing a strong, positive image for a central business district. Sensitive retention of traditional urban scale (note the new building under construction at right rear) and maintenance of juxtaposed older buildings of different shapes, patterns, materials, and textures

Fig. 3–15. Göteborg, Sweden. Covered-street network of the redeveloped Östranordstan section leads from parking garages to the historic core.

Fig. 3–16. Copenhagen, Denmark. The famed Strøget, main axis through the historic core, shows advantages of conserving existing architectural fabric.

have proven invariably more effective for stimulating interest and attraction than run-of-the-mill Modern Movement architecture and development. This is not to say that contemporary architecture has to be uninteresting, but rather that older buildings frequently have a wealth of craftsmanship, materials, and a variety of details that are not to be duplicated today. Furthermore, a casual and very stimulating multiformity in architectural elements has often accrued over generations. Seemingly accidental spaces in the older architectural fabric add color to a well-rounded image and contribute to an integration of functions by providing odd spaces for a variety of activities such as specialty shops, boutiques, arts and crafts shops, cafes, and other places for meeting or relaxing.

Achieving a multiplicity of functions and a well-rounded image and emphasizing unique characteristics of architecture should thus be considered prime ways of strengthening the retail vitality of a central business distict. An agglomeration of typical cookie-cutter chain-store facades should be left to the private venture suburban mall builders. But even suburban malls have come to value expressions of character and are busily working up ersatz traditions through the use of old lumber, used bricks, and various techniques of antiquing. Why is it, then, that cities everywhere—large, middle-sized, and small—so often treat their genuine architectural heritage with such disdain?

Copenhagen is a major exception, having demonstrated conclusively that there is gold in those old buildings—perhaps not the type of gold the usual speculator is used to developing through destruction and rebuilding, and certainly not the quantity of gold that can be achieved through high-rise construction, but great quantities of gold in the form of retail revitalization nonetheless. Increases in retail turnover amounting to 30, 40, 70 percent and more have been attained in many cities that have followed the early example of Copenhagen by simultaneously pursuing programs of traffic reorganization and architectural rehabilitation.

Bremen, in northern Germany, is another pioneering example, having instituted a major new traffic management scheme at about the same time as Copenhagen, in the early sixties. A view down Obernstrasse, the former major thoroughfare through the historic center (Figure 3–17), shows some of the architectural problems and ambiguities that can arise. At the end of the street is the Market Square with rebuilt historic monuments, including the city hall and cathedral, still asserting their Old World dominance over the modern urban fabric that has been deliberately rebuilt since the Second World War according to traditional height and bulk limitations. Commercially the street is a great success.

Removal of all motorized vehicles save the electric tram has enhanced environmental quality enormously, while great concentrations of commercial, administrative, cultural, and other magnets in this central area assure a constant stream of varied

Fig. 3–17. Bremen, West Germany. Obernstrasse, the main shopping artery, combines the modern with the historic, electric trams with pedestrianized street space.

pedestrian traffic along this major artery. Retail vitality is phenomenal, so much so that most shops have been taken over by retail chain stores. Although height limitations and other restrictions assure retention of a certain sense of the historic street space, the generalized modern architecture of many stores and their prominent signs clearly detract from the unique local image created by the cathedral, city hall, and other buildings that have been rebuilt in historic forms.

Of course this is a matter of degree and of taste. To some, the architecture represents a dynamic interplay of new and old, and the signs, limited in size and configuration, give an element of decorative, contemporary vitality to the space. Others would say that the historic monuments are defiled by advertising on an "American" scale and that local architectural traditions have been spurned by chain stores more concerned about their national image than about the welfare of either the street or the community as a whole. Even the new lampposts have been seen as pandering to a spirit of modernity and commercialism while detracting from the historic sense of place. Lampposts on the nearby Market Square, on the other hand, are originals by Schinkel from the early nineteenth century and were purchased out of permanent storage from a "progressive" city in East Germany. One of the most remarkable business lessons of the 1970s has been that the proper cultivation of history contributes very nicely to improving business vitality.

Just as it has finally dawned on us that reserving some streets for pedestrians is not a matter of dividing society into opposing camps of those who walk and those who drive, so it has also been a revelation of recent years that preserving older buildings and traditional street scale is not a matter of ruining business in order to please the "preservation freaks." In both cases the simplistic notion of irreconcilable opposites has proven to be a myth. Instead of conflict there can be mutual reinforcement. One of the most frequent effects of differentiating street spaces is to reduce conflicts and to improve the general flow of traffic. Similarly, to perceive cultivation of local character and historic traditions as being opposed to the goal of improving business is a grave mistake. Quite the contrary: generally, only flourishing commerce can provide the funds necessary to restore older buildings, while attraction of people and buying power can be very effectively achieved through cultivation of a strong sense of place and interesting local color.

The biggest problem probably lies in bridging the public's imagination gap between what is and what might be. Another problem lies in the greed factor on the part of most developers, who, after all, are in business to tear down, in order to build whatever they perceive will make the best return for the investment. The welfare of commerce in general and of the people in general, therefore, must be placed ahead of the perceived interests of individual developers or particular chain stores with financial clout. A pleasant, attractive environment in which one can walk and shop at one's leisure and with which one can identify because of particularly interesting aesthetics and historical associations inevitably brings benefits to both businesses and individuals. On the other hand, reduction of physically attractive qualities through strictly cost-effective development, overaccommodation of cars, or excessive commercialization brings disadvantages to everyone.

Bremen in northern Germany, Copenhagen in Denmark, the Buchanan Report in Great Britain . . . all are manifestations of practical measures initiated in the early 1960s to reinforce the long-term humanity of central cities as well as to help make them function better. Whether one refers to "traffic cells" or "environmental areas," the concept is to concentrate vehicular movement in areas best suited to its purpose so that other major portions of the street network—freed from the burdens of motorized traffic—can be put to better use serving a wide range of human activities.

Other Uses for Street Spaces

Commerce, of course, is only one of the many human activities that has been effectively promoted by programs for differentiating the use of street spaces in central urban areas. Other goals thus being served include:

Enhancement of living environments for all income groups and ages
Greater attractiveness for office spaces and other commercial places of work
Improvement of civic spirit by providing spaces for unstructured communication and interaction
Stimulus for spending leisure time in the city rather than commuting outward on weekends
Encouragement of alternative forms of mobility, including walking, biking, and the use of public transit

The secret to success lies in an attitude of caring for people, in wanting to create favorable environments to effectively encourage positive social activities. While commerce is extremely important, its health is closely linked to the vigor of many other urban functions. Transforming the busiest portion of Main Street into a commercial mall surrounded by a sea of asphalt and undifferentiated traffic is, therefore, usually a waste of money and

spirit. Not malls, not cities adapted to cars, but cities appropriate to pedestrians: that is the goal.

Internationally, creation of street spaces reserved for pedestrians has already advanced to top position as a leading device for improving commerce and improving traffic generally in urban centers. Yet this is only a transitional stage in achieving better urban environments and reducing negative environmental impacts. The goal can be neither total accessibility for cars nor their total ban, but a finer balance between people and transport and an improved ambience for all human activities. Existing pedestrian districts range broadly in size and scope of the areas they cover. Many, including some of the largest, are being expanded, and highly differentiated networks of street spaces on a scale far larger than anything attempted to date may well become common in the future.

In 1980 Munich seems to hold the record for the largest surface area converted from use by motor vehicles to use by pedestrians. The area of its center includes not only the principal west-east commercial axis from Stachus to Marienplatz, uninterrupted for its entire length of eight hundred meters, but also the north-south axis from Odeonsplatz to Marienplatz and beyond through the large market area, the Viktualienmarkt. Furthermore, a great network of secondary side streets has been transformed for primarily pedestrian use and limited delivery access. The current record is thus held by a contiguous surface network, virtually uninterrupted by cross traffic, that extends some eight hundred meters in its two principal directions.

Give Prestige Spaces to Pedestrians

Fundamental to all successful pedestrianization seems to be the philosophy that the starting place for a pedestrian district is the heart of the city, that is, historically the most important urban space: either the cathedral square, the marketplace, city hall plaza, another important plaza, or simply the intersection of the two most important through routes crossing at the center of town. Crucial to programs of creating public open spaces for social and commercial interaction is the important psychological breakthrough of turning over the most prestigious spaces at the heart of the city to pedestrians. If there are several such spaces, each should be converted into a people-place and then linked via attractive, barrier-free pedestrian routes with each other.

The name of the game is captivating people. The methodology is to exploit and enhance every conceivable attraction, to make enjoying these attractions easy, and to spread the magnetism over as wide an area as possible. Success can be measured in terms of how far people can be lured to walk, how long they can be enticed to stay, and how frequently they can be motivated to return.

Link Origins and Destinations

Planning for walking needs to be considered, therefore, on the same terms as any other form of movement—in terms of origins and destinations and of minimum conflicts and maximum benefits along the route. Considering origins means that other modes of transport also need to be planned in an integrated system so that comfortable interfaces can be provided and disturbing conflicts avoided. Too often in the past the question of origins of pedestrian trips has been considered in only the most primitive way, trying to do away with the problem by putting the origin immediately adjacent to or even right on top of the destination. This was once the last word in planning and indeed remains the fervent wish of merchants unversed in the magic of genuine urban attractions: acres of asphalt immediately in front of or behind stores; wall-to-wall parking, basement parking, rooftop parking, and wrap-around parking—enormous destruction of useful building fabric in the name of progress.

Origin means—or should mean—far more than just the place where one can park one's car. It can mean the place where one lives or where one works, the railroad station, the airport terminal, subway stops, bus stops, ferry terminals, taxi stands, or bike racks. Origins for pedestrian journeys are everywhere that people give up their stationary status or their role as a passenger or driver in order to begin to make their way by foot from one place to another. Every journey from place to place in a city is to a greater or lesser extent a walking trip. Clearly the place of origin for a great many of these walking trips can be anticipated and thus can be planned.

Destinations, too, can be anticipated and their relationships to places of origin carefully planned. Normal destinations for which a part of the journey is undertaken by foot each day include schools, places of work, shops and stores of all kinds, profes-sional offices, places of business dealing in services, government offices, churches, cultural magnets, and places for leisure-time activities. Traditionally, many of these activities have been and continue to be found in the central city. In cities where this is no longer the case, the quality of urban life is on the wane, and it should be a major goal of urban development plans to restore these vital functions to the central area.

Assuming that these major functions have not been removed to suburban locations or displaced by parking facilities, all urban development planning should include the conduct of origin and destination studies for *pedestrian* traffic. Only in their capacity as pedestrians can people enter and participate in the meaningful activities of schools, shops, offices, cultural institutions, and essentially every other type of building intended to attract people, notwithstanding all types of drive-in facilities that attempt to develop an additional market.

The public open space between the main railroad station and the cathedral in Cologne, Germany (Figure 3–18), is an excellent example of effective replanning based on origins and destinations of pedestrian movement. The railroad station serves not only long-distance travelers and intercity commuters, but workers and shoppers from the surrounding region as well. It is therefore a major point of origin for pedestrian traffic with destinations throughout the core area and, conversely, a major destination for pedestrians from the major shopping areas, offices, city hall, theaters, restaurants, the promenade along the Rhine, and a variety of other places of activity. This space, formerly a tangle of traffic with cars, trucks, buses, taxis, and streetcars all competing with pedestrians and with each other, now has been sorted out to facilitate the movement of all modes. The streetcar has been put underground, separate taxi access and bus-stopping bays with covered waiting areas have been provided, and the street has been bridged over with a generous system of ramps, stairs, and escalators that lead to a new pedestrian platform built around the cathedral at its floor level. Comfortable, unhindered pedestrian access now leads directly from the trains through this important nodal space to the most heavily frequented destinations in downtown Cologne. Not a single traffic street to cross; no dangers; no conflicts; no Don't Walk signs.

The following photo (Figure 3–19) is a view in the opposite direction showing the broad plaza that has been created in front of the cathedral. The roof

Fig. 3–18. Cologne, West Germany. The public open space between the railroad station and the cathedral provides for easy pedestrian movement.

Fig. 3–19. Cologne, West Germany. This view in the opposite direction suggests the generous space now dedicated to pedestrians.

of the railroad station can be seen just right of center between the cathedral's west facade and the grove of trees with a rebuilt historic gateway. Much effort has clearly been expended to divert vehicular traffic into areas most capable of handling it and to give major spaces to pedestrians. This large plaza is continued around the cathedral to a major museum complex off the picture to the right and then, further south, directly into Wallrafplatz and the area of hotels, offices, major department stores, and the two most important shopping streets, Hohestrasse and Schildergasse. While in other cities the open spaces around major churches, cathedrals, and other public monuments tend to become parking lots for shopping and other downtown functions, in Cologne this space has been made into a major public plaza dedicated to use by pedestrians at all times. Not only does it serve as the great urban plaza for ceremonies, festivals, and demonstrations, it also has the continual function of being the crossing point of many routes for pedestrians between many origins and destinations. Although almost entirely without retail commerce, this plaza is a major node in the continuous network of pedestrian routes.

The two views of Cologne exemplify a fundamental principle: pedestrian areas in urban centers must be considered *not* as islands in a sea of traffic, but rather as segments in a continuous network of routes for pedestrians. Even at early stages when various segments are not yet connected, their arrangement should always be planned with the goal of linkage in mind, so that this further development is not later precluded by, for example, intervening major facilities for vehicular traffic. Philosophies and methodologies concerning streets for people have developed chronologically during the past two decades in Germany in three broad stages:

1. Elimination of conflict and danger on the most heavily used commercial streets by banning vehicles from the busiest portions on a limited-time basis. In Cologne this step was taken on Hohestrasse and Schildergasse as early as 1949.
2. Connection of the most important generators of pedestrian traffic (origins and destinations) in the core area with a continuous route, eliminating all barriers, detours, and hazards. Cologne's unbroken linkage from the railroad station over the bridge to the cathedral, via Wallrafplatz, along Hohestrasse, and to the end of Schildergasse, was undertaken in 1968.

3. Establishment of priority for a continuous network of pedestrian-preferred routes throughout the central area that would gradually work out through the entire urban fabric. Such a network has to be linked specifically to public transit stops, urban green areas, waterfronts, and other areas of recreation, and should have provisions for bicycles as well. In Cologne, planning and development for this stage has occurred throughout the 1970s.

By 1978 the only city actually to have achieved this ultimate goal appears to be the small Swedish city of Västerås, although Cologne and Munich in Germany are two larger cities that continue to make significant progress in this direction.

Stress the Benefits

A space analogous to Cologne's cathedral plaza in being the city's premier urban space, the social and cultural center of the entire urban area, and the hub of a large pedestrian network is Munich's Marienplatz (Figure 3–20). While it may seem impossible for most North American cities ever to attain such attractive urban plazas in their central business districts, one must recognize that these European examples were dominated by motor vehicles until only a few years ago. An imagination gap always exists between what is and what might be. Certainly most of the citizens of Munich and Cologne were very surprised by the transformations of their downtowns: few of them would have said they preferred walking to driving their cars if asked beforehand. It is important to stress the benefits first and then follow with the consequences. In the United States and Canada, just as in Europe, effective methods can always be found if the fundamental purpose is to create better urban environments for people.

Interestingly enough, Munich itself was subjected to the oft-heard argument about impossibility of transferral. During the 1960s, when concepts of drastically changing movement and development patterns in Munich first were being considered, the success of Copenhagen's Strøget from the early sixties was frequently cited as a model. Opponents to the ideas of traffic management and pedestrianization were quick to argue: "Yes, but it wouldn't work here." The urban and economic structure of Copenhagen was quite different, they pointed out; the transit situation and dependence

Fig. 3–20 (left). Munich, West Germany. Marienplatz, in front of city hall and near the cathedral, is now a living room for the city.

Fig. 3–21 (below). Munich, West Germany. The city's great network of pedestrianized streets had its start in front of the famous Hofbräuhaus beer hall.

upon automobiles were different; and besides, the Danes have an entirely different character and relatability to urban spaces than the Bavarians do. All of these factors, it was insisted, doomed any attempts at transferring pedestrianization concepts from Copenhagen to Munich to failure. A decade later, Munich is now *the* example to the world, but opponents to changing urban environments in favor of people still say, "Yes, but it wouldn't work here."

One effective way to begin giving priority to people is to determine a historically important people-place in the urban environment and ban all motorized vehicles from it. In Munich, which prides itself on its historic breweries going back many centuries, this initial people-place was the street immediately in front of the celebrated Hofbräuhaus beer hall (Figure 3–21). Everything else spread out from there. More usually, though, this premier urban space is the intersection or plaza in front of the cathedral, the city hall, the courthouse, or another prominent monument of civic architecture. Frequently it is precisely the intersection of the main north-south and east-west traffic arteries that cross in the heart of the central business district. In fact, in Munich a major intersection of this nature occurs precisely at the city hall on Marienplatz; this point serves as the heart of the pedestrian district, now extending more than one-half mile in either direction north and west of this intersection (and lesser distances to the east and south).

Fig. 3–22 (above). Göteborg, Sweden. Merchants' initiative helped to pedestrianize Kungsgatan, Göteborg's main shopping street downtown.

Fig. 3–23 (right). Göteborg, Sweden. Kungsgatan before 8:00 P.M. on a summer evening. Excessive segregation of functions desolates streets after business hours.

Focus on the Statue

The traditional approach of widening both the primary north-south and east-west arteries through the center of town in order to facilitate the movement of cars and relieve congestion is increasingly falling out of favor. A characteristic example of this antiquated cars-before-people approach occurred in Salt Lake City, Utah, as recently as 1978, when it was proposed that the statue of Brigham Young be moved out of the intersection of South Temple and Main Streets in order to handle an increasing volume of cars expected through the center of town in coming years. A better solution, in keeping with the great urban successes of people-before-cars programs in many of the world's great cities during the past two decades, would be to use the statue, this intersection, Temple Square, and the most prestigious section of Main Street as the core of a high-quality people-place in downtown Salt Lake City. The necessity of preserving downtown vitality everywhere and the rising expectations for safe and very attractive urban spaces suggest that the only solution is to begin a network of spaces reserved for

pedestrians at the most important spot downtown and work out from there. In that way also the Mormon leader could be spared ignominious removal by the cars of his latter-day followers.

Instead of Brigham Young, Göteborg, Sweden, has a statue of King Gustav Adolph. It has a Lutheran cathedral instead of a Mormon temple and a King Street (Kungsgatan) instead of a Main Street (Figure 3–22). All of these are linked together in a continuous network of spaces for people, while vehicular traffic is close by but distinctly subordinated to pedestrian traffic throughout the entire core area. Göteborg was an early exception to the prevalent skepticism or open hostility of the business community to the idea of pedestrianizing the main shopping street. In this case the initiative came from the merchants themselves and the space was repaved wall to wall with their blessing. Subsequently, cross streets, parallel streets, and subsidiary spaces have all been linked into an extensive network several kilometers long. Important design principles that have since been used in a great many other cities are evident in Göteborg; they are equally applicable to the Salt Lake Citys everywhere, as soon as local authorities recognize that their two-legged rather than four-wheeled constituents deserve the greatest favors.

Let us recapitulate three important design principles briefly:

Find *the* premier urban space and devise a traffic management scheme to prevent all cars and trucks from crossing this place. (Hint: when you find the statue of a major historical figure, this is the place.)

Create an expanding network of spaces for pedestrians linking the premier urban space with major shopping areas, cultural monuments, and other magnets and significant destinations in the core area.

Reconceive the entire movement system of the city so that walking and bicycling are encouraged and developed into significant portions of such a system.

The creation of malls is not enough. Neither enclosed malls on the model of suburban shopping centers nor closing the busiest (commercial) section of Main Street to vehicles will revive a downtown area that has been in decline. To generate life again it is necessary to stimulate more than just the shopping function. A view of Göteborg's Kungsgatan before 8:00 P.M. on a summer evening (Figure 3–23) demonstrates that one-sided emphasis on commerce can result in sheer desolation for significant portions of each day and week. Excessive segregation of urban functions is a problem. In part it has resulted from a naive academic belief that "cleaner" urban structures could be obtained through horizontal separation of different land uses: commercial, residential, entertainment, administrative, and others, all neatly defined in separate blocks of color on a zoning map.

This segregation has also resulted in part from the peculiarities of centrifugal urban development induced by automobiles. Both intentional segregation through zoning and unintentional decentralization through cars have inflicted all-but-mortal wounds on the social and economic viability of urban centers. Much attention in the urban redevelopment planning of the past two decades has been devoted to countering these effects.

Learn from Minneapolis

In North America the example of Minneapolis has had great impact. Perhaps its greatest lesson has been that quite radical alteration of ordinary, commercial thoroughfares in ordinary, North American, grid-pattern street systems is indeed possible. The transformation of Nicollet Avenue into the Nicollet Avenue transitway-mall during the mid-1960s has been adequately discussed elsewhere.* A view down the converted street space (Figure 3–24) demonstrates the basic measures that were taken to convert an ugly and ordinary Main Street into a very attractive space for people that emphasizes amenity and encourages walking. A building-front-to-building-front distance of almost twenty-five meters (eighty feet) with four lanes of moving traffic, a lane of parking on either side, uninteresting straight sidewalks with tall mercury-vapor lamps and no trees was transformed into an aesthetically pleasing space with many trees, few vehicles, no garish overhanging signs, and a pleasing sense of human scale. In terms of acceptance, use, financial returns, and imitation by other cities, the conversion of Nicollet has been an unqualified success.

---

* See, for example, Ronald Wiedenhoeft, "Minneapolis: a Closer Look," *Urban Land*, Vol. 34 (Oct, 1975), pp. 8–17; reprinted in Ronald Wiedenhoeft, *Readings in Architecture and Urban Design* (Dubuque, Iowa: Kendall/Hunt Publishing Company, 1978).

In terms of advanced-planning practices elsewhere, however, certain shortcomings of the Nicollet Avenue conversion have become apparent. These include:

Regular interruption of the pedestrian space at every cross street by undifferentiated motorized traffic and Don't Walk signs

Intrusion and negative environmental impact on the pedestrian space by large, noisy, smelly, diesel buses

Arbitrariness of the sinuous configuration and the all-new furnishings or special events designed into the space, rather than enhancing any elements of local color or traditional character that might have survived from the past

Excessive variations in height and texture of the buildings, ranging in height from two to fifty-two stories and including a new parking garage fronting directly on the pedestrian space

Excessive concentration on purely economic goals, including reinforcement of the retail function, stimulation of construction in the commercial sector, and enormous increases in real estate values

In defense of the program in Minneapolis, the following counterarguments can be listed:

As in most North American urban centers, Minneapolis has no fixed-rail transportation system, so that there is heavy reliance on automobiles as a substitute for mass transit, even for the journey to work in downtown locations. This requires a great amount of space—both in streets for circulation and in storage facilities for parking—for all of these vehicles.

Bus transit, prior to construction of the transitway-mall, was very much on the wane in Minneapolis, and the program of encouraging a more favorable modal split—more people in public transit—included the rerouting of buslines so that all passengers could get directly onto the region's main commercial street with no more than one transfer.

The sinuous configuration of the transitway was a deliberate design device to give the original eight-block length of redesigned street greater variety, interest, and a sense of containment, thus shortening the apparent length of the street and increasing the willingness of people to walk. With frontage lines exactly parallel on both sides of the street over its entire length, the transitway's sinuous configuration contributes to an illusion of the variety present in irregular historic urban

streets and squares (Figure 3–25).

Variations of height and texture of buildings have always been characteristic of American patterns in urban development and may be considered a contribution to dynamism and variety of American cityscapes, depending on one's point of view. The new Investors' Diversified Services Center—all new development—includes within one square block buildings that cover the entire range from two to fifty-two stories.

A counterargument to the perception that there has been excessive concentration on economic goals in the Nicollet Avenue transformation is provided by examination of the long-term goals of downtown development in Minneapolis. Housing plays a major role, especially a great number of housing units for the elderly in downtown locations where community facilities are readily at hand. Extensions of the pedestrian paths, especially through the skyway system but also through expansion of the mall south into the Loring Greenway and northeast toward new housing areas along the Mississippi, are providing direct linkage between major housing areas and the central business district, hospital facilities, parks, a community college, museums, a concert hall, and

Fig. 3–24 (facing page). Minneapolis, MN. View down Nicollet, transformed from avenue into transitway-mall. The conversion has been a great success. (Photo: Courtesy of Downtown Council of Minneapolis)

Fig. 3–25 (near left). Minneapolis, MN. The sinuous configuration of the transitway on Nicollet conveys a sense of variety and containment.

convention facilities. Dynamic linkage via attractive pedestrian routes between many important downtown origins and destinations seems assured eventually.

Yet what happens today on the streets just one block away from Nicollet? Looking at street spaces immediately adjacent to the transitway-mall in Minneapolis reveals that the traffic management scheme has not been designed to reduce vehicular traffic, but rather to improve its flow through separation of modes (Figure 3–26). Here a major distinction is revealed between cities in North America, as represented by Minneapolis, and cities in Europe. While skyways and other amenities encourage pedestrian traffic in limited areas, the major effort here is clearly to facilitate vehicular movement. America still has not gotten away from the concept of rebuilding cities suitable for cars. Suitability for people is apparently an also-ran.

Reduce the Volume of Traffic

The main concept in Central Europe, as we have so

amply seen, is *Verkehrsberuhigung*, that is, "quieting" or reducing the volume of vehicular traffic. What Nicollet is to Minneapolis, then, Kärntnerstrasse is to Vienna, the capital of Austria and the former seat of the Hapsburg empire. A visual comparison is most instructive (Figure 3–27).

Vienna's main street is still called "street," not "mall."

The historic shape and scale of the street space has been retained; there are no skyscrapers, nor are there any two-story buildings.

Great care has been taken to retain and restore the older architecture that gives the space its uniqueness and identifiability.

Vienna has taken an entirely different approach to signage, controlling the size and aesthetics, but accepting overhanging signs as decorative additions to the space.

Uninterrupted flow of pedestrians takes place at grade in the street space, rather than in air-conditioned tubes above the flow of vehicles.

The pedestrianized main street is not interrupted by any cross traffic from its beginning near the opera to its major terminus at the cathedral.

Fig. 3–26. Minneapolis, MN. Within a block of Nicollet, other streets reveal that motorized traffic has been encouraged rather than reduced.

Fig. 3–27. Vienna, Austria. Kärntnerstrasse, the main street of downtown Vienna, provides interesting contrasts to Nicollet in Minneapolis.

STREETS FOR PEOPLE

The pedestrian axis is expanded into a network by incorporating other urban spaces including the Graben, the Neuer Markt, through-block passageways, courtyards, and other subsidiary spaces in an integrated system.

Public seating in the space is an important element in the design and is heavily used by people of all ages. It is particularly useful for integrating elderly people into the life of the city.

A major aspect of Vienna's program to reduce vehicular traffic in the core area is construction of a new subway system, undertaken simultaneously with the creation of pedestrianized streets.

Pedestrianize to Achieve Benefits

The point of comparing pedestrian zones in various cities is not to assign prizes for the best or the biggest, but rather to establish principles that can then be applied elsewhere. Planners and merchants seem to be better able to learn from the experiences of others than from their own mistakes. Above all, the most important lesson of the ground swell of pedestrianization that has become a powerful wave by the 1980s is that *trend is not destiny*. The post–World War Two trend of ever more cars does not mean that cities must accept as destiny ever wider roads and fewer trees, ever more civilizing urban functions replaced by insolent parking garages, and ever fewer places for people to sit or walk in comfort and at leisure. In most of the leading examples of transformed commercial street spaces, many merchants strongly opposed the removal of cars, feeling that this step would be the death of their businesses. Internationally, pedestrianization is now recognized as one of the most effective means to improve urban environments and stimulate trade in central areas. The process of converting urban areas to use by pedestrians now enjoys the full support of the Organization for Economic Cooperation and Development (O.E.C.D.), the economic United Nations of the noncommunist world, and has become a favored device in iron-curtain countries as well.

The international traffic symbol signaling areas restricted to pedestrians is a circle of blue surrounding the white silhouettes of an adult and child walking hand in hand (Figure 3–28). This welcome sign had come to be recognized by the 1970s as a sign of "citizen-lib" the world over. No other single

Fig. 3–28. Munich, West Germany. Symbolizing "citizen-lib" in many countries, this sign is helping to make cities safer and more attractive for people.

factor has contributed so much to making central cities safe and attractive places for people of all social groups as the revolution in urban land use that this sign represents. While now it may seem a bit of a truisim, we had to discover all over again that walking is the most democratic form of movement. Walking makes less differentiation among people on the basis of age, race, sex, level of income, or level of education than any other mode. It is truly the people's mode of movement in cities, one which even enhances accessibility for the handicapped.

Regulate Vehicular Access

It was once assumed that creating a pedestrian zone in a commercial area required that rear access for deliveries be established first. As providing delivery access from the rear, however, proved to be very difficult, if not impossible, in many cities, it was soon discovered that such rigorous separation was just not necessary. If only the priority for people can be firmly established, coexistence with vehicles can work quite well. In fact, experience has shown that deliveries from the front over a pedestrian area under controlled conditions is much preferable to the destruction of urban substance that frequently would be necessary if delivery accessibility from the rear were to be fully developed. Basically only the establishment of limits on three major aspects of delivery traffic is needed: size of the vehicles, times during which deliveries may be made, and character of allowable vehicular movements when in the space.

The example of Munich's main pedestrian axis also serves to set some workable norms that have regulated coexistence of vehicles and pedestrians. The size of delivery vehicles is limited to a maximum of seven and one-half tons, while the allowable times are restricted to weekday periods when the fewest pedestrians are in the space: from 10:30 every evening until 9:45 on weekday mornings, until 9:00 Saturday mornings, and not at all between 9:00 A.M. Saturdays and 10:30 P.M. Sundays. Limiting conditions for the deliveries (Figure 3–28) are translated as follows:

1. Duration of the vehicle's stay in the pedestrian zone is to be limited only to the amount of time absolutely necessary.
2. Pedestrian traffic always has the right of way.
3. Vehicles may move only at a walking pace.
4. Trucks may be driven in reverse only if a second person directs the movement from outside the vehicle.
5. Signs regulating the direction of movement at entry points must be observed; turning vehicles around is forbidden.
6. A protective distance of 2.0 meters from all buildings and 0.5 meters from all other objects must be maintained.
7. Every owner of a delivery vehicle is responsible for repaying the city for any damages or costs brought about by the operation of his vehicle in the pedestrian zone.

Coexistence is not only possible, it is the only solution. Some type of emergency vehicles, of course, always require access into and through pedestrian spaces, although regulations about the size of fire department equipment that must be able to maneuver in the space vary considerably. Regulations concerning fire equipment size must consider minimum supporting capability of the pavement and allowable configurations of plantings, furnishings, or other obstructions. Some cities specify that major hook-and-ladder units must be able to make it through, while others provide alternate access for heavy equipment and use only small vehicles in the pedestrian zone.

In 1975, Oak Park, Illinois, a western suburb of Chicago, established the Oak Park Village Mall on one segment of a grid-pattern street system. Earth berms covered with trees, grass, and other plant materials served to give a sense of containment and human scale to the space. An aerial view of the mall (Figure 3–29) reveals that vehicular routes through the space are maintained, while a pedestrian-level view of the same space (Figure 3–30) shows how the existence of a route for vehicles can be virtually obscured in order to create a series of intimately scaled places for people.

Relieve Endlessness, Provide Comfort

One of the main successes of Oak Park's experiment is applicable to a great many cities in North America and elsewhere: relieve the compelling endlessness of what was the main sluice for vehicles through the heart of town. Less distinguished architecturally than many historic main streets in Europe, the central commercial strip in Oak Park depends for its success largely on the character of spatial design between parallel store fronts. As opposed to the artificiality and questionable taste of man-made furnishings in so many of our urban malls, emphasis in Oak Park is on the timeless aesthetics of living vegetation and natural materials such as wood and granite. The universal appeal of nature always deserves to be given priority. By comparison, modern or pseudo-artistic creations in fiberglass, steel, or concrete often look rather arbitrary, dated, or cheap.

Degrees of comfort for pedestrians is another factor that varies considerably from place to place. Once the need to walk in safety and comfort has been satisfied, a walker's next most important desire is for a place to sit. On Oak Park's mall, seats may be insufficient in quantity, but they are high in quality and well located. Wood is far superior to stone or concrete as a surface for sitting, a backing of vegetation gives a feeling of security while seated, and orientation toward passing crowds provides the interest of human activity and continuous change. Comfort and interest are crucial factors in the design and furnishing of sitting places for people.

These concepts were applied earlier and to a greater extent in the pedestrian zone of downtown Munich (Figure 3–31). The benefits of not only allowing but encouraging people to sit have far outweighed any imagined disadvantages; and Munich's revolutionary step of providing numerous movable chairs with backrests and armrests in its pedestrian district, rather than fixed slabs of concrete or stone that city fathers and urban designers have considered good enough for so many of the world's public spaces, has been amply justified. One of the—perhaps unexpected—additional benefits of this magnanimous public gesture has

Fig. 3–29 (left). Oak Park, IL. Access routes for emergency vehicles are provided at the Oak Park Village Mall. (Photo: Courtesy of Joe Karr Associates, Chicago)

Fig. 3–30 (below). Oak Park, IL. A pedestrian-eye view of the same space shows how earth berms and vegetation can create a sense of human scale. (Photo: Courtesy of Joe Karr Associates, Chicago)

Fig. 3–31. Munich, West Germany. The benefits of encouraging people to sit, as demonstrated along Neuhauserstrasse, far outweigh any supposed disadvantages.

Encouragement to walk longer distances and stay longer times because of the opportunity to stop and rest

Social integration of young and old people and encouragement of social communication

Stimulation of leisure-time use of the space

Social control through the constant presence of people observing the space

Another major lesson of recent successes in converting urban spaces into more attractive places for people is that the most effective devices usually are simply rediscoveries of time-honored and well-known means for satisfying fundamental physical, psychic, and social needs of people. Among these are really comfortable places to sit, the presence of trees and other forms of vegetation, nearby sources of food and drink, aesthetically pleasing materials and textures, a reassuring sense of spatial containment, an opportunity to watch people, a choice of sitting in the sun or the shade, a chance to form conversational groups, toilet facilities nearby, and an overall feeling of well-being and safety. Why has it taken so long to discover something so obvious? Apparently the dynamic forces of commerce and mobility that so drastically transformed cities in the nineteenth and twentieth centuries seemed to be at odds with the indulgence of spiritual and creature comforts. The city was considered the place for dramatic progress, ill suited to relaxation and enjoyment. These preconceptions are now giving way to a recognition that commerce and comfort, not at all antithetical, are, in fact, mutually supportive to a high degree.

Increase Leisure-Time Activities

Goals to encourage leisure-time activities in urban centers will further increase the number of people in the area and distribute them over larger portions of the day and week. The first requirement is to design the space in such a way as to encourage a wide variety of users and uses through the attractiveness of the space itself (walls, floor, and furnishings), the interesting nature of the activities one is likely to find in the space (festivals, concerts, and public ceremonies, as well as itinerant musicians, sidewalk vendors, religious fanatics, and just plain folks), and the attractive linkages making it convenient and natural for people to enter the space (both as a destination in itself and as a route leading to other destinations). In its simplest terms

been a high degree of social control that many seated people provide free of charge in public spaces. It is a variation of Jane Jacobs's concept of "the eyes on the street," only far more effective here than a few people looking out from windows of upstairs residences. The presence of many comfortable seats in a public space such as Munich's Neuhauserstrasse thus actually serves several purposes:

Enhanced attractiveness of the space for pedestrians

the problem is reduced to (1) creating an attractive box; (2) putting interesting activities into the box; and (3) providing many easy and natural routes into and through the box.

Further encouragement of leisure-time activities can focus on satisfying the specific needs of four different groups of people: those who live nearby in the central area, those who live further out in the urban region, those who work in the area, and those who shop in the area. While the interests of all groups are not necessarily dissimilar, distinctions must be made in order to determine when one wants to stimulate enhanced activity in the space—lunch hours, evenings, or weekends—and to provide easy accessibility for each of the groups, be they from housing areas, public transportation terminals, office areas, or major department stores. Through careful design, planning of activities, and provision of attractive linkages, social behavior can be nudged into patterns entirely different from the usual frantic movement at morning and evening rush hours.

Physical design, planned activities, and generous and attractive facilities are all critical to programs attempting to attract more people into urban centers. Starting with programs to make public plazas and pedestrian streets into places for short-term recreation during lunch hours for those working in the area and for rest between shopping and other errands for those using the center for commerce and business, cities everywhere have been discovering the enormous unexploited potential of their main public areas. Bonn, the capital of West Germany, initiated an ambitious program of planned events during the summers and found that peak traffic in several areas was shifted from business opening and closing hours to lunch time and evenings. Every city in Germany with a pedestrian district—and at last count there were over five hundred of them—now has at least one annual festival to draw everyone into the public space and reinforce identity with that particular locale. Such festivals logically take place in the premier urban spaces where greatest attention has been devoted to enhancing the image of an attractive place for people.

A discouraging comparison with the detail view of Munich's Neuhauserstrasse is provided by a similar detail from New York's Avenue of the Americas (Sixth Avenue), a street that serves similar purposes (Figure 3–32). Numbers of pedestrians are high in both cases, while priorities in terms of urban design are grossly different. Maximum exploitation of land through high-rise construction

Fig. 3–32. New York, NY. The Avenue of the Americas, as contrasted with Munich's Neuhauserstrasse, reveals a strikingly different set of priorities.

and maximum flow of one-way traffic on the wide street obviously have highest priority in New York. Aesthetics and amenities for pedestrians are at the bottom of the list. Emissions and dangers from traffic are excessive. Pavements are filthy. Materials and textures are uninteresting, chaotic, and poorly maintained. Little is done to attract and hold people in the space, and if one needs to rest while waiting for a bus, the only alternatives are to lean against a wall or sit on a water pipe. Although the numbers of plazas, benches, and pedestrian passageways—provided by developers in exchange for mammoth zoning bonuses allowing increased exploitation of individual building sites—are gradually increasing, the net result is mistreatment of citizens and visitors alike.

Modern development and commercial vitality, however, do not need to foster such sleazy insensitivity. A view in a redeveloped section of central Bonn (Figure 3–33) demonstrates another approach to several detail-design aspects of modern commercial districts. Although not visible in this view, no zoning bonuses can be milked by the developers, other than the benefits of greater customer attraction that can be achieved through good design. Buildings must simply respect historic height and bulk limitations; open spaces are not meaningless plazas at the base of tall buildings but rather traditional contained street spaces. Paving materials, planters, lamps, tree grates, and benches are all part of a coordinated program of aesthetics in the public area and are provided as a public service rather than in exchange for private gain. In order to open up the narrow street spaces and create a small plaza, a corner of the department store is cut away under the cantilevered building mass above. Very comfortable benches are provided by the city with no motive save to provide for pedestrian comfort, relaxation, and pleasurable experience of the space. The steps around the tree can be used as additional surfaces for sitting. Patterns and materials of building surfaces and the quality of signage are

further contributions to aesthetic quality of the space. The streets formerly dominated by vehicles are now a part of an extensive network of pedestrianized streets covering most of the historic urban core of Bonn.

Encourage Walking

An argument frequently is heard that North America somehow is fundamentally different from Europe; that Americans have become so used to driving from an early age that it is difficult or impossible to get them to change their habits and walk substantial distances in central urban areas. This is a myth. Evidence to the contrary has been accumulating at least since the establishment of America's first downtown mall in Kalamazoo, Michigan, in 1959. Kalamazoo Mall has undergone major improvement and expansion since then and more than seventy additional cities in the United

Fig. 3–34 (below). San Francisco, CA. A weekend fair on Union Street: fulfilling Americans' desire to participate in communal experiences.

Fig. 3–33 (above). Bonn, West Germany. Streets formerly dominated by vehicles are now redesigned for the comfort of pedestrians.

States and Canada have established important downtown pedestrian areas in the interim.* From Eugene and Fresno on the West Coast to Dallas and Miami Beach in the South, Minneapolis and Ottawa in the North, and Baltimore, New London, and Portland on the East Coast, dozens of North American cities have found that their citizenry will indeed walk very willingly, if only they are given

* For a compendium of information on more than seventy North American malls and transitways, see Roberto Brambilla and Gianni Longo, *For Pedestrians Only* ((New York: Whitney Library of Design, 1977). Further information on American experiences has been published by the Downtown Research and Development Center, e.g., Lawrence Alexander, editor, *Downtown Mall Annual & Urban Design Report*, Volume 3 (New York: Downtown Research and Development Center, 1977).

appropriate environments in which to do so.

Temporary fairs, festivals, and markets held in more and more cities across the continent have been the vehicles for exercising Americans' generally unfilled desire to participate as pedestrians in communal experiences in public spaces. A view west on San Francisco's Union Street (Figure 3–34) shows the crowds that will turn out spontaneously for something as modest as a simple crafts fair in the street space over a weekend. While occasional crowds of this magnitude do not necessarily justify street closings or creation of pedestrian routes, they do demonstrate the need to incorporate sociointellectual goals in all urban development programs.

If planned correctly, urban development can contribute significantly to the development of social and intellectual bonds in an urban community. While such factors have been mysteriously neglected in the urban planning of the twentieth century, considerations of social relationships and intellectual development and communication among the populace historically have always played significant roles in the foundation, organization, and administration of cities. The public forum of urban open spaces has historically been the place where important social relationships have been cultivated and knowledge and attitudes developed. Among the uses that can be found to return the public spaces of today to their true role, we must see that they (1) foster communication, exchange of information, and formation of opinions; (2) stimulate citizen participation in the urban development process; and (3) integrate various social groups into the community, encourage good citizenship, and secure a sense of belonging.

Provide a Public Forum

When planning urban spaces we must design public open spaces as an effective forum for the citizenry. Places suitable for large political demonstrations and discussions as well as those that stimulate direct contact and discussion on an individual basis should be incorporated into designs. Hyde Park Corner in London is a fine example of a forum provided in the public realm where speeches, presentations, and demonstrations can take place and discussions among individuals are stimulated. But such spaces need to be integrated thoroughly with the urban fabric and brought into close proximity and association with other functions of an urban core. Well-planned pedestrian precincts present such opportunities.

The view of Union Street illustrates another important consideration of public spaces for pedestrians: a major reason for many people to go there is simply to observe other people and to obtain information and impressions in an undirected manner. Of course these spaces also greatly enhance opportunities to meet people, to talk, and to exchange ideas, but the simple function of encouraging people to be together as a society under pleasant and comfortable environmental conditions should not be undervalued. Environmental design can contribute much to this end.

A view down the Via Mazzini, a major pedestrian artery in Verona, Italy (Figure 3–35), illustrates another successful step in the realization of cities for people. Verona is fortunate to have retained its fine texture of integrated functions in an urban fabric of traditional scale and character. It always had been a city for people, although this fact became partially obscured through the overwhelming impact of automobiles in the fifties and sixties. Little more than the removal of these foreign elements and the repaving of the floor of the space from wall to wall was needed to restore major urban routes to their historic function of a communications network in both the physical and social sense. The photo helps to demonstrate the superiority of genuine streets for people, as opposed to the far more limited concept of a mall.

This superiority can be expressed partially in terms of pervasiveness of impact, inclusiveness of a broad range of functions, and social integration. One is immediately struck by the range of social mix found in spaces such as these: young, old, man, woman, wealthy, poor, local resident, commuter, tourist. This is the place to get in on what's happening, and it's always a pleasant stroll. One important additional result is an effective integration of different social groups.

Encourage Social Integration

Opportunity to belong just by being there is a social benefit not to be taken lightly by those who have this opportunity or by the decision makers who are able to provide it. Spaces in which social integration can take place need to be provided, but, since it is very difficult to create new spaces that will succeed in genuinely integrating all segments of society, it is far better to provide more conducive conditions in the spaces where it is already happening. Giving citizens generally a sense of identification with the community is very important, but so is in-

Fig. 3–35. Verona, Italy. Via Mazzini is not a mall but a major part of a network of streets for people.

tegration of social fringe groups and all segments of society that somehow feel themselves outside the mainstream. Youth trying to find a place in the job market, the elderly trying to maintain contact, handicapped people trying to overcome their disabilities and play a full role in society, and foreign workers trying to be accepted and lead a normal life—all of these groups and many others form together a republic in which social integration is a major goal.

The word *republic* derives from the Latin *res publica*, the public thing or the public realm. Fostering a democratic spirit and a sense of personal participation fundamental to every genuine republic requires social integration that is best achieved in the public realm—the streets. What one observes in a street such as Verona's Via Mazzini is a process of differentiating the use of valuable spatial resources. While some streets are needed primarily for the practical purpose of moving vehicular traffic, others are needed for crucial social functions and therefore must be freed from extraneous burdens. The successful functioning of a republic depends upon spaces in the public realm that foster social integration.

Fig. 3–36. Norwich, England. The narrowest portion of the River Walk along the Wensum is sensitively designed to accommodate itself to existing houses.

Removing cars, delivery vehicles, and other extraneous obstructions, burdens, or dangers from certain streets should not be considered an end in itself, but rather a means to achieve important goals. When an important street in an urban center, such as the Via Mazzini, can be treated as a route for pedestrians with spatial attractiveness and dangerous conflicts reduced or eliminated, social integration becomes possible. Business people, workers, shoppers, tourists, students, school children are all underway at the same time in the same space.

Enhance Living Environments

The degree of satisfaction of residents with their living environments should also influence urban development plans. Far too often concern for the residential function stops at individual dwelling units and their immediate context of building and site. Aspects of enhancing residential environments in cities are discussed in Chapter 6, but it is appropriate at this point to reiterate that streets for people is among the important devices currently being employed to upgrade the quality of existing residential areas.

Despite the much lower volume of pedestrian traffic in residential areas as compared to commercial districts, the importance of safety and freedom from disturbances plays as much a role here as it does in central business districts. Rising expectations for quality in the daily living environment have resulted in a mass exodus from cities wherever people have the opportunity and the financial ability to move. A major concern of planners internationally is therefore to stop "the green wave" of exodus to the suburbs and exurbs, to find ways of upgrading the quality of existing urban residential areas, and to entice people to return to the center.

Develop Separate Networks

A significant contributing factor in this program to upgrade urban living environments is the establishment of a separate network of routes for pedestrians and bicyclists. Too often, the possibilities for movement of pedestrians and cyclists of all ages are limited to sharing spaces already overpopulated with motor vehicles. Lack of horsepower and a protective armor of street leaves pedestrians and bicyclists at a perpetual disadvantage in the competition for undifferentiated street spaces. The best solution is to establish a separate movement system, to open up new routes, and to create new linkages.

A modest view of a significant example in Norwich, England (Figure 3–36), suggests how this can be done. The purpose is to maintain existing character and scale of residential environments while opening up new routes, new interesting vistas, pleasant spatial experiences for all residents and visitors. This can be accomplished three ways:

In new developments, entirely separate but parallel systems of roads and pathways can be laid out from the beginning.

In existing urban areas, sometimes alternate streets can be chosen, some to serve primarily vehicular and some primarily pedestrian needs.

In older urban spaces, frequently the best course of action is to open access to underused areas and to upgrade secondary spaces that have been poorly used, such as alleyways, courtyards, and the interiors of residential blocks.

The latter approach has been taken as an initial stage in Norwich; creation of extensive automobile-restricted zones is to follow. Regaining pedestrian access to the banks of the River Wensum through easements, redevelopment, and outright purchase has been an important project of the 1970s. As in many other cities, the waterfront had been largely taken over by industrial and warehousing uses during the nineteenth and twentieth centuries. Some of these uses have disappeared, some of the facilities have become obsolete, and some of the functions can be relocated outside the urban core. This will make room for more people-oriented functions, in-cluding housing and pedestrian routes along the river. The River Walk is simply a landscaped pathway for strolling, with lamps and benches but no other furnishings or development related specifically to the walkway. Left largely as a park environment, it is intended to be an amenity pure and simple and to provide an alternative way of moving through portions of the city.

The view shown is the narrowest segment of the walkway where it passes across a small street and through a row of houses. The sensitivity and modesty with which the pathway is made to adapt to the architectural fabric and make use of an existing alleyway is highly commendable. Important here is that the slot between the buildings has remained at all and not how wide it is, since it provides the only way to continue on the River Walk at this point. The pleasure is all the greater as one emerges from the narrow space into the beautiful landscape between the river and the playing fields of a private school behind the cathedral. All existing positive elements—landscape, water, materials, textures, picturesqueness, and human scale —have been retained and enhanced, and nothing insensitive to the natural environment has been added: a fine example of letting the best of an older established environment express itself.

A few steps to the left of the previous view and looking in the same direction (Figure 3–37), the River Wensum itself emerges as an important recreational facility providing berths for seagoing pleasure boats, an opportunity for boating in the

Fig. 3–37. Norwich, England. The River Wensum, now with enhanced public access, has become a major recreation facility.

Fig. 3–38. Paris, France. The qualities of the elegant Tuilleries Gardens convey lessons applicable to cities everywhere.

city, and tree-lined paths along both sides. The River Walk is behind the trees to the right, and the scene appears to be so well established as a recreational area that it is hard to imagine that public accessibility to the right bank was finally achieved only a few short years ago. Many cities in many parts of the world (including quite a few in England) have misused waterfronts that could be transformed into the kind of pleasure-giving amenity and predestrian route that the River Wensum has become. Only a little imagination, strong social motivation, and a great deal of persistence can turn "what is" into "what might be."

Encourage a Variety of Activities

The goal of encouraging leisure-time activities in urban areas can be translated into a design program incorporating both commercial and noncommercial leisure and recreation. Into the first category fall such attractions as cafes, restaurants, pubs, nightclubs, discotheques, cinemas, theaters, and concert halls. Certain athletic or quasi-athletic

activities can also be offered on a commercial basis, including health spas with workout rooms, swimming pools, handball courts, tennis courts, and the like, and such other facilities as golf driving ranges, miniature golf, skating rinks, and boat rental services. Even certain types of tourist attractions, such as observation towers, can add to the total variety of attractive offerings.

Of course, noncommercial leisure-time activities as well as participant sports should be promoted in central urban areas. These usually occur in landscaped urban open spaces such as squares, plazas, parks, miniparks, the grounds of palaces or major public buildings, botanical gardens, and zoos. (The zoo in West Berlin, for instance, is immediately adjacent to the central business district, while that in Rome is just north of the historic core in the Villa Borghese complex.) The coupling of such recreational functions with other urban functions through pedestrian linkages is obviously the foundation for a successful leisure-time program.

One of the world's great parks is the Tuilleries Gardens in Paris (Figure 3–38). This well-known segment of the grand axis, leading from the Louvre, through the park, across the Place de la

Concorde, and up the Champs-Elysées, is one of the most popular attractions in central Paris, drawing throngs of people in all seasons, even—as in this view—when the weather is cool, no leaves are on the trees, and the chairs present in summer are still in storage. While few cities could attempt to compete with the quality of this elegant urban space, some lessons nevertheless can be learned from it.

Among the attributes of the Tuilleries Gardens:

Great quantities of vegetation concentrated in a major park or garden provide relief from the hard and massive qualities of the built environment in the city.

Fountains, sculpture, expensive landscaping, and other grand gestures that can only be afforded in the public realm serve to give a feeling of uplift and grandeur and encourage the pride of place we have seen as so important.

Moving water, especially in the form of great splashing fountains, has a universal appeal and is guaranteed to attract people and generate interest.

The quality of a *route* reserved exclusively for pedestrians is of critical importance. One does not simply enter the gardens at one point, meander around a bit, and then exit at the same point. Nor can one drive through it, as in New York's Central Park. Walking is here the mode from one nodal point to another, and walking clearly is the only means for experiencing the broad range of attractive, sensuous stimuli offered.

It would be interesting to see where all of these Parisians go once they have traversed the Tuilleries. It is clear that they will not simply be getting in their vehicles and going back home, as would be the case in an analogous North American situation, such as Chicago's Lake Shore Park. The many acres of parking surrounding state fair grounds or Disneyland are simply not there in Paris, so that these thousands and tens of thousands of walkers do not immediately become drivers the moment they hit the edge of the park space. Instead, this edge is directly linked via pedestrian paths and subway stations to other attractions in the urban fabric. People in the Tuilleries are already on their way, and they keep going: to a restaurant or boutique on the Left Bank, to a department store or high-fashion shop on the Right Bank, to a sidewalk cafe or a movie on the Champs-Elysées, to the collections of the Louvre, or to any of a myriad of other magnets in the central city. The high-quality attractions of the route are there; the linkages are clear and appealing. How much of this urbanity could be captured for North American cities? How many North American cities have ever tried to capture these qualities?

Differentiate Streets Throughout Cities

Converting main shopping streets into pedestrian malls in order to stimulate commerce is no longer an insider's secret. The success of properly conceived and carefully executed malls, semimalls, and pedestrian districts in the central city has been incontrovertibly established in many parts of the world. What are not yet as widely recognized, because it has been applied much more selectively, are the benefits to be gained by differentiating the use of street spaces throughout cities, not just on the business portion of Main Street downtown. Reduction of accidents, reduction of air pollution, improvement of public transit service, and enhancement of the residential function are four of the benefits discussed elsewhere in this book. It is useful at this point to consider a few of the social benefits to be gained by rescuing street spaces from use by cars and giving them over to use by people.

Provide Streets for Play

Streets for play is one of the most logical alternative uses. If cities are to retain their life, people must live in them, people of all ages, of all income brackets, with and without children. Since central cities are notoriously lacking in public open spaces where children can play and exercise, and since urban land to provide such facilities is usually prohibitively expensive, a reasonable answer is to find the space in the streets. A view of Bologna, Italy (Figure 3–39), demonstrates this, and similar street closings are becoming commonplace, with American examples in Oak Park and Berkeley. And if the street in question already has mature trees little more may be needed than to secure permission from the authorities to simply chain off the vehicular access to provide an ideal permanent playground. The street itself provides a flat surface for playing soccer, while the side spaces under the trees are perfect for smaller children and for mothers to sit and converse.

Of course, not only little children and teenagers seek an outdoor place to amuse themselves. People of all ages welcome an opportunity to get out of their own four walls and enjoy the pleasures of ex-

posure to sunshine, greenery, and their fellow man in the public way, providing it is safe, nonstressful, and regenerative. Obviously no one will try to relax or enjoy himself in the company of his fellow man in an environment that appears to be hostile, uncomfortable, or dangerous. The founding fathers of Philadelphia recognized this fact and therefore spared four entire city blocks in the downtown fabric from being built upon. They were to be reserved as green public open spaces and still function today as oases for people and regenerative lungs in the architectural body of the city. One of these idyllic green islands in the sea of buildings is Rittenhouse Square (Figure 3–40).

Allow Comforts in the Central City

For adults, leisure-time activity and social communication can be intimately related to the idea of a comfortable place to sit. Rittenhouse Square provides a wealth of grassy areas, comfortable wooden benches (with backrests!), and raised edges of pools—with one's choice of either sun or shade—on which to cultivate the time-honored pursuits of eating, reading, conversing, and simply relaxing. It's all there, right in the heart of the city, with high-rise office buildings and the central business district on one side, doctors' offices and fashionable residences on the other. Prototypes for such amenities and for such vitally urbane interrelationships of spaces and functions exist back through the

generations and centuries, yet how many cities today are cognizant of the value of these humane planning concepts? A first step would be to recognize that these are indeed valid planning concepts and not simply romantic fantasies. Cities are for people; people like to sit: these two basic concepts deserve greater recognition than they have received in current planning practice.

Every example of urbanity and humanity in existing urban areas, no matter how small, deserves to be analyzed for its applicability in countering trends toward barrenness, inhuman scale, and lack of amenity in contemporary urban development. Philadelphia's Rittenhouse Square demonstrates that some of the older city planning concepts are still among the best. While ideas of what constitutes attractive design of spaces or desirable social behavior by people in cities may vary, planners and theoreticians should not overlook the obvious. The opportunity to sit on a comfortable bench in a pleasant environment with trees and other vegetation, safe from the dangers and nuisances of vehicular traffic, continues to satisfy fundamental human needs today as it did a hundred years ago. Spaces and amenities of this type need to be incorporated into all parts of the urban fabric, particularly in high-density areas where their potential impact is the greatest.

Cost and Quality

Excellence does not need to mean inordinate ex-

Fig. 3-40. Philadelphia, PA. In Rittenhouse Square, people of all ages welcome an opportunity to relax in communion with nature and with each other in the heart of a city.

pense. Inordinate is a relative term, anyway, and costs must be carefully related to potential benefits. Costs vary considerably, not only because of different qualities of materials and furnishings, but also because major work on fabric and utilities is quite often overdue and needs to be undertaken before a new pavement is laid. Ways of distributing costs of urban transformation for pedestrians also vary considerably, covering the entire range from total payment by the municipality, as in the case of Bonn, to total payment by business interests. If the primary purpose is to improve a retail street, business interests would seem to have good reason to bear the costs, but in that case, there may be too much pressure for design changes to benefit only this segment of the community. On the other hand, arguments put forth in Munich and elsewhere urge that, if city money is to be used, planning should focus more on communal rather than commercial goals. In any case, the substantial background of more than fifteen years of very broad, substantial, positive experience with streets for people has demonstrated that the benefits of differentiated use of street spaces can and should be extended over a far larger portion of urban environments than has previously been the case.

In the future less emphasis should be placed on spectacular transformations of central shopping areas, with far more emphasis placed on more modest improvements to the environment for living and walking and biking *throughout the entire fabric of the cities.* Now that Europe is at least a generation ahead of America in recapturing city centers for use by people, the main problem in Germany, for example, is where to terminate pedestrian zones and how best to extend them into areas peripheral to the central business district and beyond. In the overall picture of enhancing the quality of life for all citizens throughout the city, it is unsatisfactory merely to develop central commercial areas as islands of beauty and festivity while allowing other—often adjacent—areas to bear the burden of vehicular traffic, lose their attractiveness as places to live, and gradually sink into a sea of nondescript grayness. The most exciting advances going into the 1980s are in the realm of urban repair beyond the premier commercial areas.

Alternative Modes of Movement

Give the Advantages to Buses

The monumental bishop, all but awash in traffic, giving an ecumenical blessing to the reserved bus lane in Würzburg, Germany in Figure 4–1 symbolizes the new urban predicament: anarchic auto traffic dominating more and more of the urban center, even treading on the toes of historic monuments, and confronting the newly emerging resistance of the theorists whose goal is that of improving accessibility to urban centers for both people and goods. Once it has been recognized that burgeoning automobile ownership can never be accommodated in existing urban environments without destroying the very reasons people want to go there, something better than the private car is all but inevitable.

In general terms, the solution is to achieve a more favorable modal split, i.e., to reduce the percentage of surface travel accomplished by private automobile and to increase the percentage via other modes of transportation: bus, light rail, bicycle, foot. Since buses are currently the most widely used form of public transportation, improving the modal split obviously involves mandating advantages to buses in urban traffic.

Comfort, convenience, immediate access, speed, and privacy are among the reasons automobile owners generally prefer to drive their own vehicles. Slowness, unreliability, crowded conditions, and inconvenient access are widely perceived as major deterrents to using buses. Consequently, as automobile ownership increased, patronage of buses declined; parking facilities sprang up, bus maintenance lagged. During the 1960s and 1970s, various measures of traffic control were devised to redress

Fig. 4–1 (near right). Würzburg, West Germany. With cities increasingly dominated by automobiles, one partial solution is to create reserved lanes for buses.

Fig. 4–2 (facing page). Paris, France. One-way pairs of streets, like the Boulevards Saint-Germain and Saint-Michel, enhance the flow of vehicles. Only the pedestrian loses.

this imbalance, to promote preferential treatment for high-occupancy vehicles. (For a summary of these measures in the United States, see U.S., Department of Transportation, Federal Highway Administration, "Preferential Treatment for High-Occupancy Vehicles," April 1974.)

The most effective measures for increasing the speed and reliability of bus service are those aimed at freeing buses from the congestion of heavy mixed traffic on undifferentiated streets and roads. The simplest of these are lanes reserved for buses within normal street space. These may be rush-hour or permanent, with the flow or contraflow. The next step is to close a street to automobiles entirely, without redesigning it: the so-called bus street. These can be further redesigned: with wider sidewalks and other amenities for pedestrians and a narrower roadway, redesigned for the specific purpose of facilitating movement of buses, they become transitways. In addition, freeways or expressways built solely to handle large-volume commuter traffic can also provide reserved lanes for preferential treatment of buses, taxis, and car pools. The apparent advantage of speed is intended to serve as an inducement to other motorists stuck in the congested general traffic lanes to switch to public transit or car pooling.

In cities the concept of one-way pairs, i.e., pairs of parallel streets each made one-way in opposite directions, often coupled with reserved bus lanes,

has been the major evolution in the fuller use of streets since the 1960s. For those responsible for the movement of traffic and the relief of congestion, it has seemed an accomplishment of greater proportions, since a far greater volume of traffic at a far higher average speed can be handled on essentially the same street space, as can be seen in the formidable scene on the Boulevard Saint-Germain in Paris (Figure 4–2). The one-way system eliminates many time-consuming turns, the reserved lanes prevent bus stops from hindering car traffic, and control of access to the arterial routes eliminates many conflicts and delays. The only loser is the pedestrian.

One additional advantage for buses can be provided by transmitters or other actuating devices that will change traffic signals in their favor as they approach. Such measures, however, are still quite rare, as are reserved bus lanes on freeways. The sad conclusion to be drawn is that so far most improvement in vehicular traffic flow in cities has turned out to be preferential treatment for low-, rather than high-, occupancy vehicles.

These successful, congestion-relieving measures do have drawbacks. Streets once considered the epitome of urbanity have become noisy, fume-laden conduits for torrents of vehicles gushing through, difficult and dangerous for pedestrians to cross, lined by buildings that have become uninhabitable. The goal of increased traffic movement seriously conflicts with larger goals concern-

ing urban environmental quality. Nor, in this respect, is the heavy volume of arterial traffic the only problem, as a view south on the Boulevard Saint-Michel on Sunday morning shows (Figure 4–3). Traffic-control measures themselves, even without the traffic, have a deadening impact on the quality of the street space, as citizens in countless communities of the world have discovered. Signs, signals, barriers, road widening, removal of trees, straightening of axes, and flattening of curves all produce more efficient flow of traffic but also tend to rob a street of its character and charm.

The fountain of St. Michael at the right was once the focal point of Paris's picturesque Left Bank just near the Seine. Such a grandiose architectural monument near all the bistros and cafes and the graceful sense of containment created by tree-lined sidewalks made the space a mecca for students and tourists. This space had enormous potential and deserved further enhancement. Instead, it has been transformed into a desolate, chained-off sidewalk fronting on an efficient but menacing traffic intersection. Such a loss is particularly gross because, as one of the famed centers of Paris, the quality of its historic ambience was so high. Examples of similarly insensitive destruction in the name of progress are not hard to find. Although public transportation is the ostensible beneficiary, the public is the loser; the only winners, the motorists misusing the central city living room as a transportation corridor for their private ends.

But form follows funding, to take liberties with the famous architectural dictum. Improving the flow of traffic and facilitating public transportation have long been supported by state and national funding everywhere, so that transformations have been all too rapid and thorough. Figure 4–4 shows the characteristic results in an urban environment less historically sensitive than that of Paris. Minneapolis, all but devoid of traditional urban amenities on most of its downtown streets, still has considerable numbers of pedestrians using the sidewalks, even on a dreary day. Yet the clear space between buildings has been devoted almost totally to moving motor vehicles efficiently. The illustration points up the weakness of combining reserved bus lanes with one-way pairs if the ultimate goal is to achieve, not more and faster car travel, but increased use of other means of transportation. Since the great majority of the space is devoted to maintaining a strong flow of automobiles, there is very little inducement for anyone to switch to buses which, despite the reserved lanes, are still slower because of their stops. Genuinely preferential treatment, therefore, for public transportation needs to go much further if it is to have any effect on slowing the growth of automobile traffic.

The example of Nagoya in Japan (where there is left-hand drive, Figure 4–5) shows a more effective use of exclusive bus lanes on a ring road around the

Fig. 4–3. Paris, France. Traffic control measures themselves, like these on the Boulevard Saint-Michel, can have a deadening impact on the quality of street spaces.

Fig. 4–4. Minneapolis, MN. Even on a dreary day downtown many pedestrians are on the streets. Yet vehicles, not people, have higher priority.

ALTERNATIVE MODES OF MOVEMENT

core. Nagoya was the first Japanese city to institute comprehensive traffic management, integrating various measures in a city-wide program; it was one of the case study cities presented at the O.E.C.D. conference "Better Towns with Less Traffic." Although Nagoya, like most Japanese cities, has an older urban structure with many small streets ill suited to cars, there was no popular support for automobile restraint during the 1960s boom in automobile ownership. Increasing numbers of cars, a sprawl development of residential areas, and a relatively thin network of public transportation led to increasing traffic congestion, serious air pollution, destruction of the quality of living environments, and a traffic fatality rate of 12.6 per hundred thousand inhabitants, more than twice that in Tokyo. The major goal of the program was an acceptable level of urban traffic; the methods to achieve it included strong measures to restrain use of cars for commuting as well as to stimulate car drivers to switch to mass transit.

Without examining these methods in detail, we can see plainly how rigorously reserved bus lanes on the ring road during rush hours give a very decided preference to public transportation, whereas cars are subjected to intentional congestion as a positive deterrent. Far stronger measures were undertaken in Nagoya than have been seriously considered in any western country because it was recognized that more comfortable, more reliable buses alone will not motivate people to give up driving their own cars to work. Far more effective are parking controls at the city end of commuter trips. Part of the program was thus drastic curtailment of parking places, especially for government workers. Access and through passage for automobiles were also severely limited by closing over three hundred crossings of the ring road and creating over a hundred traffic cells. Nonetheless, strong positive improvements of the bus fleet and increased reliability and speed of bus service proved crucial to the program. If automobile use in urban areas is to be as effectively reduced as in Nagoya, attractive, viable alternatives must be available.

Uppsala, the old university city in Sweden, was another of the case-study cities at the O.E.C.D. conference. A primary goal of the program in Uppsala was to retain the human scale of the historic urban structure while maintaining a high level of accessibility to the center. Major road building or widening was avoided in favor of low-cost modifications of existing street spaces, i.e., organizational changes in traffic pattern.

Figure 4–6 illustrates the nature of some of these

Fig. 4–5. Nagoya, Japan. A comprehensive traffic management scheme gives clear priority to public transit while discouraging the use of private automobiles. (Photo: Courtesy of O.E.C.D., Paris)

changes. The view, toward the cathedral and the city's center, shows a part of Drottninggatan (to the right), the most direct route into the center, reserved for buses, thus providing speedy and reliable service to the Central Square, no longer accessible to cars. Cars and trucks are diverted to less direct routes and have access to the core only in a traffic-cell system. The tree-lined street straight ahead has been closed to all motor vehicles and made into part of a network of bicycle routes. Bicycles and buses are thus given the advantages of direct access and unhampered through movement, while automobiles are restricted in the core. In contrast to the less satisfactory approaches used in Paris and Minneapolis, not only were no streets widened, but the general burden of vehicular traffic was also significantly reduced.

The extent of the changes in Uppsala is suggested by a view of the Central Square, Stora Torget (Figure 4–7). The space is supposedly unique in being the only public square north of the Alps with closed corners. Despite its closed corners it was the historic crossing point of two major traffic routes but has now been drastically transformed through the removal of all motor vehicles other than buses. Uppsala thus provides an excellent realization of a basic precept of cities for people: convert the premier urban space at the center of the city into a people-place. Here this has been accomplished by converting the main shopping street, Kungsängs-gatan (visible at right center and in Figure 4–8), into a major pedestrian axis and converting Drott-ninggatan into a transitway, with the Central Square serving as the main interface between the two. The sheltered waiting area with trees, planting, and ample seating further induces visitors to come to the center to use public transportation.

Public opinion polls were conducted at various stages of the work. Inevitably some people complained about restrictions on car operation and difficulties in reaching parking garages, but a large majority favored the transformation. In what must be one of the most perverse lines of reasoning yet put forward on this subject, some retailers seriously argued that business depended to a certain extent on customers who entered stores simply to get away from the noise and fumes of car-filled streets. Any measures to improve the street environment, it was therefore reasoned, might actually result in a decline in business! Figure 4–8 of the pedestrianized Kungsängsgatan demonstrates the hollowness

of that argument. The modest and relatively inexpensive changes of the street space have made it into a highly attractive environment for shoppers. The design conception of making this part of a continuous network of walking routes through the city and providing attractive interface with other modes of transportation, especially buses, acts as a further strong incentive to draw people into the space. Bus priority measures played an essential role in achieving these significant improvements of the urban environment.

Consider Environmental Impact of Buses

Environmental deterioration in the late 1960s led to public recognition that unrestrained growth of automobile traffic in cities was untenable and that movement by foot, bicycle, and public transportation should be preferred. Proposals to build as many as twelve multistory parking garages in downtown Uppsala, for instance, met with strong popular objections. Planning centered around universal accessibility by car became politically impossible and had to be rejected as antiquated.

In North America, on the other hand, where environmental awareness by the general public also

Fig. 4–6. Uppsala, Sweden. Differentiating the use of street spaces is the key to relieving congestion and improving urban environments. (Photo: Courtesy of O.E.C.D., Paris)

ALTERNATIVE MODES OF MOVEMENT

Fig. 4–7. Uppsala, Sweden. Once the crossing point of two main streets, the central square now serves as the main interchange between walking and riding public transit.

Fig. 4–8. Uppsala, Sweden. Kungsängsgatan, the now pedestrianized main shopping street, is served by the public transit node on the Central Square.

Fig. 4–9 (left). Minneapolis, MN. Standard diesel buses with their size, noise, and fumes create considerable negative environmental impact on the Nicollet mall.

Fig. 4–10 (right). Minneapolis, MN. Revealing its bias in favor of cars, the mall here is fronted by a parking garage at the right.

developed in the late 1960s, we have seen no comparable political reaction to automobile excesses. Even the awareness of an energy crisis stimulated by the oil shortages of 1973 and 1979 has now dissipated and cars are being driven as if gasoline were water. Without a new transportation ethic, the development of buses as a viable alternative has been and will be very slow.

In fact, the buses themselves can have considerable negative environmental impact, depending on their size, their emissions, and the density of the bus traffic. An interesting comparison may be made between Uppsala and Minneapolis. In the former the primary street space has been redesigned for pedestrians and intersects with that for buses only at a major nodal point. In the latter primary bus and pedestrian movement are made to coexist in the same street space (Figure 4–9). This difference is very significant, particularly since most of the buses in the space are standard General Motors diesel models of considerable size with intolerable noise and exhaust levels. To mollify the retail business community, which feared a drop in volume due to lack of exposure, planners relocated major bus routes onto the Nicollet Avenue mall, largely vitiating the improved retail street space with a deadening burden of vehicular traffic. Despite a local reduction in traffic volume and a narrowing of the street, the automotive character of the roadway remains the dominant factor.

Figures 4–10 and 4–11 reveal, even more pointedly, the North American bias in favor of the private car at work in the Minneapolis scheme. Figure 4–10 is a view north on Nicollet toward the Northwest Insurance Company building, with a multistory parking garage fronting on the mall at the right and another multistory parking garage immediately behind the Northern States Power Company at the left. Figure 4–11 is a desolate view east taken at the north end of Nicollet (just visible at the right) with the Northwestern Insurance Company at the left. This wide arterial road is Washington Avenue, and no provisions for separated pedestrian crossing above or below this street are provided. Thus, although the Nicollet transitway clearly serves to facilitate transit movement in the commercial core, and a few flower posts and benches have been doled out, no traffic cells or other negative incentives have been employed to *discourage* use of private automobiles for commutation or other purposes. Quite to the contrary, extensive widening of streets and a massive construction program of (profitable) multistory garages combine to serve as a strong continuing incentive for the use of private cars for all purposes. In contrast to Uppsala and so many European cities, municipalities in North America apparently are still largely unable, politically, to initiate any programs that would actually reduce total volume of vehicular movement in their centers.

ALTERNATIVE MODES OF MOVEMENT

Fig. 4–11 (left). Minneapolis, MN. Washington Avenue, at the north end of Nicollet, serves as a major barrier to continuous pedestrian movement.

Fig. 4–12 (right). Vancouver, Canada. Although it follows the design example used in Minneapolis, Granville Mall has the advantage of electric buses.

Consider Electric Trams and Trolleys

Since it is clearly necessary to retain some form of public transportation to urban spaces from which automobiles are banned, the search continues for types of public surface transit vehicles that will have minimal adverse effects on the environment. Ironically, such vehicles have been available throughout the twentieth century but have been crowded aside almost to the point of extinction: the light-rail electric tram and the rubber-tired electric trolley bus.

In terms of noise and air pollution, electric trams and trolley buses seem to offer an ideal solution, since they can be very quiet and are entirely non-polluting. The aesthetic drawback of overhead wires seems quite acceptable in view of the strong advantages offered. The major factor behind removal of these electric vehicles from the streets of all but a few North American cities was the losing competition with automobile traffic for the same street space.

Granville Mall in Vancouver is an example of a recent transitway for electric trolley buses (Figure 4–12). Based on the example of the Nicollet Avenue transitway-mall in Minneapolis, the remodeling of Granville seems at first glance to resemble its prototype very closely indeed, with a sinuous two-lane roadway, widened sidewalks, numerous trees, improved pavement, and human-scaled incandescent lamps. But the fact that Vancouver's buses are electric rather than diesel is a difference of paramount significance, allowing the civilizing elements to do their work. The compatability of electric vehicles with space intended primarily to attract pedestrians is a very important plus here; in contrast, the environmental disturbance and sheer capacity to intimidate inherent in enormous diesel bus engines cannot be underestimated. If environmental improvement programs are truly intended to make downtowns more attractive for pedestrians, internal-combustion engines should be separated as much as possible from spaces intended primarily for people afoot.

On the east coast of the United States, Philadelphia's program for converting an important but congested downtown street into a transitway is touted as an example for other cities. The conversion of Philadelphia's Chestnut Street involves twelve blocks running from an important office and commercial district near Rittenhouse Square in the west toward Independence Mall and the more historic parts of Philadelphia near the river to the east. As in Minneapolis, the Philadelphia scheme involves a narrowed roadway reserved for diesel buses, undifferentiated cross traffic, redesigned and widened sidewalks with aesthetically designed furnishings ranging from lamps to litter baskets, and the pleasant addition of trees as softening elements to the urban landscape. The provision of sidewalk seating was vehemently opposed by merchants, but a compromise solution finally allowed for exactly four seats per block!

Figures 4–13 and 4–14 again demonstrate that such a compromise solution of combining transitway and pedestrian mall in one and the same street space is actually a less-than-ideal solution. Not only are the buses bulky, noisy, and polluting intrusions on the space, but even when they are not present, the existence of separated sidewalks, curbs, and crosswalks serves as a constant reminder that the central space exists to serve vehicles, while people, as dutiful consumers, are supposed to cross only at the corners and follow the straight and narrow path along the display windows.

Portland, Oregon, demonstrated yet another convolution of the sorry adage that form follows funding by creating not one but two parallel transitway-malls in its downtown area. The ostensible progress in the Portland situation is that both Fifth and Sixth Avenues have been largely freed from the burden of automobile traffic in order to become attractive malls for pedestrians. But once again the malls are designed according to the precept "What's good for General Motors is good for America." Diesel buses play the predominant role and not without justification: fully 80 percent of the total costs of street improvements were provided by federal funds intended to encourage reserved lanes for buses.

The reason for two, not one, transitways is the same simplistic one as that for one-way pairs of normal streets: higher capacity for peak periods. Sixth Avenue carries two lanes of buses in one direction, while Fifth Avenue carries two lanes of buses in the reverse direction. Capacity of the transitways was designed to be 180 buses per hour, or 3 per minute in each direction, from the beginning. This capacity, according to the director of transitway-mall construction, can be expanded to 270 buses per hour in the future! The sweet music and rare perfume of 270 four-inch exhaust pipes every hour will surely delight the great numbers of pedestrians hardy enough to use the widened and landscaped sidewalks along Fifth and Sixth Avenues. To quote *Downtown Program* (promotional material for the City of Portland, 1976),

> The Portland Transit Mall separates cars, buses and pedestrians *for more efficient travel through downtown* [italics added]. Cars will run smoothly on their own streets as the Mall removes buses from 4th and Broadway and provides two exclusive bus lanes on

5th and 6th Avenues along the eleven blocks from Burnside to Madison.

Figure 4–15 is a view north along Sixth Avenue, with a portion of the historic Pioneer Courthouse visible at the near right. Not to take too much from Portland's planners, the parking structure called Park, from which the photograph was taken, is soon to become a landscaped public open space called Pioneer Courthouse Square, diagonally across from Meier & Frank's, one of the leading department stores in downtown Portland. Clearly, the rehabilitation of downtown street spaces in Portland is a strong positive step toward enhancing the use of the city by its people, although serious questions remain concerning the improved flow of motor vehicles, in particular the great numbers of diesel buses on the so-called malls.

Consider Minibuses

In view of the continued outward migration of those who can exercise choice away from urban centers in all developed countries, it has become imperative for city administrators and transportation planners to find ways of luring higher income residents back to urban centers. Offering superior goods and services is undoubtedly one of the best means, but this must include superior infrastructure. An attractive and efficient public transportation system offering convenient access to and

ALTERNATIVE MODES OF MOVEMENT

mobility within downtown areas can serve a very effective public relations role, generating attention to and interest in downtown. Portland, to give it its due, is one of the cities that has used its bus system to great advantage in this regard.

Portland's Tri-Met, the transit authority for the tri-county region, has as its motto "Better Service for More People" and clearly aspires to get more people downtown as well as to get more people to ride the bus. The transit service thus becomes a means of achieving other urban goals rather than just an end in itself. Therefore, in order to make downtown Portland more attractive, free bus service is provided in "Fareless Square," the entire central district, an area covering more than twelve by eighteen blocks. People are encouraged to board buses anywhere within this area and pay absolutely nothing, as long as they get off again within the district. Free transit is used as a means of encouraging activities downtown.

While the Portland scheme and others like it are quite farsighted, there are certain disadvantages in having normal city buses serve as a free shuttle within the congested downtown area. Perhaps the biggest disadvantage is simply the ponderousness of the vehicle, its noise and smell. Furthermore, for those who need the services of a shuttle most—the elderly, the infirm, the heavily laden—the difficulties of climbing the high steps of a normal city bus can be a significant deterrent, especially for short trips.

The search for an appropriate vehicle that would also be economically feasible has been very frustrating. Vienna, for example, now has a new small city bus that seems to satisfy all the physical requirements quite well. The hope that it could be battery powered with a maximum speed of less than fifty kilometers per hour was dashed, however, by existing battery technology. A clean propane-burning engine was tried next, but this too proved economically unsound for the conditions and power required. To everyone's disappointment the production model was consequently equipped with a standard diesel engine. Nonetheless, the search continues.

The current state of the art for shuttles of "people movers" in high density areas seems to be some form of small bus or tractor-drawn train of rubber-tired cars with benches. Power is provided by gasoline or diesel internal-combustion engines with exhaust-control devices to minimize emissions. Vehicles are usually given special "personality" treatment for public relations purposes, as in the case of Sacramento (Figure 4–16), where a small, low shuttle bus with an internal-combustion engine has been given an appearance intended to evoke San Francisco's famed cable cars (with an inappropriate, nonoperative trolley pole added gratuitously). The shuttle bus operates back and forth along the length of the K Street Mall and has a fare of ten cents, which may or may not be paid at the rider's discretion.

The need for shuttle service on downtown pedestrian malls is actually far less than most people had

Fig. 4–13 (facing page). Philadelphia, PA. Chestnut Street transitway, with a smaller street space than Nicollet in Minneapolis, is more burdened by diesel buses.

Fig. 4–14 (near left). Philadelphia, PA. Chestnut Street, despite trees and other furnishings, is planned largely to serve the needs of vehicles.

Fig. 4–15. Portland, OR. Fifth and Sixth Avenues, a one-way pair of transit-ways, are intended to carry 180 diesel buses per hour.

predicted. In the varied European experience that has accumulated over the past fifteen years and more, the anticipated need for shuttle vehicles, even on such extensive systems as the 800-meter axis from Stachus to Marienplatz in Munich, has not materialized. In fact, the larger networks of pedestrian walkway systems have been so successful that there is now general agreement that any type of passenger vehicle in the space would be too great a disruption and potential danger even to warrant any experiments with their use. Frequent rest on numerous benches and chairs has unexpectedly proven far more useful than any type of shuttle vehicle.

The goal of decreasing people's dependence on automobiles for movement in cities through an improved public transit service can hardly be faulted. Attempts in this direction have included provision of shuttle-bus service in downtown areas of cities that have not yet pedestrianized major shopping streets, such as Milwaukee and St. Louis. In St. Louis this service, called "Scooter," is comprised of two interlocking figure-eight routes in the downtown area, charges a minimal fare of ten cents, and is advertised as being "for short hops around downtown" (Figure 4–17). The promotional material illustrated is displayed prominently on litter baskets in downtown streets.

Yet, strangely, the "Scooter" in St. Louis and minibuses like it in other North American cities found far less public acceptance than was reasonable and usually ran their routes nearly empty. The reason would appear to be that which was recognized in Sweden around 1970: no positive inducement of attractive public transportatation—comfort, convenience, speed, reliability, or low cost—will convince large numbers of people to abandon their private automobiles as long as the latter remain a viable alternative. The use of cars must have strong restraints if measures to promote significantly greater use of public transportation are to realize their potential.

Improve Waiting Facilities for Public Transit

Few aspects of human psychology are so universally ignored in urban areas as the need and desire of people to sit. Waiting for anything, including public transit, can be counted upon to elicit in almost everyone a strong desire to sit; yet how many transit stops in how many cities are provided with this basic amenity? A further need is shelter from rain and cold winds during inclement weather, and yet another is safety. A view in downtown Portland, Oregon (Figure 4–18), demonstrates how simply and elegantly these needs can be served if only they are recognized by responsible authori-

ALTERNATIVE MODES OF MOVEMENT

Fig. 4–16. Sacramento, CA. An easy-access shuttlebus along the K Street Mall provides a sense of character and ease of movement.

Fig. 4–17 (bottom left). St. Louis, MO. A handy, inexpensive minibus downtown is useful but largely ineffective if use of cars is not dampened through negative incentives.

Fig. 4–18 (bottom right). Portland, OR. Waiting facilities for public transit should include seating surfaces of wood and shelter from the weather.

ties. Wood is far superior to other materials that conduct heat away from the body more quickly, and in this case a wooden surface for sitting has been fastened very simply to a decorative wall. The shelter, which of course is not needed during pleasant weather, is a model of elegant simplicity. The open side is oriented not to the street but away from the prevailing weather, a remarkably rational thing to do. The shelter is also transparent, which makes approaching buses and passengers visible to each other and discourages the shelter's misuse, an important consideration for both the real and perceived security of waiting passengers. These simple devices for satisfying basic human needs deserve to be widely emulated in transit and urban planning everywhere.

Waiting facilities vary greatly, even on specially constructed transitways. Philadelphia's Chestnut Street transitway, for example, provides roofs but no wind shelter and no seating at bus stops. Minneapolis, on the other hand, has substantial shelters on the Nicollet transitway-mall, each with an interior wall that prevents winds from blowing through and radiant heating units in the ceiling to warm passengers in winter (Figure 4–19). But seating in the Nicollet mall design is provided only in the immediate vicinity of bus stops. American merchants still fear that comfortable seating only encourages loitering by undesirable types. The fact that generous seating amenities attract many desirable groups of people and contribute to the memorable qualities of a public space has been discovered in many other countries but has not yet gained currency in North America.

In the United States, where for so many years the automobile has been the favored means of transportation and occupied progressively increasing percentages of street spaces everywhere, Boston, Cleveland, Philadelphia, and San Francisco have remained lonely exceptions in maintaining light-rail transit as functioning elements in the overall transportation picture. Separate rights-of-way were largely responsible for retention in the first three cities; only in San Francisco have light-rail vehicles survived in the competition with automobiles for the same street space.

A cable car terminus in San Francisco on Powell Street in the block before its intersection with Market Street was redesigned during the construction of the underground Bay Area Rapid Transit (BART) System (Figures 4–20 and 4–21). Powell at this point is closed to all vehicles other than the cable cars, the space is attractively paved, and new furnishings and trees have been added. The street space is safe for people to gather in great numbers, watch the turning of the cars by hand, and wait for an opportunity to ride one of these traveling museum pieces. Perhaps because the crowds tend to be so large, or perhaps because the cars themselves provide so little shelter and so few seats, neither shelters nor seats are provided for the waiting passengers. Closure of the street, however, satisfied very well the need for safety from vehicular conflicts at the boarding point.

The cable cars, drawn by moving cables under the pavement, enjoy unique status because of their beloved quaintness and their importance as tourist attractions. Had it not been for these factors, they might well have been removed from the streets of

Fig. 4–19. Minneapolis, MN. Bus shelters on Nicollet include radiant heating and seating, although the latter is in short supply.

ALTERNATIVE MODES OF MOVEMENT

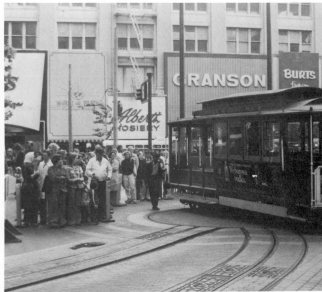

Fig. 4–20 (left). San Francisco, CA. The last block at the eastern end of the Powell Street cable car line is attractively paved and furnished but has no seating.

Fig. 4–21 (right). San Francisco, CA. The turning of the cable cars by hand at Powell and Market Streets is part of the appeal of the old system. Riders must wait in line unprotected from the weather.

San Francisco long ago. The continued useful service of this interesting antique, however, suggests that light-rail transit may very well have significant advantages.

Consider Advantages of Light-Rail Transit

Light-rail transit is the new name for an old conveyance commonly known as a streetcar or electric tram. Vehicles with steel wheels driven on relatively light steel rails by electric power drawn from an overhead wire played an enormous role in the development of American and European cities in the early twentieth century. All but totally replaced by automobiles and buses with internal-combustion engines, light-rail electric mass transit enjoyed a renaissance in the 1970s. At the beginning of the century the majority of tracks in cities were located on streets and not separated from general traffic. Today light-rail transit is considered most appropriate for reserved rights-of-way.

The great advantages of light-rail transit are being recognized today because of heightened public sensitivity to the dangers of pollution and energy waste. Clean and quiet electric transit vehicles are conducive to high environmental quality, compatible with pedestrians in automobile-free areas, and extremely efficient in the use of energy.

With so many good attributes, light-rail transit is again generating great interest among transportation experts in many countries. In the United States, the Transportation Research Board has formed an Advisory Committee on Light-Rail Transit, which conducted a National Conference on Light-Rail Transit in June, 1975, in Philadelphia. Its report, "This Is Light-Rail Transit," was published by the U.S. Transportation Research Board.

One of the committee's principal findings is most ironic: "The diversity and flexibility that light-rail transit affords are its chief attributes." It was precisely the argument of *inflexibility* that all but spelled the demise of light-rail transit the world over. Rubber tires and internal-combustion engines were considered the epitome of "diversity and flexibility" throughout the first two-thirds of this century. The streetcar, forever tied to its wires and its tracks, was considered hopelessly outmoded by traffic experts and a damned nuisance by car drivers. Even the compromise that emerged, electric power through overhead wires combined with rubber tires—the trolley bus—was considered too inflexible and a hindrance to traffic. Now, suddenly, both rubber-tired and steel-wheeled electric vehicles are again very attractive.

San Francisco, in any case, is one city that has retained both trolley buses and streetcars, as can be seen on Market Street in Figure 4–22. This is a view

Fig. 4–22. San Francisco, CA. Market Street, with the BART system beneath, reveals the diversity of San Francisco's integrated transportation system.

of the redesigned Market Street *after* establishment of the heavy-rail Bay Area Rapid Transit (BART) line beneath this street, and it symbolizes the rich spectrum of public transportation facilities for which San Francisco is very much envied today. While other cities dismantled electric systems and put all of their eggs into the "Detroit" basket, sponsoring automobiles and expensive freeways, San Francisco kept all options open and retained and developed an integrated system consisting of highways and roads for cars and conventional buses, plus systems of routes for cable cars, trolley buses, light-rail transit, and heavy-rail transit. The degree of diversity in such an integrated system greatly enhances its attractiveness in providing viable alternatives to commutation by car.

Munich, Zurich, Mannheim, and Kassel are among central European cities that have found advantages in retaining light-rail transit within urban areas that are now otherwise dedicated entirely to pedestrian traffic. The newly discovered flexibility the Transportation Research Board's committee has found inherent in light-rail transit implies that the same standards for right-of-way do

not need to be applied to entire routes or entire systems. Speeds of the operator-driven electric vehicles, and therefore the nature of the roadway, can vary over a broad spectrum, depending on local conditions. Although maximum volumes of as many as 12,000 passengers per hour per direction on a single line can be attained only on reserved rights-of-way developed to a standard essentially equal to that of heavy-rail transit, service can be varied entirely in keeping with particular requirements. A view of the main street in Heidelberg, Germany (Figure 4–23), during the transitional period—after having banned cars but before creating a space entirely for pedestrians—demonstrates how little people need be disturbed by a slow-moving tram, even on narrow streets. An interesting sidelight concerning the potential importance of trams as a major social service was provided by Heidelberg. In June 1975, violent demonstrations erupted in this space in protest to a raising of fares to the equivalent of seventy-five cents.

Flexibility also means that light-rail transit can be run in tunnels to avoid conflicts with other traf-

ALTERNATIVE MODES OF MOVEMENT

fic in congested areas, as in Boston, Bonn, and Cologne, and to penetrate major geographical obstacles, as with San Francisco's Twin Peaks Tunnel of 1917. Light rail, however, usually means lighter, narrower, and less expensive roadbeds and greatly reduced costs compared to heavy-rail transit or highway construction for equivalent numbers of commuters. A separate right-of-way at grade can be defined merely through curbing with street spaces, by using the median strips of avenues or separated roadways, or by using abandoned railroad lines or existing utility corridors. An example of a modest but effective, separated light-rail transit right-of-way is provided by Heidelberg where a line also serves as a buffer between general road traffic and a park (Figure 4–24). This view demonstrates how unobtrusive both overhead wires and rights-of-way can be. Because the spatial needs are so modest and the potential volume of traffic so high, the creation of separate roadways for light-rail transit can truly be one of the most effective land uses in urban areas.

A resurgence of light-rail transit in Europe during the past decade has also brought development of sophisticated vehicles that can be operated singly or in multiunit trains. An example is the new vehicle used in Germany's capital, Bonn (Figure 4–25). Technological advances have both enhanced energy savings and improved environmental controls. The new vehicles are extremely quiet, stylish in appearance, very comfortable and spacious within, and can be boarded both from the ground and from platform stations.

Provide for Attractive Interface

The advantage of light-rail transit flexibility extends to design of stations and terminals, since it is possible to design these fixed facilities to whatever standards are appropriate for the particular location and passenger-handling requirements. Simple shelters and benches suffice for stations segregated from other traffic, including those located in pedestrian zones. For stations located in subways or on elevated rights-of-way, it is important to provide easy and attractive transitions to grade level. A detail from the university subway stop in Bonn demonstrates one aspect of this principle (Figure 4–26). The interface between grade-level pedestrian space and underground station is made attractive through the openness of glass, bringing daylight and a view of vegetation and buildings into the below-grade space. Brightness and openness, as well as generous stairs and escalators, help to make the interface attractive.

Frequently, if the subway level in central areas is deep enough, a pedestrian concourse level can even be interposed between the subway and roads at grade level. This opens up the possibility of developing attractive and extensive pedestrian linkages between major nodal points in downtown areas: railroad stations, public transit stations, parking garages, taxi stands, major shopping streets, etc. Such areas can be made all the more appealing, given the high pedestrian counts, by shops and eating facilities at this concourse level. Such con-

Fig. 4–23. Heidelberg, West Germany. Before this street was fully converted to pedestrian use, slow-moving electric trams coexisted well with pedestrians.

Fig. 4–24 (right). Heidelberg, West Germany. Light-rail electric public transit can be effectively located between a park and general road traffic.

Fig. 4–25 (below). Bonn, West Germany. Sophisticated light-rail vehicles with great flexibility of application have been developed for use in Europe during the past decade.

courses form a particularly attractive interface between walking areas, public transit, and other modes of transportation.

Many European cities have developed such concourse spaces to provide direct pedestrian linkage from their railroad stations to the central city. Munich is perhaps the best known of these. Beneath the Stachus intersection of the Inner Ring Road, and located between the main railroad station and the pedestrianized core area, the large underground shopping-eating complex provides a logical route for great numbers of pedestrians. The complex has become a major nodal point, with direct access to the subway below, connection to parking garages, plus toilet facilities and numerous telephones. Grouping many important urban functions and facilities at the interface of major modes of travel—public transit and walking—also effectively discourages the use of cars.

In 1977 Stuttgart opened a similar interface-concourse space linking its main railroad station, the newly pedestrianized main shopping street, Königstrasse, and the light-rail transit stop, which is in a subway at that point. The point of egress from this concourse to the Königstrasse is shown in Figure

Fig. 4–26. Bonn, West Germany. Providing for attractive interface between light-rail transit and pedestrian spaces is a significant consideration.

Fig. 4–27. Stuttgart, West Germany. Making the transition from underground easy, gradual, and well-lit encourages use of public transit.

4–27. The street or ground surface normally is a membrane or barrier penetrated only by steep and narrow staircases connecting the world underground with the normal world above. Here that membrane has been broken to admit great quantities of daylight into the subterranean realm; the sense of being in the "underworld" is alleviated. Even the escalator contributes: converted to a moving ramp, it makes the transition ever so easy, even for those confined to wheelchairs. By determining major desire lines and designing the routes that follow them into generous, interesting, and attractive spaces for people, problems of high-volume traffic in urban centers have been mastered in a manner that provides powerful inducements for people to abandon the once prized automobile.

The Place Ville Marie in Montreal is probably the best-known example in North America of an extensive concourse system that serves as an attractive pedestrian interface between public transportation and major commercial and office spaces. Its pedestrian concourse system linking subway stops is almost five kilometers long. The distinction as compared to Munich and Stuttgart is that the Ville Marie is largely new architectural space built as part of a new development complex, whereas the German examples could be considered as "found space," i.e., nonbuilding architecture developed underneath existing streets. Developing underground spaces in this manner provides an excellent opportunity to provide needed space for new functions without destroying the traditional aspect of urban areas.

Philadelphia has followed the example of Montreal in developing an extensive concourse network linking subway stops with major new buildings in the downtown area. Figures 4–28 and 4–29 reveal techniques for breaking the surface membrane—making below-ground seem more like aboveground by admitting daylight, a view of vegetation, and awareness of current weather conditions to the pedestrian level beneath the street. The tendency in future development will obviously be toward ever greater integration of below-grade and above-grade spaces: larger courtyards, more vegetation, and more extensive use of glass. Compared to the claustrophobic atmosphere of New York subways, the new developments in Philadelphia represent great strides in the right direction. Sunlight, views of nature, and enhanced opportunities for orientation are among the elements that can make transit interface spaces more attractive.

Devise Programs for Coexistence

The primary quest is to devise ways of making cities into more attractive places for people. We have seen that places reserved and designed exclusively for people, such as pedestrianized main shopping streets, have proven to be enormously attractive; yet redesign of cities should not be limited to just those spaces that can be completely segregated from all vehicular traffic. The goal is rather to restore a better balance and to give people greater priority in every urban space. Therefore, a viable

Fig. 4–28. Philadelphia, PA. Large expanses of glass at the concourse level below-grade provide sunlight, views of nature, and better orientation.

coexistence of vehicles and people in urban streets is also an essential aspect of restoring the city to its inhabitants.

Coexistence implies a minimal disturbance between the two or more modes of travel existing in the same space together. It is unhappily the antithesis of conditions on normal major streets of undifferentiated general traffic, where pedestrians are given a minimum of space and are subjected to a maximum of hazards and disturbances. Figure 4–30 shows a good example of coexistence, where pedestrians enjoy virtual priority on Maffeistrasse, a street in the central business district of Munich. Automobile traffic has been eliminated and only light-rail transit passes through, with stops at this point. The light-rail transit is not a disturbance but an added advantage to shoppers and workers who are able to board within a major downtown area. The dangers of injury to pedestrians by automobiles at streetcar stops on undifferentiated streets is eliminated, and the light-rail transit operated at slow speed poses no threat at all to pedestrians. Priority is very clearly established by law and also reinforced by the design of the space.

Fig. 4–29 (left). Philadelphia, PA. Transitions between subways and surface areas can be far more appealing than the once common narrow stairway.

Fig. 4–30 (below). Munich, West Germany. Devising programs for coexistence between pedestrians and electric public transit can enhance urban spaces.

Fig. 4–31. Mannheim, West Germany. Planken, the city's main shopping street, on the day of its opening as a transitway-mall.

Fig. 4–32. Mannheim, West Germany. Heavy, pedestrian flow between attractive urban spaces suggests the need for a bridge to carry pedestrians over the main traffic artery.

ALTERNATIVE MODES OF MOVEMENT

Fig. 4–33. Mannheim, West Germany. If biking is to be encouraged, it requires a network of continuous routes separated from other modes.

The German city of Mannheim on the Rhine has also made coexistence a major factor in replanning its central area to be more attractive, both for pedestrians and for use of public transit. The main shopping street, known as Planken (Figure 4–31), was opened as a redesigned coexistence street in April, 1975. A view of this space during the opening celebration shows an apparent conflict in the use of the light-rail transit at times of extraordinarily heavy pedestrian traffic. Yet the electric tram, moving at a slow walking pace, was able to make its way through without using any warning bells and apparently without arousing anyone's ire. While it would appear here that total separation might have been preferable, a question of judgment always exists between the desirability of spaces designed entirely for pedestrians and the convenience of immediately accessible public transit.

Figure 4–32 shows the same street from the opposite direction seen in Figure 4–31. From the monumental water tower, the transitional areas between the Planken and other urban spaces can be seen. The major traffic street is the Inner Ring around the historic core, and the light-rail transit from the Planken enters a separate right-of-way in the median strip of the Ring at this point. Pedestrian travel to the Planken from the park and urban area behind the water tower, lamentably via a grade crossing controlled by traffic signals, is relatively heavy, deserving perhaps an uninterrupted crossing via bridges or a concourse.

Encourage Biking

In Mannheim and other German cities, differentiation of traffic is not limited to pedestrians, public transit, and cars. Biking too is given encouragement and greater safety by providing an extensive network of often totally separate bike routes but is more usually provided in the buffer space between sidewalks and streets. Figure 4–33 shows bicyclists using a lane between the general traffic space of the Ring and the transit right-of-way in the median strip. If bicycling is to be given necessary encouragement to develop as a genuine mode of transportation for many people, a network of bike routes should be developed as a *continuous system* rather than merely disjointed paths. Opportunities must be provided for following major desire lines without coming into conflict with other modes. Intersections in particular must be carefully regulated, and in Germany the devices for regulating intersections frequently include separate coordinated traffic signals for bikes.

In general, methods and devices appropriate for

facilitating movement in other modes, such as bus-priority measures, will also have analogous applications for encouraging the use of bicycles. Planners in Uppsala, for example, have adopted the attitude that, in striving for a more favorable modal split, it is just as important to encourage walking and bicycling as it is to give preference to public transit. The essential goal is to reduce use of cars. Therefore, along with a traffic-cell system, pedestrianized streets, and transitways, continuous routes for bicycles have been created and linked together to form a network. This network includes some streets that have been closed to all other vehicles, some segregated bikeways, and also some contraflow lanes for bikes, which can be seen in Figure 4–34. The desire to avoid the disruption of the architectural environment that creating new routes would cause has led to careful differentiation in the use of existing street spaces. The contraflow lane application for bikes suggests that many more devices could be put to effective use once the concept of biking as a legitimate mode of transportation is accepted.

Among European countries, Holland perhaps more than others has encouraged bicycling as a privileged mode of transportation. In new developments as well as old, design for safe and unhindered movement of bikes and their appropriate storage is always an important factor. Figure 4–35 is a detail on the perimeter of Hoog Catharijne, a major mixed-use development associated with the railroad station in Utrecht. Mixed-use developments are often notorious for their neglect of linkages to surrounding urban fabric and the severance effects of major roads and approaches to parking structures that they usually generate. In this case at least one adjacent street has been closed and a major approach to the complex developed exclusively for use by bicycle. This is particularly interesting since the complex is the location of both the railroad station and the regional bus terminal. An interface is thus provided for people who commute from the surrounding region by either bus or train and then use a bicycle stored at the terminal as their mode of transport within the city.

This view shows storage racks at the entrance to the complex and two types of separate bike routes: one separated only by a curb from the main street space and the other an entirely separate route in place of a former street. The two instances of people riding double indicate not only the liberal attitude of Dutch police, but also the safety afforded by separation of bike routes from general traffic.

A further advantage of inner city bicycle linkage

is that of speed, since numerous studies in different countries have shown that in congested city traffic, bicycles are considerably faster than cars. The common upper distance range for commutation by bicycle lies between six and nine kilometers, although longer distances are traveled on a daily basis by many bicyclists.

In many countries, including those with severe winters such as Sweden, bicyclists are less discouraged by adverse weather conditions than they are by the threat of motor vehicles domineering the route. Particularly in winter, when visibility is often reduced and the danger of skidding is greater, the lopsided competition of bikes against cars for the same street space can often prove to be fatal. The weather itself, unless it results in deep snow on the bikeway, usually will not deter most bicyclists who use their vehicles as a mode of transportation. It is thus extremely important to provide the appropriate encouragement of separated bike routes built to proper standards of safety and comfort.

In the United States considerable attention was

Fig. 4–34 (facing page). Uppsala, Sweden. One device for encouraging biking is a separate lane against the flow of motorized traffic on a one-way street.

Fig. 4–35 (near left). Utrecht, the Netherlands. Holland continues to pursue a policy that encourages biking as a privileged mode of transportation.

drawn to the fact that 1973 was the first year since early in the century during which more bicycles than automobiles were purchased. A flurry of interest was generated by a federally supported program to create bike routes in urban areas. While undoubtedly much enhanced public awareness derived from the program, the physical results left much to be desired. Instead of continuous networks of bike routes built to a standard that could be expected to encourage more biking, many of the results were an unmitigated farce. Figure 4–36, a view of a main arterial leading into the center of St. Louis, demonstrates the "saying-so-makes-it-so" approach. One is hard pressed to see just where the bike route is supposed to be located. With sidewalks, high curbs, parking meters, and parking lanes on both sides and six lanes of moving traffic in the center, there scarcely seems room for any type of space that could be considered encouraging or even moderately safe for bicyclists. Bike routes clearly do not mean the same thing to different people in different locations.

In New York City, 1980 was the year of the "bike-lane farce," a melodrama of short duration but great expense. The idea was to create separate routes for bicycles along one side of major midtown avenues in Manhattan, with the bikes flowing with the motorized traffic downtown on one avenue and uptown on another. Based on classic principles of separation of modes, the scheme was intended to provide greater safety for cyclists and to encourage this means of transportation so eminently suited to the high-density urban environment of the Big Apple. It was announced with great fanfare by the mayor in July.

Yet, even before the system of barrier islands creating the bike lanes could be completed, there was a great outcry of opposition from various groups, notably managers of shops and hotels who saw the new device as a barrier interposed between them and their automobile-borne customers or patrons. Taxi companies, a very powerful political lobby in New York, predictably opposed the plan, just as they had opposed the plans to pedestrianize

Fig. 4–36. St. Louis, MO. When is a bike route not a bike route? A demonstration of the "saying-so-makes-it-so" approach.

Madison Avenue and to deliver executives from uptown residential areas to Wall Street via express buses. And, just as those rational and intelligent schemes were defeated, so too was the new amenity for cyclists. Specious arguments of increased mortal conflicts between cyclists and pedestrians and tales of bikes wiping out unsuspecting old ladies as they alighted from taxicabs were used in the hysterical arguments that led to court battles, injunctions, and the precipitous dismantling of the bike lanes within only a few months. While it may be speculation that the death knell was rung by powerful interest groups viewing their financial interests as threatened, it is quite obvious that the new system of bike lanes was not given a fair trial and that no time was allowed for problems to be worked out.

Are there any lessons to be gained from the New York experience other than that politics usually is the most powerful factor in determining the shape of cities? Granting that there remain unresolved problems of competition for use of the same street space in many cities, it should be clear that prior planning of routes works far more effectively than retrofitting existing streets already heavily used. Since there is no question of the many benefits to be gained from encouraging bicycling—including health, efficiency, energy conservation, reduction of noise and pollution, elimination of congestion, and more appropriate uses of valuable urban land—

the logical solution in a case such as New York's would be to find some streets from which motorized through traffic could be banned, so that bikes at last would have a fighting chance.

If quality of route is the most important factor in encouraging movement by bicycle, an appropriate place to store a bike at the city-end of one's journey also plays an important role. This problem has two major aspects: first, the problem of physical space where a bike can be left without interfering with other functions or someone's property rights; second, the problem of security for the entire bike and its component parts. This is a matter of ethics and local custom. In some places bikes are such common utilitarian objects and the ethics concerning theft are such that one can simply lock a bike to a fixed object and be fairly certain that it will still be there with all its appurtenances when one returns. In other places one could be just as certain that all separable parts—often, the entire bicycle—would have disappeared in minutes. Thus, simple bike racks tend to suffice in Sweden, Holland, Germany, and other European countries, while locked bike garages are coming into wide use in certain parts of the United States. In an interesting combination of modes, such garages for bicycles are now being made available for rent at Park & Ride facilities for transfer to public transit into cities.

Whatever the local security needs, at some point

the interface between being a bike rider and a pedestrian must be provided, as with other modes. Indiscriminate parking of cycles is a misuse of urban space that should be anticipated and prevented through provision of more appropriate facilities. A view of Münster in Westphalia, Germany (Figure 4–37), demonstrates a simple and straightforward solution of providing bike racks at the beginning of a downtown pedestrian area. Here the facilities are already overcrowded. In Holland and Sweden one is likely to find bike racks spread more frequently throughout a pedestrian district, allowing people to walk their bikes and store them closer to their final destination. In any case, since the creation of pedestrian zones should always be part of a larger program to achieve more favorable movement in cities, planning for bicycle storage should always be linked to the planning of pedestrian areas as part of an overall strategy for attractive interface.

Improvement of safety, convenience, and environmental quality are the basic goals necessary to encourage biking. Among the reasons why bicycling should be encouraged in cities are the following advantages, summarized at a special session of the O.E.C.D. conference, "Better Towns with Less Traffic":

Cheap for the individual user

Easy to use for groups such as school children, young people, and those with low incomes

Quicker and more convenient than other modes for many short-distance urban trips

Flexible for the user in slow, congested traffic situations

Health-giving for the user

Not noisy and not polluting

Economical in the use of space

Economical in the use of energy

Make Waterfronts into Paths for People

Since two of the most universal attractions for people are nature and waterfronts, every city fronting on a river, lake, or other body of water should attempt to develop its waterfront as a landscaped path for pedestrians and bicyclists. Frequently the most difficult problem will be obtaining access to a waterfront that has been preempted by industry, railroads, highways, or private interests. So important is public access to the water that even capitalist countries have passed laws requiring that expro-

Fig. 4–37. Münster, West Germany. Bike racks provide a simple storage solution at the beginning of a pedestrianized shopping street . . . if theft is not a major problem.

priation or easements be used to regain public access to all waterfronts. Once a right-of-way is assured, development can be quite simple and relatively inexpensive.

The west bank of the Rhine River at Godesberg provides an attractive example (Figure 4–38). Two simple asphalt paths are provided, a higher one for pedestrians (from which the photo was taken), and one closer to the water for bicyclists. Trees lining the paths, the river and its traffic, and views of buildings and landscape opposite make this park eminently useful both as a promenade and as a route from one point on the river to another.

At Cologne, further north on the west bank of the Rhine, (Figure 4–39), ships at dock prevent immediate proximity to the water at some points, so that a landscaped linear route is provided higher on the bank. A wider path and more facilities are provided to accommodate greater numbers of people in the major city, and the parallel bike path is also separated a bit more for greater safety. It is interesting to note that the railroad bridge seen crossing the Rhine, which has no roadway for cars, does have a route allowing pedestrians and bicyclists to cross. Facilities to encourage walking and bicycling depend not so much on high investment, but rather on proper priorities and appropriate planning at the right time.

On the Danube at Regensburg (Figure 4–40), development of a linear route for pedestrians along the waterfront is even simpler: one path near the water, another at the top of the dike, some grass, and some trees. Most important is the simple fact that the waterfront has not been preempted for the movement of vehicles. "People first" needs to be the principal design criterion.

The same guideline holds true at every scale in every size city: recapture the waterfront for public pedestrian use. British planners at Norwich, for example (Figure 4–41), have pursued the same goals in smaller compass as German planners at Regensburg, Cologne, and Godesberg, turning the banks of the River Wensum into a park for leisure-time activity in the city. Developing a River Walk—an essentially nonproductive use—from many previous uses that had denied access to the water at many points was fraught with difficulties, but it was an investment of great significance in enhancing central Norwich as an attractive place to live. Provision of public green spaces as areas for recreation and regeneration is relatively low-cost infrastructure when the benefit is the recapturing of older urban residential areas.

Water and trees are essential park ingredients frequently present in abundance but quite often inaccessible or undeveloped for public use. Devel-

Fig. 4–38. Godesberg, West Germany. Making waterfronts into paths for people should be a fundamental goal in every city.

ALTERNATIVE MODES OF MOVEMENT

Fig. 4–39. Cologne, West Germany. Where immediate access to the water cannot be provided an attractive path further up the bank is a good substitute.

Fig. 4–40. Regensburg, West Germany. A simple path, some grass, and trees are enough to say that "people first" is the principal design criterion.

Fig. 4–41. Norwich, England. Water and trees are frequently present but often inaccessible. River Walk is the result of a concerted campaign to regain public access.

oping waterfront areas as paths, both for access and for connection between nodal points in the city, will induce people to live in central cities and discourage the use of automobiles. The possibilities are quite varied, since a walking route can be interestingly adapted to existing terrain and even buildings. For instance, a waterfront path may quite acceptably lead directly through old mill buildings that may still stand along the waterfront. In Ulm, on the Danube in southern Germany, the top of an existing fortification along the riverfront has been developed into a continuous path (Figure 4–42). It is a favorite place for strolling, even in February, and the raised elevation has several advantages, including interesting points of view and easy linkage into different parts of the city. Paths along waterfronts have always been among the great assets to making cities more attractive places for people.

Create a Complete Network for Walking and Biking

Clearly, cities *are* better when the burden of vehicular traffic is reduced, and alternative modes of movement *are* readily accepted by the public if attractive facilities are provided. It therefore follows logically that comprehensive programs of urban traffic management should be integral to all efforts to improve urban areas. The most dramatic improvements in enhancing access to city centers,

reducing harmful environmental effects, and reversing the trend toward depopulation of cities have been accomplished by comprehensive, large-scale planning rather than scattered ad hoc measures. Creating a complete network for walking and biking belongs in any comprehensive program.

While concerted efforts to counter the automotive destruction of urban environmental quality date largely from the past decade, some cities began such programs twenty or more years ago. It comes as something of a surprise to find the little-known city of Västerås in central Sweden has, over the period of the past two decades, developed a comprehensive network of paths for walking and biking, the final linkages of which were completed only recently. The example is very instructive and worthy of a close look.

Västerås prides itself on being a town with a totally coordinated traffic system for buses, cars, bicycles, and pedestrians. The city has a population of 118,000 and an automobile ratio (in 1975) of 3.4 cars for every 10 inhabitants. In the late 1950s a program was begun to incorporate separate paths for bicycles and pedestrians in every new development. Since car ownership at that time was much lower, it is a tribute to the foresight of the planners and builders to have incorporated such facilities at such an early date. A tradition of commuting to work by bicycle existed to a certain extent, but most of this was done on the existing undifferentiated road system. Gradually, throughout the six-

ALTERNATIVE MODES OF MOVEMENT

Fig. 4-42. Ulm, West Germany. The top of the old riverfront fortification makes an ideal place for strolling, even in February.

ties, a comprehensive approach to traffic was developed, while the provision of separate bike paths continued at a steady pace.

Developments of the 1960s included new parking garages, development of an Inner Ring Road, and building of a 350-meter delivery tunnel in the center of the commercial area. The conversion of driving from left-hand to right-hand required considerable attention by traffic planners in 1967, and from then on completion of the comprehensive traffic scheme was given top priority. In what has since become the model approach to improving urban centers for people, the two major radials that intersected at the city hall were simply closed to automobile and truck traffic.

These routes were reserved for pedestrians, bikes, buses, and taxis. Adjacent major shopping streets were converted for use by pedestrians only, and the network of separate routes for bicycles was expanded, both along existing major roads and on entirely separate routes. For a time division of these routes into halves—one side for bikes and the other for pedestrians—was attempted, but when this led to confusion and arguments over right-of-way (the dividing line was frequently taken as a center line by bicyclists), the simple expedient of eliminating the line and requiring both modes to coexist provided a satisfactory solution. All cycle paths are therefore also pedestrian paths, although the reverse is not the case.

The banks of its river were a logical choice for part of this network, and its treatment in the central area is shown in Figure 4-43. Benches, trees, flowers, and telephone booths are among the amenities related to the pedestrian/cycle network. Everything has been done to encourage the use of bikes for daily commuting and all other types of journeys. Consequently, bike racks are everywhere, including the main shopping street (Figure 4-44). A great advantage of the system for winter use is that snow is automatically melted from the pavement of these spaces in the central area. District heating plants supply more than 90 percent of all commercial, public, and domestic heating needs, so that the return circulation system could be run through coils underneath these streets, providing the melting capability.

The comprehensiveness of the cycle network throughout the urban fabric of Västerås is difficult to conceive without riding through it. The total length of exclusive main cycle tracks exceeds eighty-five kilometers in this relatively small city. The network extends everywhere, linking schools and residences, places of work, shopping areas, outlying residential developments, and places of recreation (Figure 4-45). Perhaps even more surprising than the continuity of the network is the degree to which it is free of grade crossings with motorized traffic. In the eighty-five kilometers some seventy-five bridges and tunnels permit bike traffic to continue unhindered over or under general traffic. The increase in safety due to separation of modes is enor-

Fig. 4–43 (top left).
Västerås, Sweden. A continuous network of bicycle and pedestrian paths is a major feature of the comprehensive traffic scheme in Västerås.

Fig. 4–44 (top right).
Västerås, Sweden. To encourage the use of bicycles, storage racks are placed throughout the central city.

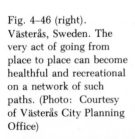

Fig. 4–46 (right).
Västerås, Sweden. The very act of going from place to place can become healthful and recreational on a network of such paths. (Photo: Courtesy of Västerås City Planning Office)

Fig. 4–45. Västerås, Sweden. Fundamental to the network of bike routes is their mandated inclusion in all new housing areas. (Photo: Courtesy of Västerås City Planning Office)

mous. Since the traffic reform in Västerås, the number of accidents within the Inner Ring Road alone (including the Ring Road itself) has fallen by 40 percent.

But reduction of accidents, elimination of congestion, and high air quality are only measurable benefits of a total movement strategy emphasizing walking and bicycling. Figure 4–46 suggests some of the less tangible benefits this overall improvement in environmental qualities brings with it. The very act of going from place to place takes on a healthful and recreational quality that greatly enhances the quality of living in the city and tends to bind residents to this community. The paths go through woods, across meadows, and to all outdoor recreation areas, so that everyone of every age has full opportunity for exercise and outdoor recreation close at hand.

For the most part, the paths in the Västerås pedestrian/cycle network have been quite inexpensive to provide. The biggest problems have arisen with filling in the gaps to complete linkages and especially with providing vertical separation at crossings with traffic arteries. Bridges and tunnels are the most expensive parts of the system, but if they can be built gradually over a long period of time, their expense can be included relatively easily in the municipal traffic budget. In the case of Västerås, the most elaborate structure for this purpose was the underpass linking the railroad/bus terminal with City Hall Park and thus with the rest of the central business district. Figure 4–47 is a view from the city side and Figure 4–48 is a view from the sta-

tion side of this underpass. The passage is wide, airy, and inviting. Quality materials were employed in the structure, there is a good level of lighting, and the approaches are well landscaped. Clearly this pedestrian/bicycle approach has been designed to be a worthy entrance to the city. Alternative modes of movement in Västerås are not merely weak appendages to the primary circulation system for automobiles but have become fullfledged components in an overall movement system.

Expand Possibilities for Nonmotorized Movement

The essence of improving environmental quality through a reduction in total volume of motorized traffic thus lies in developing modes of movement alternative to the automobile and especially in expanding possibilities for nonmotorized movement. Experience in many countries strongly suggests that the potential demand for all forms of movement without motors is far greater than existing facilities will allow. Unfortunately for the United States, heavily one-sided emphasis on road construction has meant not only failure to develop appropriate paths and linkages but even the disruption and severance of existing paths for biking and walking, in much the same way existing extensive rights-of-way for interurban rapid transit lines were cut up and sacrificed for highway construction.

Fig. 4–47. Västerås, Sweden. The city side of the bike path between the railroad station and downtown reveals the great care taken to make the tunnel open and inviting.

Fig. 4–48. Västerås, Sweden. The station side of this same passageway has been designed as a worthy entrance to the city.

ALTERNATIVE MODES OF MOVEMENT

Many means of movement are possible in cities, some that are widely recognized, others that are scarcely considered. The advent of skateboards and the rapid spread of their popularity is a phenomenon that no one could have predicted. Already skateboards have become a popular mode of transportation, not simply recreation, on many college campuses. As a form of transportation a skateboard has some unique advantages, including portability and ease of storage; yet it also raises classic questions of conflicts with other modes. Like bicycles, however, skateboards and, even more recently, roller skates, are more compatible with pedestrian traffic than with motorized traffic, raising yet another argument in favor of a network of routes separate from roads and streets.

Another suggestion of the relatively unexplored field of nonmotorized traffic is suggested by Figure 4–49. Nothing more than an upgraded tricycle, this vehicle indicates the range of style and self-expression that could blossom if this mode were given the encouragement of attractive routes. Actually, tricy-

Fig. 4–50 (left). Graz, Austria. Octogenarian Franz Wagner with his ten-speed: such triumphs of independence for older citizens depend on differentiation of traffic spaces.

Fig. 4–49 (below). Victoria, Canada. This stylized tricycle suggests possibilities for imaginative forms of transportation if attractive routes are provided.

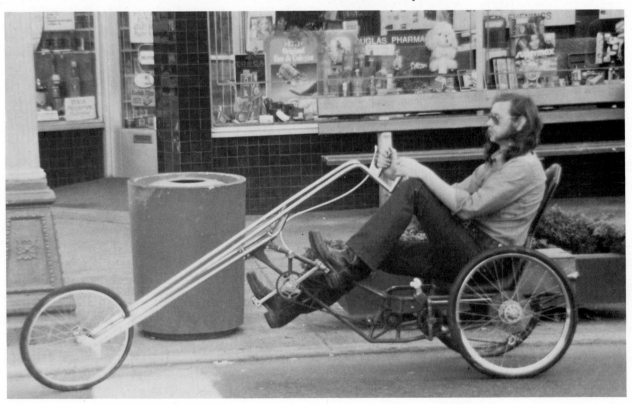

Fig. 4–51. Utrecht, the Netherlands. Ron Wiedenhoeft with his one-speed two-wheeler: even heavy baggage can be managed without motorized vehicles in a properly designed high-density urban area.

cles have already experienced a great renaissance as practical adult vehicles in retirement villages of the Sunbelt, and space-age materials and technology have recently produced a commuter trike able to move at fifty miles per hour whose stability and carrying capacity make it very useful for all types of short trips.

Mobility of the elderly is very often overlooked in transportation planning. Stairs into buses are too high, the Walk phase of traffic signals is too short, and insufficient seats prevent taking a rest where needed. Programs for encouraging alternative movement and differentiating the use of street spaces can take all of these considerations into account and thereby contribute greatly to reintegrating the elderly into society. With limitations, older folks are far more mobile than the rest of us assume.

In the Austrian city of Graz, the octogenarian Franz Wagner is quite a celebrity (Figure 4–50). On his modern ten-speed bike, he serves as a sym-

bol of elderly independence that should be welcomed everywhere. But a Franz Wagner on his bike is only possible through appropriate differentiation of traffic spaces. Limitation of motorized traffic in Graz makes it possible for the young at heart, no matter what their age, to give free rein to their urges for mobility in the city. Certainly that is a social benefit not to be taken lightly.

Finally, in a chapter on alternative modes of movement, it is perhaps not inappropriate to point out that the great majority of cities illustrated in this book were reached by the author via railroad and were then investigated essentially on foot, with some help from public transit. The burdens of baggage and heavy camera equipment were mastered with the simple device of a two-wheeled hand cart (Figure 4–51). By this means it was possible, for instance, to stroll through Paris and examine streets all the way from the Gare de l'est to the Louvre, seeing more than in the tunnels of the Métro and being able to absorb it far better than at the hectic pace of street traffic. Needless to say, some cities facilitate and encourage this form of movement far more than others; but it is important to note that not one example among the cities visited would not benefit significantly from greater differentiation of street spaces and greater reduction of automobile traffic. It is simply a matter of the survival or demise of cities as viable places to live, which is to say, in fine, a matter of the survival or demise of cities.

A Future
for Our Past

The twentieth century has been characterized as a century of continuing crisis. A sense of alienation and malaise has been widespread and seems in no small measure to have resulted from changes in the physical environment. Destruction of traditional values and associations have robbed people of old associations, old assurances. Things not only are no longer what they used to be, but the changes in quality and scale are of a vastness unprecedented in previous centuries, making individuals feel like rootless, anonymous units in a faceless society.

What, we may well ask, has been the role of architecture in this erosion of tradition? Must our age destroy every environmental tie with its past, squandering time-honored forms and values in buildings and urban design? Drastic changes occurring in some cities so often seem to threaten total abandonment of our environmental heritage; yet

countermovements have gained strong momentum within the past ten years. Preserving and reinforcing urban architectural qualities from the past is more and more seen as the way to build a better future.

A view of downtown Philadelphia (Figure 5–1) symbolizes some of the ways in which the face and character of many cities have been changing under the pressures of speculative land development: changes both in the scale and the use of urban land. Where two-story rowhouses once knotted together a residential neighborhood of intimate scale, now occupants and users are gone, and the scarred site awaits total clearance. For what? The high-rise building in the background, itself prematurely old and no longer commanding the best rents, suggests vulnerability to greater intensity of use and higher return on real estate investment. But for well or ill, the continuity is gone, removed more thoroughly than if the area had been bombed. What happened to the people? What has become of the interrelationships of neighbor to neighbor, shopowner to client, employer to employee?

Important questions about the functions considered desirable in cities may not safely be left to developers. How much change is necessary? How much is desirable? What is the desired mix of residential and commercial, for example? What are the possibilities of integrating a broad variety of human activities in urban centers, and what type of physical setting is necessary to encourage the desired mix of activities and functions? What are the desired distributions and intensities of land use? How many people per acre, what degree of land coverage, what ratio of floor area to site area? Is it wise to ignore or discard the rich inheritance of established social and commercial patterns or of inhabitants whose pride of place is the essence of a living urban environment, the very reason for the existence of cities at all? One of the grave mistakes made with modern architecture and urban development surely has been the presumption that the past has no future.

Among the many lessons to be learned from long-established urban environments is that fundamental human needs and reactions change very little. The social desire for communication with other people in an unforced environment, the physical desire for comfort, for shelter from sun or rain, the desire for visual stimulation, the intellectual desire for change within a context of permanence: these could all be characterized as basic human needs. In the accompanying view from the heart of Padua, Italy, we can recognize historical architecture and urban design going back several centuries (Figure 5–2), yet its public and semipublic designed spaces are as effective today in stimulating human interchange and personal identification with the community as ever. Programs for architectural design need to encourage supportive social behavior, a purpose that historic architectural environments seem to serve better than so many modern designs.

That is not to say that there should not be normal and reasonable modern building and development or that major parts of every city should be transformed into architectural museums, but it does mean that we need to be more careful with our cultural resources. We do need to guard against senselessly destroying the structure, character, and scale of neighborhoods and urban centers that have developed over generations.

The primary danger, of course, lies not in bad intentions. Most destruction has been done with good intentions to achieve well-articulated, positive goals. Conflicts between goals, on the other hand, need to be better recognized, so that thoughtless destruction in the name of progress can be stopped while there is still time, whether this destruction is taking place in the name of street or highway construction, development of new housing areas, urban renewal to stimulate new investment, or simply the desire to create "healthy" neighborhoods. It is crucial that we stop spending money to crush our architectural heritage, to decivilize our cities.

The aesthetics of the Modern Movement in architecture have lent themselves exceedingly well to the development of what has been aptly termed cost-accountant architecture. Elegantly simple

volumetric envelopes enclosing highly efficient skeletal frame structures have been an enormous success in maximizing profits for investors. Even where zoning limitations restrict height and bulk of buildings, cost-accountant architecture has provided the means by which to squeeze the last rentable piece of floor area out of the allowable spatial envelope. A startling contrast in central Frankfurt, the most American of Germany's commercial centers, demonstrates the mockery made of well-intentioned building codes (Figure 5–3).

Maximum building volume and high return on investment are not evil of themselves, of course. The only question is whether they are not upon occasion overbalanced by the need to preserve substantial, older architecture of greater intrinsic interest or to preserve the character and image of a

city. Economic compromises must be found to maintain the richness of texture, pattern, and human associations of the older, more interesting architectural forms that contribute to local character. We must replace irresponsible exploitation with conscientious development, and we must do it soon, while there is still something left to save.

It is a political responsibility to save the substance of the past, to care for it and improve it, and to pass on its heritage to the future. The obvious truth of such a statement is evident to the most dimwitted of us in the case of such monumental compositions of classic architectural grandeur as the Place de la Concorde in Paris (Figure 5–4). But how monumental must a composition be before it deserves some recognition of its worth, before some farsighted person or group makes the responsible political decision that it is worthy of being preserved for the present and future generations?

Yet even the Place de la Concorde, great and universally acclaimed as it is, is an embattled zone, as Figure 5–4 shows. Not only is its very fabric being steadily eaten away by airborne chemical pollutants, but more desirable social and commercial activities appropriate to such an august multifaceted outdoor living space have been all but totally displaced by the tyranny of motorized traffic.

Such mindless following of trend to accommodate perceived modern needs created by technological developments can preclude the continuity of human uses vital to urban spaces. While ways to optimize relationships between new and traditional uses of urban spaces are not always easy to find, the continued search remains a political responsibility of the highest order. Protected and revitalized historic urban environments may well prove to be the best hope for humane cities of the future.

Fig. 5–3 (right). Frankfurt, West Germany. The aesthetics of the Modern Movement have lent themselves well to creating cost-accountant architecture.

Fig. 5–4 (below). Paris, France. The great and universally acclaimed Place de la Concorde is threatened by pollution and ever increasing motorized traffic.

Our Underrecognized Resources

One of the great problems is how to satisfactorily define what constitutes historic urban environment and determine to what extent and how it should be protected. Becoming accustomed to old buildings that have gradually gone out of fashion and suffered neglect, we tend no longer even to see them. The old can too easily become the old-fashioned in our perceptions, resulting in a neglect that may be entirely unintentional. Old buildings are among the most underrecognized resources in our cities, only entering into our conscious perception when it's too late, when the gaping holes left by their removal make us conscious of the color, texture, sense of scale, and comfortable recognizability that they once provided. The bank buildings on Yonge Street in downtown Toronto (Figure 5–5), for instance, are of an architectural type all too frequently considered disposable by modern planners. To those unfamiliar with the development of western architecture over the last five hundred years, it really was a rather strange and quaint concept of the nineteenth century to make banks look like Roman temples. Why should we want to perpetuate this conceit? Polemics of modern architecture, with emphasis on structure, function, clarity, simplicity, and machine-made materials, have tended to give many of our older architectural resources a bad name: out-of-date, obsolete, tasteless, the "morphology of dead styles." Yet, if we consider the aesthetic elements in architecture that stimulate our psychological responses of pleasure and interest, we must recognize that the old buildings, often commissioned with a great sense of civic pride and responsibility by business leaders of the past and constructed by the hands of skilled artisans, have a great deal to offer, regardless of what the particular period style may have been.

For reasons of stimulating the viewer's psychological responses alone, the rich exteriors of old buildings deserve very careful consideration. Particularly in major public urban spaces, every effort should be made to retain some sense of continuity with the past and every opportunity taken to use aesthetic contributions of earlier generations. The mere preservation of facades, however, is not enough. Maintaining functions conducive to visitors behind the facades, controlling the scale and aesthetic quality of adjacent new facades, and integrating the functions of the buildings with the public purpose of the street are all significant ways to assure continued benefit from important works of architecture. As long as the street space con-

Fig. 5–5. Toronto, Canada. These older bank buildings on Yonge Street represent our underrecognized architectural resources.

Fig. 5–6. Toronto, Canada. Many of the architectural monuments of earlier eras should be valued today for their character and sculptural qualities.

tinues to be used primarily as a major vehicular thoroughfare, however, their potential is likely to go unrealized, and they will inevitably disappear to make room for larger, more interior-oriented buildings, such as the increasingly popular enclosed malls that turn their backs on existing street spaces.

Another view in downtown Toronto (Figure 5–6) illustrates the gross changes in scale that so often take place in contemporary development of urban sites. With more and more projects extending to cover one full square block or more, the street facades tend to become inward-looking closed envelopes, while all activities are focused on enclosed courtyards, galleries, atria, or other forms of through-block passageways. Since these can provide weather protection and a great many of the amenities that people have come to expect from shopping malls, such interior public or quasipublic spaces have gained wide acceptance. A basic disadvantage is that they are totally artificial and generally unrelated to the ambience of the city in which they happen to be built. The enclosed downtown mall becomes just as much removed from the real time and particular urban space as any suburban shopping mall, and the result is loss of urbanity and loss of urban image. The genuine public spaces of the city—streets, squares, and intersections— bereft of all functions but the moving and storing of vehicles, gradually die and lose their function even as linkages.

On the other hand, if the no-man's-land of parking lots and traffic lanes is to be diverted into more productive human activity, a very positive new role can be played by such eclectic sculptural monuments of a previous era as the Bank of Montreal in Toronto. Seemingly forgotten in a void, patiently waiting until someone notices and calls in the wrecking crew, such smaller older buildings can make a new contribution in the expanded contemporary urban scale. Now, instead of being simply another purveyor of interior space along the street, this highly sculptural beaux arts monument becomes an object existing in and articulating a much larger urban space defined by the huge modern projects as much as a block or two away. Like a piece of sculpture, it can generate and organize space around it. It needs only refurbishing and a designed relatability to other urban functions and circulation patterns to become a very positive contributor to people's sense of identity and tradition, a humanizing element.

It is not a matter of *which* style we prefer, whether beaux arts, neo-Greek, neo-Gothic, or any other, but a matter of preserving style as such, from any era, in order to retain interest and human scale, reorchestrating the piece rather than destroying the score. In the face of ever more styleless, scaleless, faceless urban environments made of ever more cost-accountant glass boxes trying to cover up with their shininess the enormity of site exploitation, we have a desperate need for *some* style, one is tempted to say *any* style, as long as it has the ability to provide something to attract and stimulate the eye and the mind. Frank Furness, the Philadelphia architect of a hundred years ago, was long considered the bad boy of architectural taste because of his wild eclecticism, strong contrasts, and intentional aesthetic conflicts of colors, patterns, rhythms, textures, and materials. His Pennsylvania Academy of the Fine Arts (Figure 5–7) adds jarring notes of disharmony and ambiguity, even in such matters as structure, massing, and fenestration. Yet, precisely because of its rarity today, his strong and unique architectural character is now much beloved by enthusiasts. When the American Institute of Architects and the Society of Architectural Historians held their respective annual conventions in Philadelphia during the

mid-1970s, there was a rash of lapel buttons proclaiming "Forever Furness" in recognition of his powerful contributions. Yet how many of the forcefully expressive buildings of Frank Furness, and of so many others, have been torn down in the name of progress?

An architectural heritage can only survive if it is valued by the general public, by the business community, and by the youth of a society. Otherwise it is doomed. Education and programs of public awareness and appreciation are thus of utmost importance for all age groups. The vituperative antitraditional and antieclectic campaigns of the Modern Movement may be directly blamed for the demolition of countless superbly built and highly valuable examples of older architectural styles. Not that architects themselves always called for the destruction directly, but, if the profession itself had

Fig. 5–7 (left). Philadelphia, PA. The idiosyncratic architecture of Frank Furness, as demonstrated by the Pennsylvania Academy of the Fine Arts, is now highly valued.

Fig. 5–8 (right). Victoria, Canada. The amazing and irreplaceable Provincial Houses of Parliament: architecture as sculpture.

little respect for older buildings, certainly there could be no harm in tearing them down to be replaced by more efficient, aesthetic, modern structures of, as so often was the case, considerably increased size or by parking lots in order to save on taxes. Recognition of the value of our heritage by experts is a necessary first step; education of the public to value and protect this heritage is of crucial importance.

Of course, not all buildings of the past can be expected to be as rich in aesthetic stimuli as the Pennsylvania Academy of the Fine Arts or the Provincial Houses of Parliament in Victoria, British Columbia (Figure 5–8). The efforts that went into these buildings were extraordinary and extremely expensive. The unusual amount of craftsmanship and art gracing them is a measure of the great cultural value placed in them at the time of their construction; yet high-grade materials, hand craftsmanship, and significant artistry in design can be found in buildings of many different types, from very expensive to quite humble. Preservation efforts should encompass the entire range and include all buildings and all areas of cities, towns, and villages that have historic or cultural meaning.

Modern urban design has finally rediscovered the value of contained spaces. Many buildings have particular significance not because of their own intrinsic value but because of their contributions in a particular context to a larger ensemble. Urban squares, such as the Market Square in the Swiss city of Basel (Figure 5–9) frequently constitute ensembles highly deserving of preservation. The space in Basel is directly in front of the historic city hall and thus represents a major focal point of the city and its region. The market, of course, has a highly traditional function, so that its maintenance into the present represents a strong element of continuity. The buildings are not only elements of sculptural interest and local character but also serve as

Fig. 5–9. Basel, Switzerland. Individually these buildings on the Market Square may not be of great note; as an ensemble they are highly valuable.

A FUTURE FOR OUR PAST

Fig. 5–10. Prague, Czechoslovakia. Historical associations and rich detail make this skyline, viewed from the Charles Bridge, a national monument.

decorative backdrops setting the scene, containing the space, providing the ambience with which citizens and visitors can feel a strong sense of identification. Integration and overlapping of functions in the urban space, as well as the feeling of social and cultural vitality conveyed by a functioning market in the heart of a city, can be very important elements in conveying a sense of a city's livability. The particular local color of the architectural ensemble makes a significant contribution to establishing these cultural values.

Maintaining such an older architectural setting helps sustain a sense of continuity in time. People feel they are participating in traditions with which they can identify, traditions that transcend the present; participation in annual festivals such as Basel's pre-Lenten Carnival is all the more enthusiastic because of these feelings of identity. Everyone feels he can belong, and the studied casualness of the older building forms seems to play a significant role in encouraging such feelings. The only uniformity is the pervasive hospitality to the human scale.

The Importance of Spires

Spires and domes are architectural signposts marking culturally significant places. An abundance of spires and domes means an abundance of culturally significant places, but it also produces a very interesting and stimulating skyline, a fact which has not been lost on Walt Disney Enterprises in creating the enormously successful Disneyland in California and Disney World in Florida. So successful have Disney's designers been in their thorough exploitation of the pleasant scale and delightful variety of historic architecture that a view over the center of the Czech capital of Prague from the Charles Bridge over the Vltava River (Figure 5–10) might seem at first glance almost a Disney creation. "Learning from Disneyland" is not such an inappropriate title for a book on urban conservation, since the lessons learned long ago by Disney and his designers seem to have been all but forgotten in so many cities today. What is the secret of success in the Disney entertainment environments? Two elements stand out: the interest of historical associations (even if manufactured from scratch), and the stimulation of rich detail to which people can relate (even if made of plastic). The advantage of a preserved historic environment such as that in Prague is that the historical associations are real and on the actual spot where things happened and that the materials of the stimulating detail are original and genuine (albeit restored). The skyline of Prague is a national monument, highly treasured by the Czechs and Slovaks for its historic associations, particularly in this period of oppression under the Soviets.

For similar, though perhaps less emotional reasons, creation of a strong urban image to which citizens feel bound and with which they feel a sense of identification should be among the highest goals of urban planners and city fathers. Satisfying this goal requires that, first of all, a very specific inventory of historic and cultural resources be taken. Only such an inventory can reveal the full wealth of resources available and lead to their preservation from haphazard destruction in the process of development. Specific plans need to be devised to use and reinforce these resources; simple adaptation of normal planning measures or practices will not suffice. Entire districts need to be surveyed: street spaces, groups of buildings, individual buildings, interiors as well as exteriors. A solid basis for planning is obtainable only when it is known what is at stake.

Prague is a fine example of what can be achieved through careful preservation and restoration over long periods of time and through the vicissitudes of various forms of government. But in Warsaw and Danzig in Poland, where war devastation was excruciatingly thorough, the solution was far more radical. Restoration was not even possible, and the amazing decision to *replicate* large sections of the historic cities was made as a matter of national image and identity. Other, more normal cities the world over are increasingly recognizing that the solution lies in *integrated conservation*, an approach that makes the idea of conserving cultural heritage an issue of serious consequence in *all* urban development.

In Prague, as in other cities, the goal is not just to conserve history but to reinforce it, and if possible, to pass on the heritage to future generations in improved rather than diminished condition. Thus the Charles Bridge, which until recently served as an artery for motorized traffic, has been converted into a pedestrian oasis and a linkage in a network of walking routes throughout the historic portions of the city. The bridge, built in the fourteenth century, has sculptural groups largely from the eighteenth century, while the towers, domes, spires, pediments, and other architectural adornments visible in Figure 5–10 are largely from the four intervening centuries. Despite war, famine, plague, floods, and other deprivations, the fabric of the beloved city has always been restored, refurbished, respected as a reminder of the past, a solace for the present, and a means of assuring continuity into the future.

No American city is as fortunate as Prague in having had such a rich heritage and so many generations lavishing so much care on preserving it, yet all cities everywhere do have a cultural heritage, buildings worth preserving, and the option of either drawing attention to or ignoring the contributions of previous generations. Frequently there are spires, towers, or domes that give clues to what these earlier generations valued most and what, therefore, might be appropriate to conserve for the future. The university city of Fayetteville in Arkansas is one such example, and a view on College Avenue (Figure 5–11) shows monumental architectural forms of a generic type one might expect to find in many places in the United States.

The masonry spire or clock tower in this case belongs to the courthouse and clearly was intended to serve as a monument to civic service, order, and pride. It has been restored in a program to renovate the courthouse in its historic form, but the tower now has to compete with monuments to commercial pride, including several new, tall bank buildings at the center of town and the Hawaiian-style Downtown Motor Lodge across the street. The many stately trees that once graced College Avenue and gave it such charm were removed to facilitate traffic. What was once quiet and stately is now hard-edged, fast moving, and nondescript. The preserved courthouse has a hard time holding its own.

The rich stonework of the shorter tower in the foreground belongs to a building long left unused for want of a good idea of what to do with it: the old jail. For Fayetteville even the jail forms a precious aesthetic and cultural resource within the fabric of the city, a monument of civic pride that needs to be recalled as a benchmark for future development. The colors, textures, and familiar monumental forms of these buildings provide important bases for reference and identification as newly powerful commercial interests remake the city, old stores and homes are removed by renewal, the trees disappear, and the asphalt equalizer oozes

Fig. 5–11 (above). Fayetteville, AR. College Avenue, once lined with stately trees, now barely hangs on to its history.

Fig. 5–12 (left). Münster, West Germany. Devastated during the Second World War, the buildings here have been replicated in the postwar period.

over an ever greater percentage of the urban face.

Ironically, the sudden shock of the brutal destruction of a city's cultural heritage through war has stimulated far more dedicated preservation and replication than the insidious yet more thorough destruction brought about in the name of development and urban renewal. The Principal Market in the northwestern German city of Münster is an interesting example of a city neighborhood that saw very heavy destruction of its major architectural space by Second World War bombs (Figure 5–12). The houses at the left, richly ornamented merchants' houses of the fifteenth through seventeenth centuries, were all but totally destroyed. Major portions, however, of the city hall at the right and the Lamberti Church at the end of the space remained standing, and so the brave decision was made in the immediate postwar years to replicate the historic character of the space.

The Gothic spire of the church provided a focal point, but without the scale and general character of the merchants' houses, the quality of the space would have been lost. Economic considerations made it impossible to reconstruct the historic ornament of these facades, so that the general effect is only an approximation; the desired effect, however, is achieved and the historic continuity preserved. Fortunately, a six-volume inventory of the architecture of Münster had been completed just prior to the destruction by the war. Clearly there is a direct link between the thoroughness of documentation and the recognition of value in the local architectural heritage.

It is a mistake, however, to assume that urban conservation or replication of this type is carried out only for nostalgic reasons. Recapturing the scale, the rhythm, and the spatial relationships of urban spaces is also motivated by very practical considerations of wishing to retain an underlying spirit of order and continuity in time and in society. All preservation efforts must start from a realistic consideration of the problems of contemporary architecture and contemporary society.

The romantic German city of Heidelberg was preserved from destruction by bombs in the Second World War and survived with its urban substance essentially intact. Conservation has thus meant, first and foremost, preservation of the total city picture, and the massing, relative heights and the character of street spaces have all been carefully maintained. The space of the main street (Figure 5–13), for example, retains all of its traditional spatial qualities and the general character of the building elevations. Though many important historic buildings are restored both inside and out to retain the genuine architectural substance, other buildings along the main street have been renovated on an individual basis to bring them up to modern standards while still retaining the original character of their street frontage. This has also meant for many of them a retention of the all-important residential function, so that not only the appearance but also the substance of the building uses retain the traditional character.

Density remains traditionally high in Heidelberg, although the upgrading of dwellings frequently means that more older units are joined to form fewer, more spacious modern ones. This density means that more people are closer to functions, events, facilities, infrastructure, and the university, so that now dwellings in the center are very much in demand. Despite the relative uniformity of size, shape, height, and bulk of the buildings, there is interesting variety, furthered by the bending configuration of the street and the strong articulation and orientation of the church tower. Clarity and identifiability in a vibrantly alive urban setting is the result.

Towers and turrets inevitably help not only to

Fig. 5–13. Heidelberg, West Germany. Conservation means retaining the whole city picture, including heights, massing, and character of street spaces.

frame streetscapes and identify major nodal points but also, from a distance, to provide orientation, as one sees towers appear and disappear and appear again in new relationships to each other, to facades, and to street spaces. A particularly interesting example of the importance of spires is

Fig. 5–14. Munich, West Germany. The urban living room of Marienplatz has had this "old" bell tower reappear in the 1970s.

Marienplatz in Munich, the urban living room at the heart of the Bavarian capital (Figure 5–14). The stepped gable at right center in this view belongs to the old city hall, a medieval structure many times restored; in front of it stands the Column of the Virgin Mary, a votive offering for relief from the plague in the seventeenth century. At the left is a portion of the new city hall, highly decorative architecture in a neo-Gothic style from the early twentieth century, while in between, providing an effective architectural backdrop because of its contrasting simplicity and regularity, is a commercial establishment. The great surprise is that the turreted bell tower of the old city hall at the right was built in the 1970s.

As discussed earlier, this space was once teeming with vehicular traffic. The main east-west axis through the center of the city went through the old city hall and its tower at street level. Since the entire core area was almost completely destroyed by bombs in the Second World War, the severely damaged tower of the old city hall was removed to bet-

ter facilitate movement of vehicles. The opening proved extremely useful as long as the axis was used as a traffic artery. But the opening was no longer needed after it was decided in 1969 to close this route to vehicular traffic, have a subway run underneath instead, and create one of the world's largest urban pedestrian precincts. In a referendum, the people expressed the wish to have their historic tower back, and it was given to them: a replica largely in reinforced concrete, now housing a museum. Construction was completed in 1974, giving the Marienplatz its quality of a contained room once again.

The concept of *ensemble* is all important. Munich has other historic towers in the immediate vicinity: that of the new city hall is predominant on Marienplatz, the monumental twin towers of the Cathedral are nearby to the west, and just south and east of the Marienplatz are three more church towers. There is no other high-rise construction allowed in the core area. The people of Munich are thus given the opportunity of identifying strongly with qualities of history and tradition. The evidences are everywhere visible, and yet the city is a pulsating hub of dynamic commercial and cultural activity. There is no sense of the city's being a museum at all: it is a vibrant, modern capital. It is a good bet that Munich's traditional architectural framework plays a major role in the vitality, binding the people and organizations to its powerfully attractive urban image.

Urban Living Rooms

The transformation that has taken place in Munich represents a major change in philosophy of urban development that has been in the making since at least the early 1960s. It is a philosophy best articulated in the 1963 Buchanan Report, *Traffic in Towns*, for the British Minister of Transport: the urban open spaces of streets, squares, and highways should be differentiated into urban rooms and urban corridors, instead of letting them all be used for circulating motor vehicles. One of the principal benefits of this form of differentiation is the opportunity to create outdoor urban living rooms at the hearts of cities, instead of having every historic core bisected, quadrisected, and sliced into dried-up bits by arterial roads. Virtually every city has developed around an intersection of two or more major routes; it is usually at this point that the inn, the city hall, the cathedral, or some other major civic monument was located. Since it is no longer possible to have all regional and supraregional traffic crossing at this point, many planners converted the preeminent urban space at the center into an urban living room: returning the heart of the city to people on foot who have a moment for glancing at their surroundings, savoring spaces designed to encourage all human activities except operating motorized vehicles.

An aerial view of Salzburg (Figure 5–15) conveys some notion of a city that is made up of buildings and urban living rooms. The urban fabric of Salzburg, which has never lost its attractiveness as a place to live, provides an outstanding example of designed urban open spaces that are intended to augment the living spaces inside the buildings. These spaces are not simply leftover voids or traffic sluices, but planned, roofless rooms for private, semipublic, or public human functions: cloisters, courtyards, forecourts, marketplaces, plazas, and street spaces. In a very small amount of space there are thus a great number of highly differentiated spaces for a broad variety of activities in close proximity to each other. That in itself is perhaps one of the best definitions of the word *urbanity*. This type

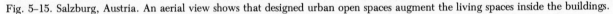

Fig. 5–15. Salzburg, Austria. An aerial view shows that designed urban open spaces augment the living spaces inside the buildings.

Fig. 5–16. Malmö, Sweden. The changing prospect of different historic materials, colors, patterns, and textures heightens enjoyment of the city.

of planning, so effective in the past, continues to provide very useful spaces for modern functions today.

Malmö is the third largest city in Sweden, and the view shown here is from a period of active urban conservation, before the pedestrianization of this important commercial street (Figure 5–16). As the towers against the sky, so the pavement underfoot and the changing prospect of different building materials, different colors, patterns, and textures provide an intensity of tangibility that heightens the experience and enjoyment of the city.

Yet the politics of conservation always require that use of the architectural heritage remains closely tied to the contemporary life of society. The buildings shown here are all inventoried and each site is classified in terms of height and bulk limitations and the desired mixture of functions: residential, commercial, light industry, etc. The variety and quality of interrelationships is more important than aesthetic qualities of individual buildings. In the aggregate, the interesting variants of modesty and historic styles from different periods add up to great richness of detail and sensory experience.

Many older European cities provide a wealth of spaces that continue to serve as urban living rooms today. The most characteristic aspect of the northern Italian city of Bologna, for instance, is its miles of covered sidewalks and galleries (Figure 5–17). These provide not only welcome shelter from the weather but seem to stimulate a greater degree of social life, a desire to linger in public places. Urban

design here has made walking into a respected and publicly supported social activity, and the inviting ambience seems to generate the type of behavior it is meant to support. Whether or not this is true, it is quite apparent that no street widening to facilitate the movement of vehicles is going to encroach on these sidewalks. The priorities in favor of pedestrians over vehicles are clearly established. Strong measures instituted by the municipal government are gradually eliminating negative environmental impacts of traffic and reinforcing the residential function in the urban center. The galleries and other public open spaces free of the burdens of traffic are making the central area far more attractive as a dwelling place than the old buildings alone would warrant. Land-use planning and traffic management are enabling many people to take advantage once again of the amenities available only to those living in the city's center.

Covered passageways, galleries, or loggias, as they may be called in different places, are a form of amenity traditional to many older cities in southern climates, where the need to get out of the heat of direct sunlight is more frequent. They are equally welcome in northern regions, however, where they provide an opportunity to avoid inclement weather and still gain one's destination. Such galleries also urge a designed route, with interesting things along the way, leading from one nodal point to another. The fact that they exist at all is a magnanimous gesture to the public welfare; thus the materials and architectural forms are usually of an aesthetic

Fig. 5–17. Bologna, Italy. The miles of covered sidewalks and galleries stimulate a desire to linger in public spaces, encouraging social activity.

character. It is, therefore, no accident that such spaces are usually attached to some monumental building complex or important urban space. They represent important parts of the concept of urban living rooms for the public.

In Madrid the main urban living room is the Plaza Mayor, the completely enclosed major plaza built in the early seventeenth century where major political events of the nation's capital took place alongside markets, fairs, jousts, tournaments, and races (Figure 5–18). It stands as the central symbol of the city, and everyone knows where this city's heart beats the strongest. Public events focus on this major space, significantly and entirely free of motorized vehicles. Here is the place to be visited by every tourist, the place to come see what's happening, to escape loneliness by being where the action is, to have coffee, read a newspaper, watch the passing scene. Monumentality and permanence of the architectural forms provide an automatic link with tradition, while shops, restaurants, and boutiques stimulate continuous activity. The passageways are linkages between other important parts of the city and provide an uplifting monumental experience that transcends the mundane everyday world, giving citizens an opportunity, however fleetingly, to identify with grandeur. So many lessons here could be applied to modern urban design.

In Florence, an analogous place is the Piazza della Signoria in front of the old city hall, the Palazzo Vecchio (Figure 5–19). Here, the great wealth of sculpture in the space balances the imposing mass of the building. No thoroughfare bisects the space; though irregular in shape, it constitutes a contained environment with only small streets impinging on the space at various corners, in essence a grand space devoted to people and suitable for great public events. The powerful and unique image is a combination of striking architectural materials and forms, major works of art, and the pageantry of the people themselves, who are clearly an intended part of the composition. Colors, patterns, textures, and a sense of grandeur all play significant roles, but perhaps most significant is the unerring design of the urban open space as a vessel for human activities.

During the past two decades an increasing awareness of such concepts has grown in most countries, north as well as south, east as well as west, communist as well as capitalist. The redesign of architectural "stages" for human activities in public spaces has become a significant concept in current urban planning. Public or semipublic, these contained open places serve as urban living rooms, attracting people and generating a sense of identity and affection for the city. In Great Britain the Buchanan Report, *Traffic in Towns*, contained the best early formulation of the concept in English. Simultaneously the northern German city of Bremen also devised a new plan for reducing the impact of traffic and guiding new development in

Fig. 5–18 (above). Madrid, Spain. Monumentality of the enclosed historic Plaza Mayor provides an opportunity to identify with grandeur.

Fig. 5–19 (below). Florence, Italy. The Piazza della Signoria, with the Palazzo Vecchio and a noble complement of sculpture, provides a grand setting for human activities.

the historic urban context. In Central Europe and Scandinavia, Bremen's example drew considerable attention, giving rise to the cluster of concepts that came to be known as the Bremen Plan.

In essense the scheme is a combination of traffic management to reduce environmental impacts and land-use management to exploit the qualities of attractive streets and squares. If the normal central city is looked on as a circle cut by the radial lines of major streets intersecting at the center, the basic idea of the Bremen Plan was to divert motorized traffic from the radials onto the less disruptive circumference road. As in so many other cities, the former intersection of radial routes at the center was the main Market Square with important architectural monuments, including both the city hall and the cathedral (Figure 5–20). Recovering this historic space from the needs and pressures of heavy general traffic made it available for more conducive functions and restored its possibility of once again serving as the main public living room.

The decision to make this major shift came at an important juncture in the early 1960s, just as the major recovery and rebuilding following devastating war damage had been achieved and an ex-

plosive boom in automobile ownership occurred. Had not the loss of so much historic urban fabric happened with such suddenness and had the transformation to accommodate automobiles taken place more gradually, undoubtedly the normal tendency would have been to continue modernization and transformation of the urban fabric on a piecemeal basis. More of the older buildings would have been removed to make way for more efficient, larger modern buildings, and the streets and open spaces undoubtedly would have been widened, paved, and filled with vehicles as in so many other cities. In Bremen the shock of these destructive tendencies impacting on a treasured historic environment clearly in mortal danger was sufficient to create a political atmosphere conducive to stopping the trend and finding a solution that would conserve more of what had gone before.

A system of traffic cells was devised, defined by the principal radial routes entering the core. To remove through traffic from these radials, including the main commercial street and the Market Square, each cell or quadrant of the core could be entered by vehicles approaching a destination from the ring road. Instead of being able to cross through

A FUTURE FOR OUR PAST

to another cell, vehicles have to go back out to the ring road and drive around. This simple yet revolutionary change achieved the seeming paradox of enhanced accessibility coupled with reduced traffic. Removing vehicular competition in the main spaces through the center also enabled public transportation (in the form of trams) to move freely and reliably once again. Undoubtedly the greatest change was in the street spaces themselves, now no longer perceived as congested arteries and parking lots but as living architectural spaces that could be experienced as rooms and thus serve as containers for human activities. A view of a crowd gathered to listen to a visiting Mexican band in the Market Square demonstrates this role.

In a contained space of comfortable scale but monumental grandeur, the highly decorative qualities of brick, stone, roof tiles, windows, arches, and sculpture all contribute to a strong sense of quality and character that stimulate civic pride and active use. Although music can easily draw a crowd anywhere, the attractiveness of the environment and the popular activity are mutually supportive. Sensitive, conserving redevelopment efforts here have been directed toward maintaining

and restoring the scale, color, texture, and structural qualities of the architectural heritage so rich in historic associations. Details of furnishings, including paving, lamps, benches, vegetation, and sidewalk cafes, add to the intended impression that this is a major place to come for enjoyment and social communication. The effect is all the more impressive when one realizes that most of these historic qualities had to be re-created following the destruction of the war.

What now appears perfectly evident in Bremen is a concept frequently opposed and still hotly discussed in many cities, particularly in North America: maximum attraction of people and efficient accommodation of motor vehicles in the same urban spaces are irreconcilable. The traffic-cell system devised in Bremen, with a distributor ring around the core and loops of traffic access routes from the ring into the core, has become one of the most persuasive models for reducing environmental impacts of motorized traffic and enhancing the value and attractiveness of urban centers.

Graz is one of the largest cities in Austria. In seeking a strategy to revitalize the historic center, Graz adopted a scheme similar to that in Bremen,

Fig. 5–20 (facing page). Bremen, West Germany. A traffic-cell system removed the cars and allowed the historic Market Square to realize its potential as an urban living room.

Fig. 5–21 (near left). Graz, Austria. Restored older architecture and removal of cars and trucks made the Market Square the focal point for the urban region.

including conversion of the main public square from a traffic intersection to an urban living room for people (Figure 5–21). The elements of a monumental central square are similar to the situation in Bremen: location at the hub of activity, a historic market function still alive and viable, a prominent architectural monument set off in scale, aesthetic treatment and position, an architectural setting of more modest but aesthetically designed urban architecture forming decorative walls containing the space, and a distinct, attractive focal point for the city and the urban region. The shift from accommodating cars to accommodating people in the street space seems amazingly simple: where cars and trucks once rumbled and belched exhaust in uncomfortable proximity to the sidewalks and buildings, there are now the tables and chairs of a relaxing sidewalk cafe. Yet, of course, this philosophical decision to give priority in the principal urban space to pedestrians rather than vehicles had to be supported by a well-prepared urban development and traffic management plan. Among the goals of this plan was the creation of a functionally differentiated overall traffic system and the implementation of this sytem to reduce impact on the urban environment.

The detail view at the center of the city suggests how well the system works and how successful the improvement of environmental quality has been. As in the case of Bremen, the decision was made to retain the electric streetcars through the main urban space in Graz. Driven at a walking pace through the square, light-rail vehicles represent no essential danger and minimal disturbance in the space while providing the valuable service of direct accessibility to the center for workers, customers, and others seeking services or entertainment in the center.

Removal of cars, by itself no panacea for declining central business districts, can, however, be one of the key factors in removing environmental burdens from older neighborhoods. Sometimes that is all that is needed to make an unattractive location commercially attractive again and to make refurbishing of old buildings a feasible investment. Downtown is, after all, the traditional center of all urban activities: commercial, political, cultural, educational, and even recreational. The essence of most central cities is the densely woven fabric of spaces and facilities where all of these things take place and where one can find more goods and services in a concentrated area than anyplace else. The buildings and established urban spaces, therefore, carry with them longstanding associations

that can be revived through timely restoration. Refurbishing the architecture can serve to reinforce latent perceptions that downtown is still where all the action is and that the same degree of concentrated offerings cannot be found elsewhere. To this end, restored older architecture can be much more effective than new construction.

Too often, though, as new growth and development have gone on elsewhere, older commercial buildings in central cities have been allowed to slide into disuse and decay, leaving a negative association of older buildings with a stagnating economy. Destroying the buildings in the hope of getting a fresh start, as has been done in so many American cities, can be simply a matter of confusing cause and effect. A far more effective approach (even more cost-effective!) is to employ regional planning to analyze the situation and discover weakness in the economic structure. Then plans can be formulated to generate activities in areas that have been left in the shadows. Through intelligent distribution of nodal points in traffic, employment, and urban infrastructure, for instance, such areas as the central market square in Graz can be reestablished as focal points and the buildings returned to a position of demand on the real estate market. When refurbished and reused, such buildings serve as strong visual indicators that an urban entity of considerable tradition can draw on its own resources for renewed vitality.

Creating urban living rooms is an effective way of nurturing this ethic, since traditional relationships of scale, monumentality, and containment of main streets and urban plazas seem to appeal to basic psychological needs. While environmental conflicts must be resolved if the positive psychological effects of an architectural environment are to be realized, the concept of creating an urban living room does not always require total elimination of all motorized traffic. Particularly the retention of nondisruptive public transportation, such as the trams in Graz and Bremen, may be conducive to stimulating a flow of people into major public spaces. Or it might be possible to have a normal traffic street cross one side of a major urban space while the remainder of the square or park is undisturbed and available for relaxing and communication.

Such is the case in Oslo, which demonstrates the idea of an urban living room developed as a park on one side of the city's main commercial and governmental street, the prestigious Karl Johans Gate (Figure 5–22). The older architecture defines and contains the space, giving it sculptural char-

Fig. 5–22. Oslo, Norway. A park on one side of Karl Johans Gate makes the commercial street an urban space of great appeal.

acter and decorative surfaces. Trees contribute further to an arcaded sense of containment of the space, as well as adding the gentle movement of sun and shade. Fountains, trees, and the well-maintained historic architectural forms together convey the sense of integrated three-dimensional planning that is sensitively tuned to the needs of people. Integrating such comfortable and attractive spaces into the planning of downtown areas is of critical importance in improving the image and appeal of urban centers.

The Usefulness of Passageways

Very efficient for land development and supply of services and appealing for its intellectual clarity, the ubiquitous grid system of laying out city streets has a serious drawback: it frequently forces people to walk in patterns contrary to their inclination. It is natural for a person to seek the shortest route linking two points, and if his origin and destination happen to lie along the same street, the designed route corresponds with his desire line and everything is fine. But if origins and destinations are on different streets, it becomes necessary to follow a series of zigzags, in effect being forced to walk both legs of a right triangle rather than its hypotenuse.

In situations where choice is available, such as on college campuses, in city parks, or on urban plazas, the beaten path of desire lines inevitably runs diagonally across rather than along the aesthetically planned system of right-angle walkways. There are significant lessons that can be learned from this homely observation.

The obvious lesson is that, in an urban environment as much as anywhere else, people, perversely economical, will go to some trouble to follow their desire lines as closely as possible in moving from place to place. A second lesson is that one of the best ways to encourage walking as a mode of movement is to anticipate the desired routes and construct pathways along these routes for walking. And it follows that if these passageways can be made attractive, interesting, safe, and pleasant, their degree of acceptance and use is likely to be very high. Planning pathways in this manner can contribute immeasurably to enhancing the usability of cities for people.

Pathways or passageways can follow existing streets, or they can be through-block cutoffs that either go through buildings themselves, in the manner of the commercial galleries that have become so popular in the 1970s, or they may make use of relatively unused spaces between buildings or in the centers of blocks. In the case of London Street in

Fig. 5–23. Norwich, England. Though hard to imagine, London Street once served as a major vehicular route through the city's center.

Norwich, England, the principal passageway has been created out of the main shopping street which once served as a main traffic artery running diagonally through the heart of town (Figure 5–23). Owners and managers of shops and banks along the route were vigorously opposed to closing the street to vehicular traffic initially, but its commercial and popular success has since made the conversion a delight for everyone. Almost incidentally, the high quality of its design and the care taken with preservation have won wide recognition.

Desire lines in the case of Norwich merely run to existing functions and buildings. The locations of shops, housing, and places of entertainment, education, and other aspects of culture in a city are usually predetermined. The designer's job is to find a meaningful way to link them together. Much modern planning, however, also involves development of land use plans or arrangement of various functions into a pattern of meaningful relationships. In either case, relationships and linkages need to be designed specifically to encourage lively interactions that, as we have discussed, give cities their character and quality.

The design elements that have made London Street into a lively passageway are essentially of two kinds: those already existing in the street space which require only reinforcement and those that have been added, such as vegetation, benches, pavement, and lamps. The sensitive reinforcement of existing qualities would seem to have been of greatest importance here. The curving configuration of the existing street also conveys a comforting feeling of containment without confinement that makes more sense to a walker than a driver. The contained vista promises something of interest ahead and the suggestion of even more interesting things to come just around the corner. With their undulations, such older streets provide constantly changing vistas, an interesting series of experiences as one moves through the space.

Older buildings also make an aesthetic contribution to the quality of the visual experience, even beyond whatever emotional associations they may evoke. Within a comfortable range of height and bulk limitations, there is great variety of materials, textures, colors, and sculptural relief of surfaces. Such variety and interest in visual stimuli would inevitably be either neglected, or self-consciously mannered in new construction. The exciting contrasts of light and dark, rough and smooth, open and closed, straight and jagged, bright and shaded have been respectfully, even lovingly refurbished, rather than modernized or misused for advertising purposes. This contributes enormously to a sense of interest and satisfaction in walking along London Street. Modesty and care in designing such elements as signs and lamps allow fullest enjoyment of the interesting old building forms.

Not far from London Street in Norwich is a

passageway of far humbler scale that demonstrates vividly the importance of both convenient passage and the delights of historic texture and scale (Figure 5–24). The clutter of small-scale residences and shops crowded against an old flint church would be a prime situation for clearance and renewal in most cities. How many planners and administrators have the perception to recognize such human-scaled passageways and the lively intimacy of such modest spaces as genuine assets that deserve preservation and reinforcement? Integration of a variety of walking routes in a high-density, tightly woven fabric of mutual reinforcement is essential for an interesting and attractive city. One of the best ways of using existing density and encouraging that mutual reinforcement is to stimulate individual movement on foot throughout the central city. Opening up passageways is a significant device to this end, but the routes must give the appearance of being well lighted, active, and open to observation by people in shops or dwellings. If this narrow passage in Norwich had closed walls on both sides, it probably would not be a suitable pedestrian path; yet the fact that the shortcut along the side of the church coincides with a desire line in the inner city undoubtedly was the reason for establishing shops in the first place.

A further example from Norwich illustrates the contributions of older architecture in making such pedestrian passageways attractive (Figure 5–25). Tombland Alley is a modest triangular space, a tiny former churchyard in the interior of a block opposite the cathedral. As a part of the rehabilitation of the picturesque old half-timber structure that now houses the Tourist Board and Tourist Information Center, the little buildings facing onto this modest court were refurbished as well, and pavement was added to turn the space into an interesting shortcut for pedestrians to the center of the city. A bench and tree add to the visual delight of the old stone church wall, as the timber and plaster construction and the quaint modesty of the small utilitarian structures at the rear. It is a simple case of letting interesting architecture coincide with desire lines to make a literally sensational walking route. Such sensitive awareness of the potential for human delight in modest elements of the townscape can go a long way toward encouraging pleasurable use of the central city.

Qualities of age and density in the built environment of historic downtown areas are too often looked upon as tarnish on a city's dynamism and vitality. The simplistic solution in too many American cities has been to eliminate the old merely

Fig. 5–24 (left). Norwich, England. Human-scaled passageways and the delights of historic texture add quality to modern urban life.

Fig. 5–25 (right). Norwich, England. Tombland Alley, a modest churchyard, has been refurbished to become a delightful walking route.

because it is old, to clear sites wholesale to promote more efficient, more modern development and spacious monumental plazas.

On the island with the oldest development in central Stockholm, the historic Old Town (Gamla Staden), the opposite approach has been taken. The cramped appearance of tall buildings on narrow winding streets has been purposefully kept within walking distance of the redeveloping commercial center of the capital city (Figure 5–26). The castle, famous old churches, and other historic buildings are nearby, but the individual buildings seen here are all undistinguished in their appearance and general architectural character. Only a desire to preserve the ambience, the architectural ensemble of the historic core, prompted retention of these structures. Amazingly, it works: people—perhaps somewhat bored with the efficient and sanitary qualities of their well-planned modern housing developments on the outskirts of the city—feel attracted and stimulated by the contrast. In any case, boutiques, souvenir shops, clothing stores, restaurants, art galleries, and other small specialty activities all flourish, and a demand for housing units exists in this area. The main attraction here seems to be simply the quality of age itself, and the street has become a central mall in an area of stimulating activity. Entertainment and tourism, as well as commerce and the dwelling function, seem to fit comfortably into the old buildings, which line an ideal passageway linking other city functions.

A difficult aspect of conservation advocacy is the problem of demonstrating benefits in monetary terms. Yet, if the potential costs of losing the vitality of historic areas are counted, the equation balances differently. If cost-benefit analyses are prepared in order to assess the consequences of alternative development proposals, it is of crucial importance that the social costs be assessed as well. Personal and commercial relationships disrupted by the clean-slate approaches of urban renewal can result in a very high social cost, while the benefits of building upon existing relationships can be very valuable indeed. More and more cities such as Stockholm are recognizing that the unique appeal of the architectural givens in an older urban environment can be used to great advantage in reestablishing the vitality of central cities.

Integrated conservation, however, seems to be the key concept, rather than a piecemeal approach to individual monuments. The character and quality of an entire district, including especially the character of street spaces seen as rooms and as passageways, is essential to this integrated approach. A view of the heart of Austria's Graz serves to illustrate the point that the whole can be equal to much more than just the sum of the parts (Figure 5–27). Although, considered individually, particular style choices made at different times in the past may be open to serious questions of taste or practicality, taken together they add up to a very lively visual experience that conveys a sense of strong character and unique image. Such spaces lend themselves readily to being identified as "my city" by shopkeepers as well as shoppers, by long-time residents as well as new arrivals. *Enticing people to want very consciously to walk or sit in an urban space because of its attractions should be a conscious goal of all urbanists.* Respecting and conserving the established architectural qualities of street spaces are very effective means to this end. Clearly there is a high-priority need to create more legal, administrative, financial, and technical means to provide more effective support for concepts of integrated conservation.

Contributions of Old Buildings

The most common reason for tearing down old buildings is economic. Dated appearance, structural unsoundness brought on by neglect, lack of modern facilities, and failure to meet modern building code requirements are among the reasons commonly cited, but taint by association with economic decay of a neighborhood or an entire district quite often plays a central role. What is fashionable in building styles and neighborhoods determines what is well maintained and preserved, as opposed to what is neglected and ultimately torn down. That old buildings of all styles and in all settings can make significant contributions to the aesthetics, social stability, and productive land use of their particular environments is seen too late or not at all.

Central Amsterdam is one of the finest demonstrations in Western Europe of successful rehabilitation and beneficial use of hundreds of older buildings (Figure 5–28). Amsterdam's protective legislation and active support programs for rehabilitation efforts have resulted in one of the highest percentages of conserved architectural fabric of any city in the world. The photo suggests many of the benefits achieved. Aesthetically these conserved older buildings provide a rich visual contact with craftsmanship in the use of building materials. Within a very fine-grained environment of roughly uniform scale and texture, a great variety of skillful surface treatments in different materials provide a rich blend of colors and patterns. The visual stimulus of the architectural forms encourages walking while the rededication of the former street space to use by pedestrians makes leisurely enjoyment of that aesthetic experience possible. Conservation and redesign of the area with the interests of the users foremost in the minds of the planners have made this into a very lively space, even, as here, on a rainy day.

Fig. 5–26 (facing page). Stockholm, Sweden. The quality of venerable age in the historic Old Town adds a stimulating contrast to modern life.

Fig. 5–27 (near left). Graz, Austria. Enticing people to walk or sit in an urban space should be a conscious goal of all urbanists.

Fig. 5–28. Amsterdam, the Netherlands. Even on a rainy day, the pedestrianized street, with all its rich historic texture, exudes great appeal.

Socially the area has a great sense of vitality because of the close integration of a variety of functions: clothing stores, variety stores, boutiques, restaurants, bars, discos, and residences. The fine-grained texture of the restored architecture is reflected in a similarly fine-grained texture of integrated uses, giving the area a lively sense of interest related to the human scale. Distribution of land uses here is also an important issue. The particular section of street shown is part of the pedestrian route of Niewendijk and Kaalverstraat leading through the heart of central Amsterdam, and the uses of the buildings at street level are closely related to a heavy flow of pedestrians passing by. Since there are a great many commercial ventures that can benefit from heavy pedestrian contact without extensive floor areas, their incorporation in a small-scaled downtown space of this nature is ideal.

The same happy conjunction of pedestrian-intensive commercial functions with older buildings of striking architectural character can be seen on Union Street in San Francisco (Figure 5–29). Although the location is not quite analogous to that of Amsterdam and the elimination of vehicles here was only a temporary measure, the particular character of restored older buildings has attracted people and stimulated commercial success. What previously was considered merely old has been transformed through preservation into a very tangible commercial, cultural, and social asset. The selling of antiques, jewelry, shoes, clothing, crafts, and other items that benefit from historic associations but do not require large area fits in very well with bars and restaurants that openly exploit their architectural character. Occasional street fairs with temporary stands selling handmade jewelry, leather goods, candles, and similar items contribute to the ambience, but the real strength of these commercial areas in both San Francisco and Amsterdam is the substantial quantity of attractive older housing available in the immediate vicinity. An inherent problem is that successful revitalization of such areas tends to inflate prices and rents at a rapid rate, thereby undermining one of the great advantages of older buildings: their economy.

Too much success with rehabilitation leads to excessive increase in property values and taxes, thus forcing out established residents and low-volume commercial activities. This is a very important but distinctly separate problem that requires other, probably legislative, measures for its solution. The essential point here is the proof that preservation and enhancement of the historic character of older buildings are goals that are highly compatible with reinforcement of commercial vitality in cities. The cheap argument, "We don't want to make a museum of our city," does not apply. It is not a question of historic preservation versus commercial vitality. As we have now seen demonstrated in countless examples, commercial vitality and historic perservation through recognition of older architecture as cultural assets are highly compatible with contemporary urban life.

A small example from the extensive pedestrian network in the central business district of Germany's capital, Bonn, serves to sharpen the point made in San Francisco, Amsterdam, and other cities (Figure 5–30). A formerly rather nondescript old building, much smaller than a replacement on the site could have been, when carefully refurbished with its half-timber frame exposed, becomes a most effective, unmistakable symbol for a high-fashion shop. The restrained letters of the firm's name and sedate display windows set within the timber frame of the structure suffice to draw attention to the company and its products, completely stealing the show from its nondescript modern neighbor on the left. A sense of quality, responsibility, and long establishment is effectively conveyed by the architecture. For public relations

Fig. 5–30. Bonn, West Germany. Sensitive refurbishing of an older building demonstrates respect for local traditions and for patrons' sensibilities.

Fig. 5–29. San Francisco, CA. Refurbished buildings and a street fair on Union Street provide a pleasant and stimulating environment for pedestrians.

purposes alone, a commercial establishment should have as one important virtue an attitude of respect for local traditions. A restoration of this quality is one of the best demonstrations of the firm's respect for the sensibilities of its patrons.

Certainly the technical means are now available to save even the most dilapidated old buildings if the perception of a compelling rationale to do so is present. The lesson of so many successful examples internationally is that there is strong inherent demand for qualities of continuity and tradition in urban environments. Maintaining a sense of continuity with the past in the physical environment of a city seems to satisfy fundamental psychological needs, particularly in an era when so many have been uprooted from the immediate environment of their childhoods. A period of great social fluidity would appear to create particularly strong desire for stability in the physical environment. This may even be the primary explanation for the enormous popular success of preservation and restoration efforts of recent years.

Perhaps the most extreme examples are the architectural re-creations of the war-torn cities of Danzig and Warsaw in Poland. Replication of facades, street spaces, and entire urban districts, based on old photos and art works, was seen as so crucial to the national identity that this was given an even higher priority than solving the critical postwar housing problems. The devastated centers of these cities were virtually reconstructed from scratch, with an exterior appearance as close to the former condition as possible. Replication is the re-creation of past architecture that has fallen down, has been destroyed, or has disappeared for whatever reason. Replication has long been decried by architects as "plagiarism," "a sham," "shameless lack of imagination," and worse. One probable motivation for such arguments has been protection of the professional's central reason for being: to build, and better yet, to create. Notwithstanding such understandable motives of self-preservation, the actual history of the building art holds replication and reconstruction in varying degrees, including complete reconstitution of something which had entirely disappeared, as perfectly legitimate aspects of architecture.

We tend to overlook too easily the fact that many of the most meaningful historic monuments enjoyed today, from palace to primitive village, can only be experienced because of a high degree of past reconstruction, quite often done during the twentieth century. Devastation caused by the First World War and the Second World War necessi-

tated enormous amounts of reconstruction, often from scratch, and the corrosive effects of pollution in the 1950s, 1960s, and 1970s have necessitated a continuous process of replacement of stones in major cathedrals across Europe. But how many people realize that the Bell Tower of St. Mark's, on the Piazza San Marco in Venice, is a twentieth century replica following the spectacular collapse of the original structure in 1902? Even now the memory is beginning to fade that the tower of the old city hall on Marienplatz in the heart of Munich is a replica built from scratch in the early 1970s, some twenty years after the stump of the bombed original had been removed to facilitate the flow of vehicular traffic in the reconstruction following the war. Since it fills a psychic void, the fact that it is an imitation in entirely different materials and serving an entirely different purpose than the original is completely forgotten. Replication may serve some significant purposes and serve them well indeed.

Change within a framework of continuity has always been a major aspect of architecture and urban design. No other basic theme has a more venerable history in the field of building than the art of fitting in, of developing the context of the present within the framework of the established heritage. From the Roman sack of Carthage before the time of Christ to the firebombing of Dresden, belligerence and violence have resulted in programs to eliminate all built vestiges of an enemy's culture, but it has remained for the last half of our century to devise programs, in peacetime, for the systematic destruction and obliteration of our own nation's architectural heritage for reasons of short-term profit.

A striking alternative, continuing a tradition of more than 99 percent of the world's building, is shown in a recent construction photo from the north German city of Celle (Figure 5–31). Immediately adjacent to a building constructed in 1662 and subsequently restored and preserved in essentially its original form is a building of enormous differences in materials, methods, facilities, and interior layout but of virtually the same size, shape, and general character. In other words, it is indeed possible in a commercial society of today to respect the past, to accept the established parameters of an urban environment that has been functioning for generations or centuries, and to fit in without destroying the established scale. Have modern spatial needs changed that much, after all, that they could not fit into parameters established in previous generations? Are there not any modern functions that could fit into this newly constructed

Fig. 5–31. Celle, West Germany. A marvelous example of sensitive in-fill, the new building follows the example of its neighbor built in 1662.

but historically scaled architectural space? Modesty is, apparently, one of the available options.

Altruism and respect for history, of course, are insufficient motives for urban development. Powerful financial interests as well as the spatial needs of contemporary society and contemporary commerce will always be among the most forceful determinants. All efforts at conserving older architecture and established urban environments must do so from the basis of serving current needs, solving contemporary problems, if they are to be successful. Fortunately, the proof that old buildings are extremely adaptable to new needs and changing value systems is everywhere around us. What once may have been built as a major factory or mill may now serve better as housing or as a large commercial center combining shopping, restaurants, and entertainments, as in the case of San Francisco's famed Ghirardelli Square (Figure 5–32). Originally built as a woolen mill, it was later converted to manufacture chocolate. In the 1960s the chocolate factory, Ghirardelli sign and all, became America's most famous example of adaptive reuse. By the late 1970s Ghirardelli had become the development inspiration for countless other squares and adaptive reuse projects, as well as one of San Francisco's most frequented tourist attractions. Most important of all was the recognition that the old structures provided not only substantial building shells that could be profitably adapted to new uses, but that the particular qualities of materials, textures, and architectural ornament from a previous era were among *the most valuable assets* in creating an ambience, a quality of intimate human scale, and a unique image with which everyone could identify.

These qualities have become highly marketable and extremely profitable in the 1970s, as exemplified by the great success story of the Faneuil Hall-Quincy Market perservation and adaptive reuse project in Boston. Following more than a decade of cautious skepticism, commercial investors are finally accepting the lessons of Ghirardelli Square and recognizing the potential of older building complexes in central cities.

But it is not only the venerableness of the buildings themselves that causes the great interest and enthusiasm. The secret lies in their potential to be adapted, modified, and changed. One might call them kickable, malleable buildings with plenty of room to incorporate a great variety of human activities. The accidental qualities of the givens are among the most interesting aspects. Adaptive reuse is a very different process than the careful restoration of a historic monument. A detail view of Ghirardelli Square demonstrates the importance of designing places for people into the older structures (Figure 5–33). In this particular view almost nothing of the specific qualities visible depends on what was there before. Landscaping, paving, lamps, benches, fountains, spatial relationships, and the arrangement of paths and plazas are all newly designed elements added in anticipation of human needs and responses. Sensitivity to the needs of users is an essential ingredient to successful adaptation of old structures to new uses.

To summarize, the three criteria fitting older buildings for new purposes are:

Found space, that is, an existing spatial envelope that normally can be purchased for far less than an equivalent volume of space normally would cost if constructed anew

A sense of continuity with established urban environments, a strong image, and identifiability with the local scene

Adaptability to new uses while contributing qualities of unique character to the new space

Trolley Square in Salt Lake City, inspired by the success of Ghirardelli Square, is a prime example of the application of these principles (Figure 5–34). Although this particular view does not show the impressive sense of character and atmosphere created within this commercial complex in the former municipal streetcar barns, it does demonstrate the feasibility of finding a decorated shed in an urban

Fig. 5–32. San Francisco, CA. Recycling of older architecture, pioneered at Ghirardelli Square, can be a great financial and social success.

environment, letting its particular qualities of materials and structure contribute to the expressive image, and then filling this box with new functions. This view, limited as it is, also serves to show some of the potential weaknesses of this approach.

First of all, this complex is highly introverted, with very little landscape or plaza development on the exterior. Parking is brought as close to the doors on all four sides as possible. Second, a desire to have as much color and texture as possible led the developer to have the painted surface of the brick sandblasted, resulting in a heavily textured surface that has lost much of its original character as well as its durability. Last, the spatial quality the barns once had has been totally sacrificed in order to fill up the various levels of rentable floor area. While retaining its handsome old structure and achieving great commercial success with it, the Trolley Square project raises the question of just how far exploitation should be allowed to go. What are to be the criteria in drawing the line between conservation and exploitation?

Now that it has been amply demonstrated that history in the form of old buildings is a highly

Fig. 5–33 (left). San Francisco, CA. This detail view of Ghirardelli Square shows the sensitivity to its users' needs that is essential to successful architectural recycling.

Fig. 5–34 (below). Salt Lake City, UT. Streetcar barns proved an ideal found space, and the decorated shed was converted into a commercial complex.

Fig. 5–35. Seattle, WA. Pioneer Square was an early success story in recapturing traditional qualities to enrich the contemporary environment.

marketable commodity, perhaps it is important to raise questions of propriety regarding the degree of transformation for reasons of commercial expediency. While it is clear that old buildings, in order to be able to survive, must serve useful roles in our contemporary society, there undoubtedly need to be other criteria applied in addition to the analysis of commercial returns on a square-foot basis.

Recapturing Traditional Qualities

"How will we know it's us without our past?" asked John Steinbeck. Surely associations and memories are among the important civilizing elements that keep a society functioning harmoniously; without traditions, society begins to disintegrate. Alienation and anomie so characteristic of urban life in the twentieth century have been directly related to the disruptive impacts of hostile, disorienting physical environments. In a very real sense, conservation of older architectural environments can mean protection of people.

In the United States a steadily increasing number of cities now recognize the value of older buildings and established street spaces, neighborhoods, and districts. Seattle has been one of the leaders of this movement, with the Pioneer Square district as one of the focal points for renovation in the historic core (Figures 5–35 and 5–36). The approach there is not simply to use the old shells for new functions, but consciously to recapture the originally intended environmental qualities. Traditional commercial structures, such as the one il-

lustrated, are being allowed to reappear in all the design elegance originally conceived by their patrons and architects. Rather than transforming the older structure into something different from what it was, its inherent strengths and beauty of materials and composition are emphasized through careful restoration and planning of uses that are compatible with the structure. Shops, restaurants, offices, professional offices, and a great many other modern spatial needs can fit into a wide variety of spaces, so that compatible adaptation of the old structure to new uses is more a matter of accommodating modern heating, light, and other facilities and satisfying modern code requirements than it is of solving difficult spatial problems. In structures such as this, the formerly neglected basements frequently offer some of the most exciting new spaces for public access.

Certainly the addition of new trees and landscaping is a major contribution to creating a pleasant environment in what had formerly declined to a very undesirable level of neglect. Refurbishing or reintroducing historic streetlights, benches, doors, and paving contribute to the sense of conserving a significant portion of the city's heritage. In Seattle this approach has included the reintroduction of policemen patrolling on foot in historic uniforms, complete with sideburns and moustaches (see Figure 5–36). The extra care of a city administration willing to go to such lengths to recapture valuable social and environmental qualities from the past encourages merchants and the public alike to support the efforts to reverse decline and make the area vital again.

SILLY

Fig. 5–36. Seattle, WA. Reinforcing the city's heritage at Pioneer Square has included the reintroduction of patrolmen in historic uniforms.

Although there will always be disagreements over details, establishing an ethic of affection and respect for the past is something vitally healthy, particularly among the young. Even an apparently useless building can serve an important function as a point of orientation for a people to their particular location in time and place. Therefore, considerations of economy and expediency alone must not be allowed to dictate whether or not particular buildings are to be saved and restored. Broader considerations of worth to the community and its sense of continuity should play an overriding role. Tax laws and other legal and administrative devices ought to be adjusted to reflect this ethic, so that powerful economic forces working against retention of older buildings are not overriding.

A view of the main street of Trier in Germany shows a somewhat illogical juxtaposition of sizes, shapes, patterns, and styles of buildings that can accrue in a historic street space (Figure 5–37). Purely rational considerations would have led to using the opportunity of war destruction to achieve more logical order and system in the street space, but more important social considerations dictated that unique local character was essential and justified not only retention and protection but extremely expensive restoration work by the community. The intangible benefits include a vivid image of Trier that benefits both commerce and tourism and a strong sense among citizens of this place as *their* city rather than just an anonymous place to live, shop, and work. Such benefits are of great significance in preserving a sense of community.

Examples of recaptured traditional quality of ur-

ban space through architectural preservation and restoration are legion, particularly in Europe, where recognition of the social and economic benefits has become widespread through the great efforts associated with European Architectural Heritage Year 1975. But it has been no easy task. A great deal of conviction and dedication are necessary, first, to achieve sufficient public education and awareness, and second, to muster all of the legislative, administrative, technical, financial, and design skills that are necessary to complete a program of this type.

Compromises with the Present

More frequent, sadly enough, than concerted effort to achieve a comprehensive development plan are ad hoc measures that involve compromising the past in order to achieve short-term goals in the present. Two views of the historic high street in Guildford, Surrey, in southern England, demonstrate the nature of two very common compromises with the present (Figures 5–38 and 5–39). These compromises involve badly resolved conflicts between architectural character and current uses of the buildings and spaces. Though no one would argue with the necessity for shopkeepers to show their wares and for customers (and others) to drive and park their vehicles, there is now sufficient reason to seriously question the wisdom of cutting off the bottom story of historic buildings and of filling the street space with traffic. Just as there are clearly preferable means of handling traffic prob-

lems, so too there are far more satisfactory ways of handling the need for display space than simply cutting off a venerable urban structure at the knees and leaving it suspended on a few sheets of plate glass. A skillful, highly sensitive, differentiated approach is needed that would be more in keeping with the admirable preservation of these traditional buildings and the commendable restraint expressed in the signage. Through greater care and a total design approach, the remarkable aesthetic and cultural potential of this space could be used to far greater advantage than by continuing to follow the path of expedience.

A view of downtown Utrecht in Holland, on the other hand, points up the magic of modesty (Figure 5–40). Or, to paraphrase the late Louis Kahn, "I asked the street what it wanted to be, and it said it wanted to be a people-place." How incredibly simple it seems to adopt the environmentally conservative approach in order to achieve major new benefits for people. What delightful, funky charm in the stylistic idiosyncrasies of the old, humanly scaled buildings! They have been allowed to be themselves, contributing to the liveliness and gaiety of a street now freed from cars and totally dedicated to use and enjoyment by people. Utter lack of danger or other hindrances to freedom to walk about or simply relax and enjoy the urbane experience contributes greatly to the opportunity to appreciate an ambience that could hardly be called historically significant in anyone's book. It is, very simply, uniquely characteristic of Utrecht and

Fig. 5–37 (above). Trier, West Germany. Rational considerations might have removed this mixture after wartime destruction, but local character triumphed.

Fig. 5–38 (bottom left). Guildford, England. Cutting off historic structures at the knees and floating them on glass is an unfortunate compromise.

Fig. 5–39 (bottom right). Guildford, England. The remarkable aesthetic potential of this space conflicts with its use as a sluice for through traffic.

A FUTURE FOR OUR PAST

therefore unconditionally worthy of conservation. The space obviously is well suited to self-expression on the part of both shopkeepers and the public at large. Such spaces automatically become places for social communication and lend themselves very well to demonstrations and the exchange of ideas and information as well as of goods and services. Such buildings have many upstairs rooms that still can be used as very desirable dwelling units located exactly where the action is. Could such variety and life ever be designed into new, larger-scale, efficiency-oriented, modern architecture? In Utrecht apparently the answer to that question is, "Not very likely," and the logical conclusion has been to preserve as much as possible the traditional qualities that remain.

Yet, despite increasing recognition that previous generations have conveyed to us something worthy of conservation, mistakes and compromises continue to be made every day. They crop up sometimes in places where one might least expect them. The southern German city of Regensburg on the Danube, for instance, is one of the most venerable of historic urban environments, having over two thousand individual architectural monuments worthy of preservation. Hardly damaged at all during the Second World War, Regensburg is going through an exceedingly long and painstaking process of maintaining its major cultural monuments and gradually restoring and upgrading individual buildings of the ordinary urban fabric. Although the process is proving to be extraordinarily expensive and drawn out, the feasibility and viability of housing contemporary functions in an organic urban structure that has grown over many hundreds of years has been amply proven in Regensburg.

The mistakes and regrettable compromises that have taken place are all in the realm of excessive removal of older buildings in the name of progress, which in various cases has meant accommodation of cars, opening courtyards for light, air, and sun, and the accommodation of commercial users. A partial view of the Horten department store complex on the Neupfarrplatz in Regensburg demonstrates how misguided the compromises can be (Figure 5–41). A department store of one thousand square meters had been built in this area at the end of the nineteenth century, in 1955 it was expanded to approximately twice this area, and in the early 1970s, at the loss of some six adjacent buildings, the total area of the department store was expanded to five thousand square meters. Despite the retention of a historic neoclassical facade and an attempt to ease the impact of this enormous monofunctional mass on the small scale of the urban setting, the disruption of urban continuity is severe. Even the visual treatment of parts of the whole as discrete blocks cannot mask their impact as concrete blockbusters with little sense of scale or relatability to the urban place. The role of the colonnaded but doorless portico is apparently little more than that of a fig leaf to cover the shame of this insensitivity. Accommodating functions that bring on gross changes in the scale of land uses can have devastating effects

Fig. 5–40. Utrecht, the Netherlands. Modesty has a distinct magic. Preservation of historic idiosyncrasies achieves a delightfully humane quality.

on historic architecture. Simply because the most potent investors tend to be corporations with gross spatial needs does not mean that only such needs should be served or that the central city is where such needs should be satisfied.

In American cities the architectural boom that has accompanied economic development of cities usually has left little of historic value in the current central business district. Older architecture usually remains in areas that have been left in the development backwaters as commercial centers of cities have shifted to new locations. Sparked by the Bicentennial celebration of 1976, a wave of nostalgia has inspired new appreciation for older architecture, frequently just in the nick of time. What is left to be preserved may no longer be of the finest quality or in the best locations, but it may be all we have.

Thus Denver, jumping on the bandwagon of creating nostalgic squares, has had to settle for an isolated remnant of older commercial buildings along a street that is now a major one-way artery leading traffic from downtown parking garages onto an urban expressway (Figures 5–42 and 5–43). Larimer Square might more accurately be called "the Larimer Expressway Ramp." Nonetheless, this one-block collection of older buildings in a sea of empty land cleared by urban renewal (and now being gradually filled with skyscrapers) has been successful in attracting people to its interesting mixture of shops, restaurants, and places of entertainment. The activities and contents of the buildings are augmented by the patterns, textures, and materials as well as the trees, flags, and fancy cast-iron benches.

Prospects for the Future

Adaptive reuse is a newly fashionable concept in architecture much touted by members of the profession. Apparently there is a current awareness that in the future less and less architecture will be built from scratch on cleared sites and that architects will have to concern themselves more and more with retrofitting—adapting older structures to new uses. Of course, this is a new awareness rather than a new practice, since it has been done for hundreds of years. Somehow until our era it always seemed natural that valuable resources of existing structural fabric not simply be thrown away to be replaced by something else. Classically, additions, modifications, renovations, and adaptations have

Fig. 5–41. Regensburg, West Germany. Within a venerable historic environment, the department store flexes its concrete, yet hides behind the fig leaf of a preserved facade.

Fig. 5–42. Denver, CO. Larimer Square, a successful preservation effort, is bisected by heavy traffic and surrounded by urban removal.

Fig. 5–43. Denver, CO. As Larimer Square illustrates, what remains to be preserved may not be the best, but it may be all we have.

always been the rule—that is, until our century, when it became possible to change drastically the scale of buildings. Now even a lavishly expensive structure can be sacrificed very early in its life if it suddenly becomes economically feasible to construct a building of considerably larger volume on the same site.

The present trend in American cities is, however, no longer toward ever greater populations, ever greater urban densities. A net loss of population, of business, and of industry continues unabated in many cities as suburban growth continues apace. A very real challenge exists in determining what to do with buildings designed originally for high-density settings that are left standing in what have become low-density urban areas.

A shocking reminder of prospects for the future, if certain trends continue, is provided by an instance of adaptive reuse in downtown Los Angeles. Clearly expressing a trend toward more parking and fewer activities in central cities, the conversion

of the Adolphus Theatre to a parking garage symbolizes the great dangers of losing urbanity as ever larger percentages of urban land are devoted to the expediencies of accommodating motorized traffic (Figure 5–44). This too is adaptive reuse, but is it the direction we desire for future development of our cities?

The urbanist Albert Mayer stressed a concept that could well serve as a motto for current urban development: "Trend is not destiny." There are design measures, administrative measures, new ways of thinking, and new value systems to be instituted that can slow down or reverse trends. Perhaps the most critical first step is to develop an appreciation for human values as criteria for urban development. Perhaps taking into account the needs and desires of people can begin to be a standard of an importance related to that of purely economic considerations. Perhaps the examples of cities succeeding extremely well in holding people through environmental quality and achieving

economic vitality of their centers through reinforcement of traditional urban values can have widespread impact and start a new trend toward urban conservation and measurement of success in human terms.

At present it would seem that too many cities are still measuring their successes in numbers of skyscrapers built in the shortest period of time. Is Philadelphia, perhaps, among this number? The Chestnut Street transitway (Figure 5–45) represents, on the one hand, a kind of progress in the direction of making a major commercial street downtown more attractive to people by relieving the bumper-to-bumper congestion that once caused chaos in these spaces. But a major question remains: who benefits?

The delightful old buildings contributing so much character and local color in this view, while still visible in 1976, were doomed. Far more money had been spent on the gimmicky theme lamps for the bicentennial than on painting the trim of these colorful and delicately textured facades. The opposite corner already had been cleared and the fate of these structures was sealed, doomed. If maximization of rentable floor area is to be the highest value in transforming our cities, the fate of traditional urbanity is sealed.

Another view of the processes of change in action is provided by Mariahilferstrasse, a major radial route leading to the heart of Vienna (Figure 5–46). Booming with commerce, throbbing with life, but congested with motor traffic, the space requires that the fundamental question be asked: which trend will win out in the future?

6

The City as Habitat

Our cities are in a state of crisis. The causes may vary, as may the degree of severity, but there is a widely felt sense of urban problems requiring solution. The nature of these problems is complex, with economic, social, educational, political, and physical factors all playing major roles. Yet, whatever are perceived to be the most serious physical problems in a city, one underlying question is always present: what can be done about the disaffection of people for their own urban environments? This issue may be seen in terms of net loss of urban population, in decreasing real estate values, in higher percentages of people on welfare, or simply in a drop in the perceived desirability of the city as a place to live, shop, or work. Whatever the name, the fact is that too many cities have become unattractive to too many people. Something must be done about it.

The challenge to urban designers, city planners, and the movers and shakers of urban development, then, lies in establishing new priorities centered on people's needs and desires. Cities, simply enough, must be made hospitable again. A city's feeling of hospitality, in turn, is largely determined by the qualities of its physical environment: do its buildings, streets, and squares provide a congenial, supportive ambience, not to say an allure, that enhances the lives, work, and play of its citizens?

For clarity, perhaps the task of defining the elements of supportive urban environments can be divided into two general areas, economic and physical, although the two are closely related. Goals for achieving economic quality include strengthening a city's economic underpinning: jobs, revenues, and an adequate supply of goods and services. Achieving physical quality, on the other hand, involves preserving or re-creating an urban tapestry: a warp of distinguished private buildings, public crossroads, and existing neighborhoods and a weft of tactfully accommodative new construction or renovation to achieve a strengthening of established social networks and employment/recreation patterns.

Uses of Traditional Scale

Let us focus, for the moment, on aspects of physical design, specifically on the qualities of urban outdoor space created by buildings and their relationships to each other. A view on the Annastrasse (Figure 6–1) in rebuilt central Augsburg in southern Germany suggests a number of ways in which traditional urban scale answers the purpose of quality. Immediately, without analyzing any details, one senses a feeling of comfort and containment: this open street space has the interest, the associations, the comprehensibility of an urban room. This comprehensibility exists largely for two

or three basic reasons. First, the amount of space that one can see at a glance is limited, contained by the curve in the street and the lateral closing of the vista by the church roof in the background. Second, the height of the buildings in relation to the width and length of this vista is comfortable; it can be taken in at a glance. A third factor is charm, the degree of discreteness and individuality of the different buildings—some lighter, some darker, some a bit taller, some a bit shorter—with differing roofs—some ridge lines perpendicular to the street, others parallel. The images, in short, stimulate the eye and initiate a visual adventure, a satisfaction in exploring different forms within an overall pattern. That this streetscape works so well is all the more surprising when one realizes that most of these buildings have little distinguishing historical character; they are all more or less rebuilt or built anew since the destruction caused by the Second World War.

Closer examination reveals that, at the base of the facades that define the space, a one-story street-level interest band has been designed as commercial space with signs and display windows of such in-

Fig. 6–1. Augsburg, West Germany. Materials, textures, associations, and a sense of containment help this street become an urban room.

Fig. 6–2. Lübeck, West Germany. Conserving the traditional human scale can be a powerful force in attracting people to live in a city.

timate scale as to appeal directly to pedestrians. Without the distraction of large or overwhelming advertisements, the architectural character of the space and the decorative character of the displays nicely complement each other. This living composition is finally tied together underfoot by a textured pavement and overhead by the color and rhythm of its awnings and streetlamps. The eye-level impact conveys a lively interest that seems in turn to generate human activity, which adds even more to the attraction of the space.

Even without studying a circulation map of the area, one can also sense that this street serves as a linkage, that it is a natural part of major desire lines leading through the downtown area. Consequently, a density of mixed uses and an environment highly conducive to walking coincide in a very successful manner.

How does such an approach, preserving and exploiting traditional scale to encourage pedestrian activity, work on a broader scope? A view over the Market Square and the center of Lübeck in northern Germany from the restored tower of the Petri Kirche suggests the answer (Figure 6–2). The conservative approach toward retaining the streetscape as demonstrated in Augsburg, extended to the entire historic area of a city (as it is in both Augsburg and Lübeck), can yield surprising results. Accus-

tomed as we have become to hearing the gospel of bigger is better, that progress means growth, and that the heart of a city can only be called alive so long as a steady flow of automotive traffic pulses through it, it is indeed exciting to discover a modern, dynamic city with as fine-grained, close-knit texture as this.

While the concept of pedestrianizing an urban center may be simple and straightforward enough on paper, the process itself is anything but easy. There are constant pressures to change land uses in the central area from residential to commercial, pressures to tear down groups of small buildings and build single larger ones, pressures to open up more space in the center to access and parking of cars. Department stores, with their demands for extensive surface area, exert some of the strongest pressure, as they tend to bring strong economic benefits and generate commercial traffic. Pressure is exerted on builders by the construction trade unions to provide a continuity of new and larger job sites. Pressure is brought to bear on city fathers, finally, to maintain full employment and the promise of growing commercial activity.

In general, though, as this view from the church tower suggests, the struggle to retain the character and scale of the Lübeck cityscape has been successful. The results are a strongly positive image of the

Fig. 6–3. Minneapolis, MN. The American alternative seems to be to banish the people to the suburbs. Such cities are for cars, not people.

of development was coupled with conscientious restoration and maintenance of historic buildings and their spatial relationships. It may be argued that many of the new buildings stand out more than they would need to or more than is desirable. Nevertheless, they are designed for the most part in compatible materials and shapes, within strict height and bulk limitations, so that the special spatial balance of the city's streets and squares has been largely retained.

Finally, the growing push toward residential land use in central cities, far from being incompatible with development patterns, actually provides essential qualities of density and integration with other activities, which are belatedly being recognized as among the greatest advantages that central city living can have. Outmoded plumbing and heating or problems of decay in the structural substance of older housing are cited by high-rise sponsors as making such dwellings less desirable, but far more frequently it is dirt, air pollution, and noise that make urban centers undesirable for living. The relationship of central city residence to other functions and the interesting configuration of many older residential buildings and their courtyards are often, as we shall see, among the most effective weapons in campaigns to recapture or reinforce the vitality of central cities.

Of course, there remains yet another alternative of simply saying, "To hell with the people!" (or perhaps, "To the suburbs with them!"), tearing down all those messy old buildings, and responding to the trend by building adequate modern traffic arteries and parking facilities. On the face of it, this appears to be the message of a view (Figure 6–3) of central Minneapolis not from a church tower but from the top of the fifty-two-story headquarters of Investors' Diversified Services. This skyscraper is only the currently tallest element in a vast new development program slated for the center of Minneapolis. Every single block in the downtown area is or will be involved. In contrast to the careful repairing, refurbishing, and upgrading of the architectural fabric of Augsburg and Lübeck, the approach here has been that of the bulldozer, obliterating with a vigor that is truly cyclonic. Where this leaves the people who once lived here and who once attended the church (upper right) visible in this view is clear: somewhere else. Yet to give Minneapolis its due, a major attractive new downtown housing complex recently has been built at the Loring Greenway, a few blocks off the picture toward the upper left.

Of course, the problems of revitalizing old resi-

city, a high degree of well-integrated commercial and recreational functions, and a sense of life and economic vigor in the central city. Both Lübeck and Augsburg, with former traffic spaces now devoted to pedestrians, have banished general automotive traffic in some areas to good effect, the cars visible being taxis that provide an interface between the traffic and nontraffic areas.

The view from Lübeck's Petri Kirche shows that the churches and city hall continue to dominate the cityscape, maintaining a strong image and conveying a sense of identity and recognizability that is very reassuring. To achieve this, careful guidance dential areas in urban centers is not an easy one. Bypassing all the problems at one fell swoop may well seem to be an attractive prospect. A block of older buildings clustered tightly together, such as one in the center of Graz (Figure 6–4), usually contains a wide variety of problems: mechanical, structural, economic, sanitary, and social. Such buildings in no way meet modern building-code standards for minimal living quality or even safety. There is far too little light and air, usually insufficient fire exits, and little protection against the spread of fire. Since the degree of site coverage by buildings is so great, the problems so complex, the architecture undistinguished and fabric deteriorating, and the current uses only marginally profitable, a reasonable solution would seem to be to tear it all down and start afresh.

Not so in Graz. Signaling a major turnabout in contemporary attitudes toward urban rehabilitation, an entirely different approach is being taken with this block in Graz. The block is in the historic core and plays a significant role in determining the character of the area. The municipal authorities therefore looked upon it as an area that required careful study and an orchestrated rehabilitation of the structural fabric and the various functions that it houses. The first essential step was to have a multidisciplinary team prepare an in-depth inventory of the entire block. This included not only a detailed physical inventory of the buildings, their state of repair (or decay), changes from original construction, and an inventory of current uses, but also a careful sociological inventory to determine who the people were who used the spaces and the nature of their use. Such new attitudes represent a drastic change in the fundamental assumptions of urban renewal but seem to be absolutely essential if continuity of vitality, indeed, viability, in central cities is to be retained.

Both people and buildings, it becomes obvious, should be considered as endangered resources in situations such as these. They need to be protected through recognition of their value to the community and careful analyses of existing activities and social linkages. The continuity of social interactions and the physical realities of an urban environment need to be respected and treated with intelligence and sensitivity if inner cities are to retain the attractiveness as places to live that caused them to be built originally. Though standards of comfort, convenience, and sanitation are of course higher today and therefore require more than cosmetic modifications, it should also be recognized that there are many physical and psychological needs of

Fig. 6–4. Graz, Austria. The first step in getting people to live in cities is to do an inventory of who lives there now and the nature of their needs.

a residential environment that were much better satisfied in older urban centers. It is grossly counterproductive to sacrifice all of these values, which are still valid and often highly desired today.

A view of an ancient residential courtyard in another block in the heart of Graz suggests even further reason to seek out an older residence in the heart of a historic city (Figure 6–5). One is immediately reminded of the *cortile* of the Renaissance palaces in Florence, the residential courtyards of the Marais in Paris or those adjacent to the Cathedral of St. Stephen in Vienna—or even of the New Orleans courtyards that have become such attractions for restaurants as well as for residences in its historic French Quarter. The inward-turning open space of a residential courtyard in the center of a city provides a rich contrast: direct proximity to all the shops, services, places of work, and cultural advantages of the bustling urban center on the one hand, and the quiet contained space for light, air, relaxation, and the more domestic forms of social communication on the other. No modern construction can ever quite capture the richness of texture and social continuity of such a space.

Clearly it is a good idea to rehabilitate a central-city residence of such unusual quality, but many more ordinary buildings in every city could make valuable contributions if rescued from decay, if freed from misuse and economic impotence. Buildings do not have to decay and be discarded: yesterday's architectural styles are by no means unstimulating to today's imaginations. Though today's heating, ventilating, plumbing, and electrical needs place additional demands on old buildings, such purely mechanical problems always find solutions. *Continued use of historic residential buildings for central-city housing should be one of the highest goals of current planning. In order for cities to stay alive, people must live in them.*

Urban population loss is a postwar phenomenon experienced in many countries and is largely a result of economic well-being. Prosperity stimulates greater expectations of material comforts and possessions and an inflation of spatial "need" per person. For this reason it has been widely assumed that the flight to the suburbs, the so-called green wave, is an inevitable corollary of and an initial result of the mobility offered by automobiles.

But are there, on the other hand, also those people who would prefer to live in urban centers if there were attractive opportunities to do so? Recent analyses of market conditions and real estate trends show that this is beginning to be the case. Indeed this countermovement has become so strong in some American cities, including our nation's capital, that we are beginning to hear concern expressed over the issue of gentrification—the squeezing of lower income groups out of affordable urban housing by the rising rents that accompany renovation or the capital requirements of cooperatives. These groups are replaced by the gentry, middle and upper income people.

Depopulation of urban centers is apparently not inevitable. To document demand for housing in this historic core of Graz, for example, urban planners there ran fictitious newspaper ads offering different sizes and types of dwelling units in older buildings. They found a surprising range of people—students, young professionals and government workers, couples without children, and older people—who wanted to escape from the boring an-

Fig. 6–5. Graz, Austria. No modern construction seems capable of capturing the charms and satisfactions of historic residential courtyards like this.

Fig. 6–6. Malmö, Sweden. The uneven development of older, unfashionable residential districts is too often the meat for the sausage grinder of highway construction.

onymity of modern housing developments on the outskirts of town. The respondents wanted to live closer to the attractions of the city, including the university, their jobs, the best shopping, cultural attractions—near "the action," in the argot of our day. Perhaps most interesting of all was one reason given for wanting to live in the old city center: the possibility of being able to avoid owning a car. Less important than price, less important than the absolute quality of the environment surrounding the dwelling, it seemed, was lack of a contiguous parking space, usually considered so essential by contemporary planners.

A basic deterrent to a more rapid buildup of housing desire in central cities is the failure to perceive just how attractive central urban areas can become. The word slum has been bandied about so much that great quantities of substantial, eminently recyclable housing have been lost as a result. After all, the conventional reasoning went, what's the sacrifice if buildings torn down were only slums anyway?

A typical view of a central urban area that had seriously declined in popularity—therefore in incomes, therefore in maintenance, therefore in popularity—was the western half of downtown Malmö, Sweden's third largest city (Figure 6–6). Uneven development, the evidence of cheap materials, a house shell left standing empty are among the characteristic signs of a core area in decline, an area

heretofore ripe for major removal of buildings and transformation into something else. For Malmö this "something else" was planned in the early 1970s to be a handsome expressway link slashing across this portion of the old core in order to relieve congestion and provide better access between major places of work in the harbor area to the north and the main suburban residential areas to the south. In keeping with the old concepts of progress and bigger is better these nondescript buildings were perfect sausage meat for road construction and the development of a high-speed corridor right through this older residential district. What this would have done to the remaining possibilities of the area for attractive housing is clear: urban removal would have been the inevitable result.

Fortunately, the early 1970s in Malmö saw the growth of citizens' groups who questioned established ways of doing things. Bulldozing and roadbuilding that previously would have been accepted as inevitable were strongly challenged. "Down with the building mafia" was one of the slogans expressing public opposition; politicians quickly took note, calling on a group of environmental professionals to study the situation and come up with recommendations. Altogether it took some three years to discuss the district's rehabilitation in public forums, formulate a new set of goals, and draw up a plan for its future development.

The final result was a comprehensive scheme for

Fig. 6–7. Philadelphia, PA. Most of these delightful rowhouses west of Rittenhouse Square are now prestigious offices for doctors and lawyers.

enhancing the environmental quality in the city and, incidentally, not building the proposed expressway connector. Conservation and rehabilitation of older architecture, creation of newly designed streets reserved for pedestrians, improved public transportation service, design of a very precise land-use plan for all future development, and a renewed emphasis on actual domicile in the city were among the features of the comprehensive plan. Malmöans began to recognize attractions of the central urban environment that they had long forgotten; architectural qualities were discovered in buildings long seen as mere shacks or slums; the qualities of street spaces, green spaces, and the banks of the canal were discovered again. With qualities of a living environment newly established as high priority considerations in city planning, people began to rediscover the attractions of living in the center. Instead of the deadening impact of a new highway, the city got a lively influx of new residents. It's all a matter of priorities.

Much can be learned from the buildings themselves in older central cities. Perhaps because their actual construction was more laborious, spaces tend to be much more intimately scaled, the textures of walls and floors of the spaces tend to be more thoughtfully designed and therefore more interesting. The sense of a cultivated ambience often filters through dilapidation to encourage feelings of comfort, safety, and identity. A street of

rowhouses in Philadelphia, adjacent to the central business district in the area west of Rittenhouse Square, represents spatial qualities that once graced many central-city residential areas both in the United States and in other countries (Figure 6–7). Whatever the nature of the original chemistry that resulted in this delightful urban living room, its attractiveness today is undisputed. So great, in fact, is the sense of a quality living environment that pervades this space and so great are the advantages of having such a quality space within easy strolling distance of Philadelphia's commercial center that most of the houses have now been converted to prestigious offices for doctors and lawyers. Gentrification, in a word, has set in with a vengeance.

Though the displacement of residential functions by more remunerative ones such as professional offices and the replacement of lower income residents by a wealthier clientele are growing social issues for American cities, more fundamental is the reborn recognition of the dimensions, textures, materials, and greenery that can combine to form high-density, intimately scaled attractive living environments in central cities. If today's architects, planners, and urban developers can, they should try to recapture such qualities in future residential construction. But whether this is possible or not, the wholesale destruction of currently viable living environments must certainly cease. Both the func-

Fig. 6–8. Basel, Switzerland. A residential square in the heart of the city points out the importance of details: trees, benches, fountains.

munity corporations have been doing some of this work already, as in the Roxbury section of Boston, but these are only small beginnings of a movement that needs to be greatly expanded.

As we have noted again and again, the problem of greatest seriousness if our central cities are to survive is what to do with the cars. If the qualities of community living spaces are to be recaptured, differentiation to reduce environmental impact and to guide the movement and storage of vehicles into less damaging patterns is essential. Street spaces must revert to community rooms, not become transportation corridors.

And we have seen why details of design, moreover, in such community rooms are critical if the advantages of high-density urban living are to be reduced to an acceptable level. The key is to reduce noise, dirt, and pollution to acceptable levels and to regenerate public spaces that can serve as high-quality extensions of the indoor living environment. An example of this from a residential square in the heart of Basel gives some clues (Figure 6–8). Trees are absolutely essential to soften this rather bleak space, to provide beauty and interest as well as shade, movement, and oxygen. Even the plainest of buildings can be softened and made attractive with trees and other vegetation, but sympathetic design and furnishing can provide additional interest, attraction, comfort, and human scale. In a high-density situation, for instance, expensive paving laid by hand can be afforded, as well as comfortable benches, play equipment, even fountains. The most successful plans, however, are often the most conservative: maintaining traditional qualities rather than coming up with new gimmicks. Thus, paving of brick or traditional cobbles in natural colors may be far more appropriate than flashy abstract patterns in modern concrete, while traditionally styled fountains can convey a strong sense of continuity, texture, and scale. And, most important, there must be seating; a dead giveaway as to whether municipal authorities are sincerely interested in the welfare of people or not is whether the seating surfaces are of wood rather than concrete and whether there are backrests or not. Being kind to the anatomy as well as the eye might well be the first rule of successful urban design.

In many cases, of course, the elements are already there, placed by previous generations whose slower-paced lives were more affected by the quality of their environment. Their pride in urban spaces designed of superior materials was a natural outgrowth of extended daily use and enjoyment. What remains is for our generation to recognize

tion and the fabric of older handmade buildings are crucial to the quality of life of the central city.

Older dwelling types are, it develops, not outmoded at all. In fact, the demand for "character" real estate of this type is currently pushing prices out of sight in Philadelphia, Boston, Baltimore, New York, New Orleans, San Francisco, and Washington, D.C., to mention only the most prominent examples. Coping with the displacement of low-income residents who had filled the vacuum when money flowed off to the suburbs is the other social problem. It can best be dealt with through public rent subsidies and rehabilitation programs supported directly by the government or undertaken by nonprofit, public interest groups. Com-

THE CITY AS HABITAT

these qualities, to free them from unfair competition with powerful impersonal environmental impingement, whether from industrial sources, motorized traffic, narrowly exploitative land use, or purely profit-oriented architectural development.

Besides rehabilitating individual buildings and individual dwellings, the process of re-creating appropriate environments surrounding the housing often involves some removal of inappropriate accretions added over the years. A view of a newly refurbished residential area just behind the historic city hall in Regensburg (Figure 6–9) illustrates this clearing-out process, known in Germany as *Entkernung*. Literally "de-coring," this concept refers to the fact that prior to the Second World War urban development concentrated housing and other buildings on the periphery of the blocks, whereas the core, frequently large areas of land in the centers of the blocks, was traditionally reserved for gardens. Subsequent development or exploitation tended to fill up these spaces with subsidiary buildings of a generally lower quality. Thus, one of the best ways to improve the living environment is to open up the gardens again, removing the less desirable accretions.

The scale and character of refurbished older buildings add considerably, of course, to the charm and attraction of these inner-block spaces. The faithful retention of picturesque arrangements of building and windows is obviously important to the sense of uniqueness of place, of character and tradition that makes living in such a place so attractive. One feels part of a continuum, both beneficiary of and contributor to an ongoing sense of urban quality. It is significant to note that, though the regained garden space with its plantings and benches may be within an enclosure of houses and other buildings, it is treated here as a quasi-public space and is part of a network of pedestrian routes through the fabric of the central city. The ability to walk through a rich variety of spatial experiences, including the drama of archways through buildings and narrow passageways between them, only to come upon such delightfully quiet green oases as this, greatly enhances the attractiveness of living in the city and provides opportunities for social communication as well. An essential aspect of this de-coring project in Regensburg is a plan to keep access for cars inconspicuous and nondisruptive. As part of the redevelopment of the interiors of the blocks, parking garages are built underground.

Upgrading the centers of blocks as living spaces, centers for leisure-time activity, and portions of

Fig. 6–9. Regensburg, West Germany. "De-coring"—removing less desirable accretions from interiors of blocks—is an important step in refurbishing older buildings for attractive housing.

attractive walking routes through the center of the city has become one of the most dynamic new concepts in European urban development. As opposed to the bulldozer approach of tearing down the old and building anew in an entirely different format and at an entirely different scale, this movement could be called the development of found space. At once a conservative yet very dynamic process, this development of underutilized space in the urban interstices provides the exciting challenge of intensifying density and activity by retaining all the old uses that give an established urban center its character while sensitively adding compatible new ones.

An example of commercial and leisure-time

development of a block interior, also in Germany and also near the city hall, is provided in downtown Cologne (Figure 6–10). The project is part of a comprehensive redevelopment plan for the central business district and the adjacent historic old town that has among its goals intensification of land uses in the core, an improved overall movement strategy for downtown, and strong encouragement of the residential function in the city's center. A portion of the resulting product is shown here. New housing retains the scale of existing older buildings and the general configuration of enclosing the block on all four sides, but large balconies and loggias visually extend the living spaces into the landscaped and attractively furnished courtyard. Trees, fountains, interesting pavement, and changes in elevation add to the interest of the new and old architecture and make this a stimulating vista for residents and pathway for visitors. It is a perfect place also for restaurants, cafes, and specialty shops that do not rely on maximum numbers of people passing by: an exemplary reinforcement of traditional urban qualities. Integration of these new pleasures and exciting varieties of urban experience with the rest of the city through a well-conceived system of walking routes is, of course, an essential element.

A fine way to enhance the feasibility of housing on expensive inner-city land is to combine it with income-producing commercial uses such as shops and restaurants. Designers can create desirable new sites for these commercial uses by building attractive passageways and oases for pedestrians in the formerly underdeveloped and underused centers of blocks. A recent example of such through-block, mixed-use development with a strong residential component is provided in Munich, just west of the university (Figure 6–11; a photo taken during construction). The dwelling units are small and expensive, but their light and airy design with balconies overlooking a new urban miniplaza taps the aesthetic delight of trees, fountains, and old gas lanterns, as well as the varied prospect of passersby having coffee on the terraces and is a great inducement for many to live here. Other factors underlying the success of the design are its advantageous location at the center of a highly desirable area and its positioning between two very active streets. What once was an unattractive space used for garages, storage, and other low-grade purposes has received the Cinderella treatment and been transformed through design and intensified reintegration of uses that incorporate a desired pedestrian route into a very positive urban amenity. Central cities everywhere can learn significant lessons from this metamorphosis.

The success of Philadelphia's Society Hill, renovated and gentrified into very expensive housing in

Fig. 6–10. Cologne, West Germany. Another example of a rehabilitated block interior at the center of a major city. Housing is combined with other amenities.

Fig. 6–11. Munich, West Germany. Yet a third example shows how using the found space of neglected interiors of blocks can extend the living space of high-density urban housing.

Fig. 6–12. Philadelphia, PA. Society Hill was renovated and gentrified into very expensive housing in the 1960s. Careful detail enhances its appeal.

the 1960s, is now an old story and all the more instructive for being on our own shores (Figure 6–12). The appeal of old bricks, Federal-style rowhouses, gas lanterns, and tall trees made the area a natural for rehabilitation, particularly since it was located so close to downtown. The small-scale, highly textured continuous fabric of such old living environments is now widely recognized as aesthetically proper, and the conversion of every last former stable, carriage house, or servants' quarters into luxury quarters for swinging singles or wealthy professionals is no longer news. Part of the area was cleared nonetheless to provide luxury apartments in high-rise buildings, but to provide balance, new rowhouse complexes were built as well. The overall effect some fifteen years later is still one of very high quality and very pleasing aesthetics. The question now is no longer whether it is economically feasible in this country to pursue rehabilitation at this scale or whether there will be a market for such properties, but whether it could not be done without removing 100 percent of the existing population, i.e., to keep from transforming the area into a

Fig. 6–13. Munich, West Germany. The texture and detail of paving contribute significantly to the quality of an urban room.

rich people's ghetto. There is a feeling that such exclusive neighborhoods, while they may be very pleasant and seem relatively secure for the wealthy people living there, are socially sterile, not to say undemocratic, particularly if government or community funds have been used for the rehabilitation. Current goals would aim toward preserving economic diversity and social mix in the residential area while pursuing both preservation of existing buildings and an upgrading of the public way.

Upgrading the quality of an entire neighborhood is an endeavor requiring an integrated approach. Undoubtedly, one of the great attractions of historic residential environments such as Philadelphia's Society Hill is the richness of the details. This includes such apparent trivia as paving details, in which color, pattern, texture, and perceived quality of material can have a richly unifying effect. Achieving such textural qualities of pavement is a painstaking process, as is suggested by the work of a paving mason in a pedestrian zone in Munich (Figure 6–13). Even without seeing any more of the urban space for which this is the new floor, one can sense an ambience of quality. Precisely the opposite impression is evoked by the careless cheapness of machine-poured, undifferentiated asphalt that covers so much of the modern cityscape. In streets and squares, as well as in dwelling restoration, care must be taken with details if people are to develop strong bonds of identity and affection for their urban environments. Details must reveal genuine care, educated tastes, and quality if the critical ingredient, pride of place, is to be present. *Whatever else may be required in a living environment, achieving a sense of pride of place is perhaps most crucial.*

What this can mean on a broader scale is revealed in a view of downtown Munich taken from the church of St. Peter (Figure 6–14). Although everything visible in this scene was either severely damaged in the Second World War or built entirely from scratch in the intervening years, these buildings reveal a very conscious decision to rebuild not only within traditional limitations of height and bulk but also within the same urban image that had existed before. While there are a great many changes in detail and in use of the spaces, a remarkable sense of urban identity and unique image emerges from this approach. A booming commercial and cultural metropolis, Munich has been called the secret capital of West Germany. Certainly there have been no negative effects on the economy through this retention of historic scale and restriction of developers to the existing framework. There has, on the other hand, been a great intensification of use of the land, which has meant a greater integration of functions and heightened quality of urbanity.

The highly successful Kaufingerstrasse, the main pedestrian axis here extending diagonally from the lower right, is only half of the main, uninterrupted, pedestrianized street running east-west

THE CITY AS HABITAT

some eight hundred meters through the downtown. A perpendicular axis of similar length begins at the Marienplatz in the foreground and extends north and south from there, while the area around the twin-towered cathedral, the entire permanent market area, and other important areas downtown, including that around the famed Hofbräuhaus, have been redesigned for pedestrians as well.

All of this adds greatly to the attraction of the city as a place to live. What can now be seen in retrospect as the incredible environmental burden of undifferentiated traffic through these spaces has been removed, stimulating development of leisure-time activities in the area. A view from this angle helps to show that improvement of environmental quality has involved far more than just the creation of a mall. It is relatively easy to create an attractive commercial spine in the manner of suburban shopping malls, but the acres of dead asphalted space for parking flanking such malls are the antithesis of urbanity. Munich's remarkable success has been achieved by simultaneously improving spatial qualities, upgrading buildings, and creating a close-knit texture of residences, business, and appealing walkable spaces. The city's ultimate goal is to extend these linkages ever further, to the point of achieving a safe and continuous network of attractive walking routes that would directly connect major residential areas all around the central business district with the various commercial, administrative, and cultural functions of the core.

Munich, like most other major cities in Germany, Europe, and other industrialized areas of the world, has lost too high a proportion of the residential population to its suburbs and the larger urban region. But this loss has been far less in Munich than in many other places because of the early and concerted program to achieve high environmental quality throughout the city. Rather than letting whole segments of the city slide into decay, a vigorous program of renovation has been pursued, including relentless elimination of environmental burdens and a sustained drive toward improvement of infrastructure and environmental quality.

High-Density Living in Central Areas

The essence of urbanity in all the world's most famous and best-loved cities has always been the people living there. A Roman, a Dubliner, a New Yorker, a Parisian, a Viennese, or a Londoner all

Fig. 6–14. Munich, West Germany. The high density and uniform texture of the rebuilt center of Munich conveys a sense of pride of place.

bring to mind distinct qualities. All other activities, facilities, buildings, and open spaces of the great urban centers traditionally mark and are marked with the stamp of one basic fact: a great many people use that city as habitat. Throughout the third quarter of the twentieth century there has been a strong tendency to ignore this fundamental consideration, all of us hypnotized by the potential of mobility and the possibility of living anywhere and being able to commute. Now, in the last quarter of the century, there is suddenly a great awakening to the old truism that cities *are* basically people. Not only is high-density living in central areas still with us, it is becoming a new fashion, lending urgency to the regeneration of the city as a psychoemotionally rewarding place to "be from."

Yet, although central-city living was relatively neglected in the 1950s and 1960s as the great migration to the suburbs took place, in some cities the provision of adequate modern dwellings in the center retained high priority in city planning. Rotterdam was one of them. All but wiped out by blanket bombing in the Second World War, the heart of Rotterdam was rebuilt in the early 1950s according to principles that took into account both traditional considerations of the richly varied life of the heart of a major city and the latest ideas of modern architecture concerning the forms in which these functions should be housed. The famous Lijnbaan with its network of delightfully scaled shopping streets reserved for pedestrians was the result (Figure 6–15).

This view suggests that the concept of the Lijnbaan was more than pleasant shopping malls with plants and benches. Fundamental to the scheme was the physical proximity of central-city commerce and administration to downtown high-density housing. The major break with tradition was that, instead of continuous street frontages of shops at street level and three- or four-story walk-ups of housing above, the rows of low-rise shopping streets were alternated with high-rise slabs of twelve-story housing open to the fresh air, sunshine, and view in the best tradition of Le Corbusier and the Charter of Athens. It was the radiant city realized: sun, space, and air, and all in the heart of the city, complete with green meadows and grazing goats.

The age-old secret of concentrating housing where the action is so that high density can justify a high level of amenities and infrastructure continues as valid today as ever before. With residence contiguous to shopping areas, there is a mutual assurance of sound commercial life and ample and varied supply. Recreation and amusement facili-

ties, public transportation, and medical services can all be within a stone's throw where there is a permanent high-density concentration of clientele. The beauty of it is that the result can be an upward spiral of mutual reinforcement. High-quality environment, services, and facilities tend to attract people to live in the area. As more people with increased purchasing power are attracted to the area, the goods, services, and amenities sold there can be upgraded, leading to more people being attracted, and so on.

The area around Ghirardelli Square in San Francisco is an outstanding example of this type of success story. An overall view of the district from the bay shows how the creation of a remarkably attractive commercial complex from the shell of an old chocolate factory can give birth in turn to a very strong residential background (Figure 6–16). Ghirardelli is far from downtown in a waterfront and warehouse district at one end of a breathtaking cable car ride and flanked by a once dingy low-rise residential area. While the story of the now widely emulated conversion of old brick factory buildings into a great shopping and leisure-time attraction at the very edge of San Francisco Bay is now well known, the mutually reinforcing relationship between a stylish commercial development and the large residential area surrounding it is less widely recognized. In fact the general appeal of the area has increased so much that high-rise residential complexes are steadily replacing the old rowhouses. It would seem that urban density and high-quality living environments can be the best of neighbors. How high the density should be is another question.

Whether, on the other hand, tall housing complexes are as good for their neighborhoods as they are for their developers remains open to doubt. Indeed, in some European cities there have been moratoriums placed on any further building of high-rise residential towers because of serious social and psychological issues which they raise, including especially a sense of isolation and a high incidence of antisocial behavior. And, if the contribution of older architecture to the character of Ghirardelli is so significant, at what point does replacement of old with new structures of different character become a danger to the very environmental quality that spawned them in the first place?

So far, such fine tuning of urban areas does not seem to be a matter of high priority in cities of the United States. Merely keeping people from abandoning the city seems to be a concern of higher urgency. The prevailing attitude seems to be that the benefits outweigh any potential detriments that

Fig. 6–16. San Francisco, CA. The area around Ghirardelli Square shows mutual reinforcement of commercial and residential developments.

Fig. 6–15. Rotterdam, the Netherlands. An entirely different scheme of redevelopment, the Lijnbaan nonetheless includes a strong component of housing in the city's center.

Fig. 6–17 (above). Vancouver, Canada. Great quantities of housing are concentrated in close proximity to the central business district.

Fig. 6–18 (right). London, England. The highly imaginative Barbican, a central-city housing scheme, combines high density with remarkable openness.

major changes in scale or building type might bring. Despite a spurt of interest generated by Oscar Newman's published studies on the relationships between high-rise housing and crime, the erection of tall buildings remains a favored way of generating greater returns from limited sites. But we must never forget that it is also an effective way of destroying the scale and character that made a neighborhood attractive in the first place.

High rise versus low rise will continue to be a hotly debated issue in housing because of the seemingly irreconcilable conflicts between financial and sociological motivations. On the other hand, the argument about whether high density or low density is the more appropriate form for housing is being resolved more and more in favor of high density. It may well be that low-rise but high-density forms of housing in areas closely integrated with other urban functions will be the most positive solution in the future, as we have seen so often true in the past.

One North American city that has valiantly resisted the flight to the suburbs by pursuing a very active program of high-density housing close to the urban core is Vancouver in British Columbia. In the period since the Second World War, when so many other cities experienced unimpeded low-density sprawl development into the far suburbs and exurbs, Vancouver managed to concentrate a great amount of its development on the peninsula that includes both its central business district and the historic parts of the city (Figure 6–17). In this view of the peninsula from the south, the central business district with its office towers is in the distance at the right, whereas all of the tall buildings at the left and center are residential towers. Although this concerted program to reinforce housing close to the core has not totally prevented suburban development in Vancouver, it certainly has helped retain the vitality of the core and made it possible for the city to use the strengthened tax base to improve environmental quality. Instead of a downtown existing as an island surrounded by a vast gray area of slums, former industrial districts, and open land cleared by urban renewal as in so many other North American cities, Vancouver's central business district is directly connected to viable housing areas attractive to all income levels. Excellent public transportation, an attractive transitway-mall modeled after that in Minneapolis, redevelopment of the waterfront, rehabilitation and restoration of older buildings and neighborhoods—all these evidences of enhanced urbanity are present in Vancouver.

One of the most imaginative large-scale residential planning achievements of recent years has been the Barbican, situated on 15.2 fiendishly valuable hectares (37.5 acres) immediately adjacent to the central business district of London (Figure 6–18). Wresting a feeling of maximum openness out of the very high density of 568 people per hectare (230 people per acre), the Barbican achieves a high degree of environmental quality through brilliant planning and clearly established priorities. All parking, deliveries, and vehicular movements are routed out of sight under a massive podium, while the view from the dwelling units and an extensive network of pedestrian walkways on top of the podium looks out over quiet garden spaces and a lake. Dwelling units are concentrated in three slender towers and bands of apartment buildings with continuous terraces, as well as a few row-houses in the podium for variety. In addition to shops and services needed to support everyday domestic life, the complex includes several restaurants and pubs, a theater, movie house, lending library, art gallery, girls' school, and music school. A subway runs beneath the project, and bus connections are immediately adjacent.

The features which make the Barbican such a stunning success represent important guidelines for the design of high-density living areas in central cities and will bear brief review here:

Easy, immediate, and attractive pedestrian access to the central city and its jobs
Public transportation to the entire city, its metropolitan region, and beyond
Convenient access to a great range of goods, services, and cultural offerings
Pleasant leisure-time ambience of open spaces with gardens and water
Elimination of the environmental burdens of parked and moving motorized traffic
Sufficiently high population density to make the above feasible

In fine, the problems of residential revitalization of the cores of our great cities can be met—have been met—successfully, pointing the way to planners, city fathers, and concerned urban dwellers alike, all those who feel for their own city that vital pride of place.

Problems and Potential

If the idea that central cities can indeed be excellent places for people to be living is accepted, a logical question arises concerning what to do with all the high-density housing that has always existed there in the past. Figure 6–19, taken from the heart of Paris just north of the new Pompidou Center, demonstrates one answer to that question: tear it down and replace it with something else.

The potential is certainly there to reuse the land for a different purpose or at least for an entirely different clientele. Total removal of the structural fabric requires in the first instance removal of the social fabric, and it is frequently at least an unspoken motive of urban renewal to remove the less desirable low-income populace from the site in order to put the land to more remunerative uses. Such was certainly the case in Paris, where an enormous area of the historic urban core on the Right Bank from the Marais to the former market area of Les Halles is being totally transformed from a scruffy working-class district into a very elegant high-rent area for the elite.

A fundamental question that next must be addressed is whether cities exist primarily for the people or the investors. It is not a matter of either-or, but it is a serious question of primacy. If indeed maximum financial return is to be the highest criterion, then certainly it can be expected that particular functions, buildings, and land users will be removed from time to time to make way for other functions, buildings, and users that can generate higher revenues. If, on the other hand, the life of the city is recognized as its people, then "removal" cost-efficiency must give way to a sensitive assessment of each neighborhood, each block, and each building. We must be able to repair and conserve the existing physical fabric of the city in order to conserve and encourage identification with it by its citizens.

Similarly, the seemingly unresolvable conflict between the desire for environmental quality and the desire for a parking space for one's own vehicle needs to be solved through use differentiation, through a new set of goals for urban open spaces, including streets and plazas. Although car ownership probably does not yet need to be restricted, certainly the anarchy of random disposition of vehicles on every conceivable urban surface needs to be brought under control.

But differentiating the use of urban street spaces to encourage the housing rather than the parking function is only one aspect of programs needed if

central cities are to become strongly attractive again as places to live. A view in the historic center of Lübeck suggests several other basic problems that often afflict older urban centers everywhere (Figure 6–20).

Dwelling units tend to be smaller or in other ways substandard (plumbing, heating, insulation, etc.) compared to newly built residential units.

Because of the lower competition and possibly lower prices, such an area may also attract a high proportion of the economically weaker segments of the working force.

As a result of these various factors, areas such as this rarely have political clout, and thus have low potential for concerted community action.

Because of these problems, the potential contribution of such areas to the urban fabric is rarely recognized. Consequently, one of two approaches is usually taken by municipal authorities: either a do-nothing laissez-faire, in which case buildings continue to decay and the quality of the neighborhood

Fig. 6–19. Paris, France. Traditionally, urban housing has been very dense, with too little open space. Replacement is sometimes necessary.

THE CITY AS HABITAT

gradually (or swiftly) deteriorates, or the clean-slate approach, in which the marginal uses and structures are simply wiped away in order to deal with a financially strong developer and a larger-scale renewal project. In either case, the potential benefits of an intimately-scaled, tradition-rife living environment for a broad range of people in the center of a city are squandered and irretrievably lost.

In Lübeck the approach is different. Although various sins of removal have occasionally been committed, the scale of the central city remains very much as it traditionally was, with a strong continuity of low-rise, high-density building strongly infused with the residential function. The traditional image and identifiability of the city are highly valued as precious assets, both in a sociological and an economic sense. Therefore, houses are being renovated and restored on an individual basis: block by block the streets are regaining their substance and quality while still retaining the best aspects of past traditions. In order to retain the established residents who wish to remain, the program is strongly subsidized by the municipal government. Comprehensive planning includes analy-

Fig. 6–20 (above). Lübeck, West Germany. Problems evident in old residential areas of central cities frequently obscure their great potential contributions.

Fig. 6–21 (left). Norwich, England. The texture, scale, and amenities of historical residential areas like Elm Hill are resources that can contribute greatly to the quality of life in contemporary cities.

Fig. 6–22. Norwich, England. One solution is to add in-fill housing of an appropriate scale behind the refurbished older dwellings.

sis of whether or not the parked cars belong to residents of the area and the provision of alternative parking specifically designed to meet the needs of the people living here.

Of course, different situations require different solutions, and it is not always an appropriate solution to provide centralized parking or underground garages. But as the highly successful *Woonerf* "living-court" program in Dutch cities such as Delft has proven, the appropriate solution may be simply to change the public's perception of the street from a place for traffic to a place for living in which automobiles may be tolerated—but only just. Elm Hill in Norwich is similar, retaining the traditional character of the street and the possibility of its use by cars in a ring-and-loop traffic management scheme but clearly changing the emphasis to give priority to the street space as an extended living environment, as a place for relaxation and communication (Figure 6–21). Through creation of a traffic-cell system the planners have left this street available for residential access but no longer for through traffic.

Older homes, trees, benches, intimately scaled signs, shops, lamps, and plantings all add up to a delightful place for anyone to live, and the quaint scale of smaller old dwellings is certainly compensated to a great degree by the quality of the living environment surrounding the buildings. Yet it is essential to recognize that residential environments

of this character and quality do not simply grow as the result of accretion over the generations or centuries. Such qualities must be carefully nurtured and husbanded by successive generations, each respecting the contributions of the previous ones. In fact, the character of the space as it is seen here is the result of a concerted program of restoration undertaken in recent years. Sensitivity and modesty have been major ingredients of that program, passing the architectural heritage on to the future in a condition at least as good as, in fact considerably better than, the condition in which it came to our generation from the past. This requires not only respect and restraint but also firmness in establishing new priorities. Overall traffic management was a necessity if the destructive burdens of vehicles on a fragile environment of this nature were to be avoided.

Changing land values and the costs of the careful restoration program itself may well require that the residential density of an area such as Elm Hill in Norwich be increased. Obviously the residential towers that crowd in on Ghirardelli Square are not a reasonable addition to Elm Hill, but a certain increase in the intensity of use, as long as it is not destructive of the character of functioning of the space, could be very appropriate. In Norwich in-fill apartment units were added in the spaces behind the older buildings shown in Figure 6–21. The nature of some of these new dwelling units is shown in Figure 6–22. It is quite apparent that the challenge of small scale and lack of space was well met. The givens were simply accepted as the parameter and the new units designed to fit in unobtrusively so that both old and new residents could get maximum benefit from the positive aspects of the neighborhood. If only more urban development in cities everywhere could be as sensitive to the built environment inherited from the past, the strength and appeal of housing revitalization in central cities undoubtedly could be reestablished more quickly. The potential is there; the problems can be solved.

Sociocultural Concerns

People choose to move from cities for predominantly tangible reasons: more space for less money, the opportunity to have a yard or garden, less dirt, less pollution, less crime, fewer annoyances. Conversely, people decide to live in cities for predominantly intangible reasons: atmosphere, interest, excitement, culture, being "where the action is." Certainly the sociocultural benefits are potentially very great in cities. If they can be broadened and if

the tangibles of environmental quality also can be upgraded, cities would be the choice of far more people as the appropriate place to live.

A view of New York City's Bryant Park, between 41st and 42nd Streets with the Avenue of the Americas to the west, faces the back of the New York Public Library, suggesting some of the great riches a large city offers in the intangible realm of sociocultural concerns (Figure 6–23). The fantastic resources of the legendary New York Public Library stand as a symbol of all the cultural riches that only a large and dynamic city with a strong tradition of support for cultural concerns can sustain. Concerts, opera, ballet, theater, exhibitions, great art collections, museums of all sorts, and an enormous spectrum of educational opportunities are among the cultural benefits of the world's great cities. The extent to which they are present in other cities frequently is used as a measure of the quality of life and the desirability of living in one place as opposed to another.

Environments conducive to development of sociocultural aspects of life, however, are by no means limited to educational or research facilities in the limited sense or to institutions of high cul-

Fig. 6–23. New York, NY. Such cultural benefits in great cities as the New York Public Library are powerful inducements for people to live there.

Fig. 6–24. Norwich, England. The benefits of such traditional social institutions as open-air markets are being rediscovered and reinforced.

ture. Every facility that stimulates peaceful communication between people can generate information and impressions in a positive manner. One of the oldest social institutions to serve this purpose, as well as one of the oldest reasons for the development of cities, is the public marketplace. The central square or the main street of most cities once began as the market where everyone of virtually every social class came together not only to buy and sell but to discuss, negotiate, exchange information, or just be seen. The state fair, the annual farmers' market, the annual arts and crafts market, and similar periodical fairs or markets still held in so many places today are direct descendants of this ancient urban function.

The permanent—or at least more regular weekly or monthly—market is being discovered again as a strong positive force in attracting people to cities and stimulating positive communication among people. Permanent *daily* markets in the open air, strange as it may seem to those who have not seen how well they work, are functioning beautifully in cities as formal as Boston (Quincy Market) and London (Covent Garden) and as high-powered as New York (Allen Street and the Fulton Fish Market) and are providing a strong example for other cities to follow. The permanent market in Munich, just southeast of the city hall square, recently underwent major design improvements, including elimination of through traffic. In England, Norwich provides an outstanding example in its Permanent Market directly in front of the City Hall, with

the historic Guild Hall just to the north and the city's main commercial district to the east and south (Figure 6–24). The central location of this daily open air market in Norwich could hardly be more prominent, emphasizing its continued central role in the functioning of the city. Not just the vegetables, flowers, meat, poultry, fish, cheeses, and other perishable and nonperishable goods that are offered for sale here, but the social ambience that is provided, are of the essence. Where else can one capture as well this spirit of informal and dynamic interchange? Certainly the antiseptic environment of the modern shopping center is only a pale reflection, with its concentration on the single purpose of creating a disoriented, artificial environment conducive to impulse buying. The genuine market is almost more a social institution than a commercial one; its wonderful ad hoc nature provides delightful opportunities for participating and observing, for learning about one's fellow citizens of all ages and all income groups, and for developing a sense of belonging with the city.

For all the advances in creating modern markets, squares, galleries, and other forms of inventive indoor shopping facilities today, historic urban environments can still teach us important lessons if we open our eyes to them. The ad hoc, somewhat sloppy, casual, but always interesting and highly stimulating quality of informal open-air markets is a civics lesson in itself. People want to feel integrated with their urban environment, to have a sense of belonging, and it should be among the

THE CITY AS HABITAT

highest goals of urban planning to give them this opportunity of identifying with their surroundings and with their fellow citizens. The beauty of the market is that everyone can participate, regardless of age, income, or inclination to purchase. Everyone present is automatically both participant and observer simultaneously.

Among recent programs to develop urban quality and citizen participation in European and American cities, one of the most spectacular successes has been the institution of flea markets. Along with the establishment of pedestrian zones in main downtown shopping districts, the new flea markets have been extremely successful in drawing people into the cities from the suburbs and from even further out in the urban regions. A view of a flea market in the central business district of Stuttgart in southern Germany conveys some sense of the atmosphere of an urban happening that seems to occur when flea markets are held in appropriate, pedestrianized urban settings (Figure 6–25).

Perhaps the spirit of nostalgia in the 1970s, the appreciation of old things, and the reaction against impersonality and lack of scale and relatability in modern architecture and commercial development that are so widely prevalent in the United States are the direct cause of the new fashion for flea markets here. Or perhaps there is a basic psychological satisfaction in the great visual stimulus provided by a wide variety of old and curious objects so different in color, pattern, texture, and shape from most of the products of our culture today. Undoubtedly the fun of coming to watch other people looking, selecting, and haggling is as much a motivation as looking at the objects themselves. Whatever the magical combination, it is clear that the urban designer's contribution lies in providing the conducive space in which such activities can take place. The open space itself merely needs to be interesting and stimulating.

Trees and other aesthetic elements of landscape and urban design are obvious means of providing

Fig. 6–25. Stuttgart, West Germany. Such an old device as the flea market acts like a powerful magnet to draw people back to urban centers.

attractive spaces to stimulate social contacts in cities. They are all too often overlooked in the rush to develop land for maximum profits or maximum efficiency. In Philadelphia the city fathers had the foresight to provide four entire city blocks located equidistant from City Hall as park spaces in which the citizens could find relaxation, diversion, and social communication close at hand. Rittenhouse Square is the park closest to the central business district, so that its attractions are particularly important for all the people who use the central city, especially during lunch hours (Figure 6–26).

Inner-city greenery is one of the most appreciated amenities, especially since it is generally available in only very limited amounts. To the normal appeal of nature is added the welcome contrast of soft and rustling shapes as a relief from the oppressively hard, cold, and unresponsive forms of modern commercial architecture. The designed appeal of a space of this quality is not only a social benefit in its own right; it tends to generate others. Chance meetings with friends are always quite possible, as are all kinds of other unexpected experiences: a street musician, a sidewalk artist, a vendor of unusual crafts, or, as here, a flower show. The appeal of the community place for relaxation and leisure-time enjoyment makes it a natural setting for a benefit sale of flowers and plants by a local garden club.

The location of quality urban spaces is also an important issue if these spaces are to serve the intended purpose of stimulating social contacts and a sense of belonging. The isolated grandeur of the monument is a wasted, hollow gesture in terms of urbanity. Integration with other urban functions is the key to success. This gives the monumental public place an opportunity to draw on a permanent constituency and to stand out as a special event by direct and immediate contrast with the everyday urban fabric immediately adjacent.

Goals for successful planning of urban spaces and the various forms of communication and interchange that should take place in them are very complex. To achieve the appropriate relationships that will be most conducive to desirable commercial, cultural, and social activities requires long-term planning of land uses, public funds, and the involvement of private investments. A great many conflicts must not be forced but need to be resolved over a long period of time through coordinated planning and concerted efforts. Among the conflicts to be resolved are those between the goals and the givens of the existing situation, but there frequently are conflicts between the various goals themselves.

Figure 6–27 should serve as a reminder that, in all of these deliberations and resolutions of goal conflicts, the factors of personal comfort, attrac-

tion, and pleasure should not be forgotten. People, after all, are intended to occupy and use the spaces; yet the somewhat depressing conclusion that inevitably arises from observation of both old and new urban centers is that modern developments are far more inhospitable to human beings than are the historic ones. Motives of efficiency, speed, and profit do not tend to make for attractive urban environments conducive to human activities.

Colonnades and arcades and marketplaces, as here in Padua, are the types of architectural environments hospitable to people's public intercourse in central cities. Open and semiopen public spaces at the heart of the dense urban environment can serve as the ideal vehicles for communication and integration if not continually disrupted by pollution, noise, and conflicting activities. And integration is not simply a matter of the adult male population, either. The urban center needs to be an environment hospitable to the younger generation, learning through observation. Children ought to be able to participate as well, while the environment ought to be so conducive that even mothers with infants can find visits to the central city not only possible but enjoyable. If preservation of historic environments, elimination of negative environmental impacts, and the design of sensitive, adaptive modern buildings and public spaces can create such receptive environments, then social integration will

be possible and the goal of cities for people achieved.

Play and Regeneration

It would seem to be a simple solution: the inhospitable character of modern cities could be easily ameliorated if only some attention would be paid to designing some spaces that do nothing more than satisfy the fundamental human need for play. How can it be that in a dense, historic, urban environment such as Paris on the Left Bank, very near the Boulevard Saint-Michel, Notre Dame, and the Seine, there can be an intimate space of trees, benches, bushes, and sand suitable for playing *boulle?* Yet there it is, so modest and yet so eminently suitable for its purpose (Figure 6–28). Space needed for play and regeneration is often so modest that one wonders why it is not more frequently provided. Undoubtedly it is a simple oversight, a failure to recognize that urban life requires a redressing of balance, an opportunity to shift from the intensity and the hard surfaces to something relaxing in a soft environment. The secret, from a design standpoint, would seem to lie in contrast: providing relief from the buildings, pavement, and intensity of the urban struggle with oases of casual, anarchic softness that provide an opportunity to get away from it all right in the midst of it all. Who needs to escape when you can have a game of *boulle* right down at the corner with the boys?

This release-valve function is, of course, inherent in central parks everywhere. The principle has long been recognized but often forgotten for the sake of expediency. Central Stockholm, in the far north with long winters, has not forgotten: the Kungsträdgården in the heart of the city is only one portion of an enormously extensive park system that reaches far out into the suburban region. While further out the park system is more natural with extensive trail networks through the woods, here in the center of the city the park and its facilities are more concentrated, more urban (Figure 6–29). Flowerbeds, fountains, children's playgrounds, a bandstand outdoor theater, and a macrochessboard are all part of the facilities in the heart of the central business district.

Why aren't these people all home watching soccer on TV, one might ask. Is there really something more participatory in watching a chess match in person? There must be something to it: a sense of social communication that can only be felt by being on the scene, no matter how momentary or tenuous the relationship. There is simply no substitute for interesting human activity, and urban design can make it all possible. The trees are also a critical fac-

tor. When, just a few years ago, some of the trees very near this spot were threatened by the building of a new subway stop, the reaction was so intense that people chained themselves to the trees in protest until the plans were changed and the future of the trees assured. That is the type of citizen love and engagement that good urban design should engender.

Trees, of course, are also among the most important design elements in children's playgrounds, as they are for any area intended for play and regeneration in cities. Yet how often are playgrounds designed entirely in hard materials, with no touch of nature at all? Fortunately, there has been an increasing awareness in recent years that playgrounds need to be more imaginative and more plentiful and that soft surfaces, earth, vegetation, and water are among the elements that ought to be included. All too often, though, these new play areas are to be found only in strictly residential areas or in new town developments. Facilities for children's play in central cities are woefully lacking everywhere and continue to be one of the main deterrents to families living in cities.

The Netherlands, Great Britain, and the Scandinavian countries appear to be most advanced in recognizing the need and alleviating the problem

Fig. 6–29. Stockholm, Sweden. Powerful lessons can be learned from the successes of central parks of high quality like Kungsträdgården.

THE CITY AS HABITAT

Fig. 6–30. Helsinki, Finland. A generous play area for children in the center of the city reveals very positive social priorities.

by building attractive play spaces in existing urban areas. A single example from central Helsinki, near the National Museum and Finlandia Hall, suggests how generous facilities for little children can be if only the need is recognized and appropriate priorities established (Figure 6–30). In addition to the conventional play equipment of swings, slide, and seesaw, there is really very little on the site other than sand and trees. But what a remarkably attractive atmosphere! The generosity of the large piece of land dedicated to nothing else but the play of small children is a most striking feature. No vest-pocket park is this. And then the trees: ample mature shade trees on all sides of the site, creating a genuine oasis in the center of the city. Newer trees have been planted in the midst of the site. The choice is always there: play in the sun or play in the shade. There are plenty of places to run, great rock outcroppings on which to climb, and yet a protective fence all around. More important than specific details, though, is the pervasive sense of care: care in providing a quality environment for the activities of children in the central city.

An interesting further development of these concepts of providing play facilities for children in the urban center is to provide them directly in the business district in conjunction with major shopping facilities and with responsible playground supervisors, so that young children can be left while mothers are free to shop. Conventional downtowns are far too dangerous, too hectic, and too inhospitable to encourage their use by any but the most hardy of the working and consuming adult populace. Central cities can be transformed into safe, hospitable, attractive environments for all, so that everyone, regardless of his or her age or physical condition, can participate in the activities and benefits of a dynamic urban center.

"But where are we to get the land?" is certain to be an objection to proposals of this type. "Downtown land is too expensive to use in building parks and playgrounds" is an old refrain. Fortunately, it is perhaps easier today than ever before to counter such arguments because of the discovery that all cities have a great abundance of underused, municipally owned land directly in the heart of the central business district, as well as in all other sections of the city. This is the overabundance of street space that has been reserved and built up over the decades on the mistaken assumption that it was indispensable for moving and storing motor vehicles. *Streets and intersections are the great open-land reserves of our cities.*

In Austria, the example of the central business district of Graz serves to show how simple the realization of this concept of regaining street space for purposes of play and recreation can be once an overall traffic management scheme had been devel-

Fig. 6–31. Graz, Austria. Using existing trees and the great open-land reserve of all cities, a street was transformed into a playground.

oped (Figure 6–31). This street in the heart of Graz formerly led to the main market square in front of the city hall (behind the camera). The program conceived to reduce the impact of traffic on the city's center determined that this street was redundant, no longer needed for the movement of vehicles. So beneath the trees and in the architectural setting of preserved historic buildings, this delightful urban space makes an ideal playground, with the further advantage of having been realized very quickly and at low cost. Astroturf is simply placed over the street surface and the benches and play equipment put in place by an adjacent shop that deals in these objects. Is it heresy to transform downtown street spaces into such humane uses?

Occasionally, people of all ages, all occupations, and all degrees of physical fitness need rest, an opportunity to regenerate in a pleasant environment. Should not such opportunities be offered in the heart of major cities? Should it not be a viable option to live in cities, to be able to choose to do without an automobile, and to be able to find sufficient change of pace and recreation opportunities within the city itself? A detail view in the Tuilleries Gardens in Paris demonstrates a resoundingly affirmative response from one of the world's great cities (Figure 6–32). Cities need to be perceived as more than stress producers, full of hectic motion and fraught with dangers. It is entirely feasible, as we have seen, for municipal governments to provide green oases in the middle of bustling urban environments, oases with trees, grass, flowers, water, sculpture, and real chairs with backrests and arm-

rests. Perhaps it could be a benchmark for planners and urban administrators everywhere: "Do we have a place in the heart of our city where the people can lie back and sun themselves in comfort and security as they do in the Tuilleries Gardens in Paris?"

Where is the joy in our urban environments? Everyone knows what the elements are: trees, water, comfortable seating, places for social communication, for relaxation, for play. Why don't we build more of them? Certainly the weather is no handicap. Scandinavian cities are richly endowed with urban parks that are absolutely delightful in their landscape design and aesthetic quality of their furnishings. The city of Göteborg even provides folding canvas lounge chairs free of charge so that people can sun themselves in downtown parks. And all of this despite its extreme northern latitude, the long dark winters, and the short summer season. We know what it takes to make cities absolutely delightful places in which to live. Many of our cities have most of these latent qualities, which lie unrealized because of goal conflicts and for lack of more humane priorities. If things were going well, there might be little reason to change, but in a great many of our cities things are not going well. *It behooves us to learn from those that have found the means of making their urban environments more habitable, more humane.*

Another view of the Kungsträdgården in central Stockholm conveys a sense of the type of urbanity everyone wishes for their own central cities (Figure 6–33): people able to communicate in a highly con-

Fig. 6–32 (above). Paris, France. Cities everywhere can provide oases of genuine appeal and quality like the Tuilleries Gardens in the core areas.

Fig. 6–33 (below). Stockholm, Sweden. Lavish park spaces and urban amenities like those of the Kungsträdgården help inculcate a sense of identity with the community.

ducive environment, a park space highly cultivated and including many trees, elaborate fountains, lavish works of art. But the first priority is to have a designed open space available for the purpose, one freed from traffic and other destructive environmental impacts. It must also be located where it is needed: at the very center of the city. Under such circumstances and with such facilities, the battle to build an urban image and to inculcate a strong sense of identity and love for the community will be all but won. *Not expediency but amenity needs to be placed at the top of the list of urban priorities.*

Design Conducive Environments

Two related but contrasting views, one from downtown Stockholm (Figure 6–34), the other from the antiurban setting of O'Hare Airport in Chicago (Figure 6–35), remind us that the changes required need not be lavishly expensive. Nor is it necessary to hope for major changes in people's habits or major breakthroughs in technology. The means are all currently available and well known; the habits and desires of people are also well established and well known. We all want a more pleasant, more conducive urban environment in which we can live in peace and comfort with direct and easy access to our places of work and to all the other places and facilities we want to visit and use in the city. This requires an integrated environment of closely related functions. It requires concentration, density, in order to be able to provide a high level of services and infrastructure. And it requires a designed relationship of elements that complement rather than conflict with each other.

Above all, these more beneficial changes in our way of doing things require a separation of different modes of movement in order to eliminate conflicts, disruption, and danger. O'Hare Field—and many others like it—have taught us that we are indeed capable of walking great distances, that in high-density situations walking, indeed, is by far the best means of transportation. Drottninggatan in Stockholm serves as a typical example of many that have shown us how the same capability and appropriateness applies to urban environments in the open air just as well as to the totally artificial, enclosed environments of airports and suburban shopping centers. Variety and interest of the sensory experience, in fact, makes it far more stimulating in the urban than in the nonurban setting. And Drottninggatan in this view has had *nothing* done to it other than the removal of vehicles.

People are already walking everywhere, even in the bitter cold on Toronto's Yonge Street in February (Figure 6–36). The desire and the necessity to live and function in the city comfortably are there;

Fig. 6–34. Stockholm, Sweden. Variety and interest of sensory experience, coupled with a removal of disturbing factors, are crucial elements in a successful urban environment.

THE CITY AS HABITAT

the desire and necessity to walk between inner-city destinations are there—in every city and in every country. Major, dynamic, vital functions, including the residential, will continue to exist in our cities and will continue to function best when concentrated and spatially related to each other.

The question remains: how long will each city continue to tolerate the gross disruption of essential linkages between these functions? How long will prestigious downtown communities, priding themselves on the finest department stores, the most elegant indoor malls, and the finest agglomerations of shops, continue to allow their street spaces to exist in a chaos of disruption, pollution, visual blight, noise, and proximate physical danger? The need for comprehensive planning at every level dictates that the no-man's-land of street spaces also be incorporated into the organization of comprehensive spatial relationships. *Exterior spaces, too, must be designed as conducive environments for human activities.*

It is necessary to recognize that, every time a citizen is imposed upon by a hostile urban environment, the city dies a little. As the city dies, so is its commerce enfeebled. As commerce sickens, so dies the fundamental reason for mankind to foregather into cities. To retain vigor and vitality in the urban environment a concerted program of humanistic goals must be pursued.

Fig. 6–35 (above). Chicago, IL. The totally artificial environments of airports and shopping centers like O'Hare Field offer both positive and negative lessons.

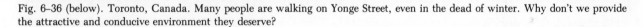

Fig. 6–36 (below). Toronto, Canada. Many people are walking on Yonge Street, even in the dead of winter. Why don't we provide the attractive and conducive environment they deserve?

Fig. 6–37. Munich, West Germany. A close equivalent in function to Toronto's Yonge Street, Kaufingerstrasse bridges the imagination gap, demonstrating the potential of such urban spaces.

A vision of the revolutionary changes in urban environmental quality that this approach is able to bring about is suggested by comparing Figure 6–37 with Figure 6–36. These two major shopping streets are exactly equivalent in their primary functions: the one, Toronto's Yonge Street, the other, Munich's Kaufingerstrasse. Both have served as the major route through downtown; both have subways running underneath bringing many people from the entire urban region; both are the locations of the city's most prestigious department and clothing stores; both have a great wealth of historic architecture of great interest and quality. The differences are all too obvious, in particular the greater volume of people using the more hospitable environment of Kaufingerstrasse. It is a simple matter of priorities. Are the people who make all of these buildings work, who keep all of these businesses flourishing, to be treated with the kindness and respect their membership in the city deserves, or are they not? *Are the urban spaces in our cities to be designed as humane environments, or are they not?*

The principles and techniques for saving our cities are both well known and well tested. Certainly it is not a matter merely of converting downtown main streets into shopping malls but of applying the principles of differentiation to the entire urban fabric on an allover scale. Priorities need to be shifted back to the people. Economic well-being, efficient functioning of traffic, satisfactory solutions to housing problems are all related to the creation of conducive environments in the open-space network of cities.

The task is not easy, and it is far too complex to be solved by one discipline or one social segment alone. The concerted efforts of preservationists, architects, urban planners, traffic managers, social scientists, economic planners, citizens' groups, and politicians are critical if this enormous task is to be handled in a satisfactory manner. The beauty of the situation is the overwhelming body of positive experience that has built up in recent years demonstrating that it can be done, that *it is being done.* Adequate resources are at hand; the fundamental urban fabric is still largely or at least partially available, so that cities still have the option of building in a continuum with the past. *We can still choose to build as if people mattered.*

But time is running out. The destructive impact of unhampered destruction and redevelopment on a larger scale and the ravaging of urban fabric by unrestrained accommodation of motorized traffic mushroom unhindered in many places as if we hadn't learned any better.

How much longer will it continue?

THE CITY AS HABITAT

Epilogue

Are things getting better or are they getting worse? This is a logical question following consideration of so many cities in different parts of the world. Clearly the answer must remain equivocal: better in some places, worse in others, but in most cities both better and worse simultaneously, depending on which area of a particular city or which aspect of environmental quality one considers. One great cause for optimism is the growing awareness that things cannot continue as they have in recent decades, that our destiny cannot be dictated by outmoded trends.

The opportunity of writing and publishing a book on a topic of such importance for the contemporary world as urban environmental quality gives one an enhanced awareness of how things are changing over time. The research, travel, photography, and inevitable length of time involved in bringing such a project to fruition has an effect similar to time-lapse photography: changes that normally go unnoticed suddenly become quite clear.

Throughout the decade spent on this work I have been impressed to find my concerns and observations widely shared. Neither as new nor as revolutionary as one might at first presume, these concepts are everywhere evident or at least close to the surface as people realize that the overwhelming impact of automobiles must be alleviated, that too much of our architectural heritage has been senselessly squandered, and that too much of the space in which we live has been formed by expediency rather than rational considerations of humanistic design. It is refreshing to find popular perceptions now frequently ahead of those of planners in demanding that trees and buildings be saved, that the juggernaut of highway construction be brought under control, that the burden of cars be removed from certain areas.

Yet improvements must be measured in increments, and different rates of progress must be individually recognized from country to country and even among cities of one nation. For example, having moved to Germany to study the advanced planning principles widely in effect there, I became deeply involved in a citizens' action group for better city planning in a town where the old practices of using urban development to enrich the few rather than benefit the many were still very much in evidence. Naturally, the advances achieved were not as dramatic as those in a more enlightened city, but changes were made nonetheless and were highly significant in their context. Nothing, it seems, is as crucial to the improvement of environmental quality as the interest, vigilance, and active participation of ordinary citizens.

International conferences, such as those on transportation and urban life held under the auspices of N.A.T.O. in Munich and on contemporary urban environments held by the International Federation for Housing and Planning in Helsinki, the widely publicized conference and forum on the human habitat organized by the United Nations in Vancouver, and the Council of Europe's major Amsterdam congress on the architectural heritage, demonstrate a ground swell of concern and a wealth of plans and campaigns to achieve significant improvement in the quality of life in cities. Although the ponderous and expensive nature of architecture and urban development dictates that changes will be slow and deliberate, these conferences and others like them clearly indicate movement in the right direction.

The good news is that this positive tendency continues unabated in many places. The preservation movement continues to grow in numbers of people, numbers of buildings saved, increasing size of conservation areas, and increasing range of the types of structures considered worthy of preservation. The idea of living in the heart of a major city as a matter of choice is gaining currency among many people of sound economic status, including many who are attracted by, among other things, the vision of not being constrained to own and maintain at least two automobiles per family. The automobile-oriented layout of suburbia that forces one to drive everywhere has lost its appeal for many; yet it is lamentable that we had to wait for rapidly rising fuel costs to produce a salutary awareness that all is not well in our current practices of sprawl development. Fortunately, however, although we still have a long way to go to achieve crucial economies, the standard gas-guzzling American behemoth seems to be going the way of the dinosaurs.

Another part of the good news: removing cars from certain city streets to give other human activities a better chance is an idea no longer met with the outrageous incredulity it once was. Imaginative conversions of main streets into downtown malls or transitways have gained wide currency and are being introduced in ever more cities in many countries. In West Germany alone, the movement to pedestrianize downtown streets has risen so steadily during the course of this study that the number of cities that have taken this step had to be raised to five hundred while this book was in galleys.

The bad news is that, despite smaller cars and greater awareness of the need to conserve everything—from water and land to mineral and energy resources—there is still an overdependence on the private automobile. Merchants everywhere still perceive their main problem as a lack of parking space in front of their stores, too much power still lies in the hands of the highway lobby, and notwithstanding some spectacular campaigns to halt major highway construction for environmental reasons, the steady ooze of asphalt continues to cover the land.

On the suburban fringes sprawl development continues unabated, although now usually with smaller lots and frequently with more compact housing types, largely as a result of high mortgage rates and the state of the economy. While the recognition by some governors and legislators of the necessity for land-use planning is a positive sign, county commissioners and the financial interests they represent still too often thwart efforts that could in any way hamper the enormously lucrative activity of developing farm and ranch land into building sites for homes.

Meanwhile, back in the cities, buildings that have been put on the National Register of Historic Places continue to fall to the bulldozers in night and weekend blitzes calculated to keep preservationists from getting needed restraining orders from the courts. Such destruction of our historic heritage too often is carried out with the tacit approval—if not active cooperation—of local authorities who have been conditioned in the past to consider old buildings as stumbling blocks on the road to progress.

Finally, in the United States of the early 1980s, the proposed severe budget cuts may have a serious impact on environmental programs for cities and countryside that, after finally having begun to have significant effects, are now apparently to be either dismantled or severely curtailed. It appears that the Reagan administration intends to eliminate federal funding from many programs what would benefit the quality of the environment for everyone. Instead, major concessions are to be granted to powerful commercial interests that have a history of degrading the quality of both urban and rural environments. We can only hope that our worst fears will not be realized.

Yet, despite ominous signs, one must remain optimistic. Perhaps economic constraints will, after all, lead to new, imaginative coalitions of different interest groups to achieve enhancement rather than debasement of environmental quality. One such coalition that suggests possibilities of great things to come is the new National Main Streets Center in Washington, formed with a grant to the National Trust for Historic Preservation A consortium of federal agencies supporting this program includes the Department of Housing and Urban Development, the Economic Development Administration of the Department of Commerce, the National Endowment for the Arts, the Department of Transportation, the Farmers' Home Administration of the Department of Agriculture, the Small Business Administration, and the Heritage Conservation and Recreation Service of the Department of the Interior. Since the program was conceived under the previous administration and initiated only in October, 1980, too little time has passed to determine how it will be affected under the new federal administration.

One of the most positive aspects of the National Main Streets Center, which is specifically aimed at revitalizing downtowns in the nation's smaller cities, is its strong support from the business community as represented by the International Downtown Executives Association. Support of state governments through the State Community Affairs Agencies also seems assured. Unifying revitalization interests with those of conserving and upgrading the heritage of historic architecture should lead to strikingly positive effects in the nation's smaller cities.

Europe still appears to be well ahead of the North America in alleviating the negative effects of development practices of recent decades and achieving positive change. It is the hopeful message of this book that the necessary steps are already well understood, in practice, and proving themselves in a great many incremental steps in many cities across the world. A logical conclusion would seem to be that these realizations and devices should be integrated, adapted to local conditions, and applied everywhere. To my knowledge no local conditions anywhere preclude the application of the principles here presented and the achievement of more humane urban environments.

As to a vision of what the next step beyond those described in this book should be, where planning truly oriented toward the welfare of all the people can lead, I refer readers to a book published by Callwey Verlag of Munich in 1977, entitled simply *Fussgängerstadt*, "City for Pedestrians" (Paulhans Peters, editor). The fundamental premise of that book is our need to reorganize the use of vast areas of the public realm in cities to make them socially more useful. The key lies in differentiating the ways in which we use urban rights-of-way. Instead of maximizing the flow of motorized vehicles, our highest planning goals should involve the creation of continuous networks of paths for pedestrians and bicyclists throughout the entire urban fabric. It is not a matter of eliminating the absolute and overwhelming priority we have given this one mode of movement, which—as we have come to realize—has so many negative secondary effects. The Dutch *Woonerf* or living-court concept, which enables people and vehicles to coexist but eliminates the dominance of the latter, deserves serious study and emulation elsewhere.

In conclusion, I would like to express my sincere appreciation to both the National Endowment for the Humanities and to the many planners who have shared so generously their knowledge and experience. *Cities for People* is not intended to present a survey of any city or group of cities, in either positive or negative aspects. It has not been my purpose to demonstrate any one locale as being better or worse than another, but rather—through selective use of generic situations as exemplified by characteristic examples—to demonstrate practical measures that can be applied to achieve measurable improvements of urban environments for people. It is worthy to note that, particularly in the case of American examples, appearances may have altered drastically since the photographs used here were originally made. I feel that the points of this book do not diminish simply because a specific example used illustratively has changed, and I leave to my readers the joys of recognition and comparison, as well as the judgments in specific instances as to whether things are getting better or worse.

Index

(Italics indicate pages with illustrations.)